Of Muscles and Men

ALSO BY MICHAEL G. CORNELIUS

The Boy Detectives: Essays on the Hardy Boys and Others (McFarland, 2010)

Nancy Drew and Her Sister Sleuths: Essays on the Fiction of Girl Detectives (McFarland, 2008)

Of Muscles and Men

*Essays on the Sword
and Sandal Film*

Edited by MICHAEL G. CORNELIUS

McFarland & Company, Inc., Publishers
Jefferson, North Carolina, and London

LIBRARY OF CONGRESS CATALOGUING-IN-PUBLICATION DATA

Of muscles and men : essays on the sword and sandal film / edited by Michael G. Cornelius.
    p.   cm.
Includes bibliographical references and index.

ISBN 978-0-7864-6162-2
softcover : 50# alkaline paper ∞

1. Epic films—History and criticism. 2. Masculinity in motion pictures. 3. Men in motion pictures. I. Cornelius, Michael G.
PN1995.9.E79O42   2011
791.43'652—dc23   2011030754

BRITISH LIBRARY CATALOGUING DATA ARE AVAILABLE

© 2011 Michael G. Cornelius. All rights reserved

No part of this book may be reproduced or transmitted in any form or by any means, electronic or mechanical, including photocopying or recording, or by any information storage and retrieval system, without permission in writing from the publisher.

On the cover: Reg Park in the title role of *Hercules in the Haunted World*, 1961; details from poster art of the films (top) *Atlas*, 1961 and (bottom) *Samson and the Seven Miracles of the World*, 1961

Front cover design by Mark Berry (www.hot-cherry.co.uk)

Manufactured in the United States of America

McFarland & Company, Inc., Publishers
  Box 611, Jefferson, North Carolina 28640
    www.mcfarlandpub.com

Table of Contents

Introduction — Of Muscles and Men: The Forms and Functions of the Sword and Sandal Film
MICHAEL G. CORNELIUS 1

Hercules, Politics, and Movies
MARIA ELENA D'AMELIO 15

Hero Trouble: Blood, Politics, and Kinship in Pasolini's *Medea*
KRISTI M. WILSON 28

"To do or die manfully": Performing Heteronormativity in Recent Epic Films
JERRY B. PIERCE 40

From Maciste to Maximus and Company: The Fragmented Hero in the New Epic
ANDREW B. R. ELLIOTT 58

Reverent and Irreverent Violence: In Defense of Spartacus, Conan, and Leonidas
JOHN ELIA 75

"Civilization ... ancient and wicked": Historicizing the Ideological Field of 1980s Sword and Sandal Films
KEVIN M. FLANAGAN 87

Homer's Lies, Brad Pitt's Thighs: Revisiting the Pre-Oedipal Mother and the German Wartime Father in Wolfgang Petersen's *Troy*
ROBERT C. PIRRO 104

An Enduring Logic: Homer, *Helen of Troy*, and Narrative Mobility
LARRY T. SHILLOCK 124

"By Jupiter's Cock!" *Spartacus: Blood and Sand*, Video Games, and Camp Excess
    DAVID SIMMONS   144

Beefy Guys and Brawny Dolls: He-Man, the Masters of the Universe, and Gay Clone Culture
    MICHAEL G. CORNELIUS   154

Developments in Peplum Filmmaking: Disney's *Hercules*
    CHRIS PALLANT   175

Hercules Diminished? Parody, Differentiation, and Emulation in *The Three Stooges Meet Hercules*
    DANIEL O'BRIEN   187

About the Contributors   203
Index   207

Introduction

Of Muscles and Men: The Forms and Functions of the Sword and Sandal Film

MICHAEL G. CORNELIUS

Cinematic classification by genre is largely derivative of particular tones or atmospheres that films themselves reflect. These tonally descriptive monikers assume and imbue other characteristics onto a film so identified — distinctive qualities related to characterization, plot development, artistic style, and other such filmic expectations, however loosely defined — but identifying film genre tends to begin from a generic quality that acts as an indicator of the prevailing emotional mood or, indeed, *tone* of a work. A horror film, for example, seeks to create a sense of fear in its audience; while there are numerous differing permutations of the horror film, aspects that operate as differentiae to the overall species, horror films in general strive to create the same type of generic tone from one film to the other, regardless of subgenre, approach, or purpose: in short, they wish to make the viewer afraid. Other films genres work from this same guiding principle: romantic films create a tone reflective of sexual love and the coming together of two individuals; medical dramas generate an atmosphere that pivots on the generic "race-to-find-the-cure"; action films use explosions, car chases, and relentless pacing to establish a "rock-'em sock-'em" style and mood. Comedies make audiences laugh, tragedies cause them to weep, and thrillers bring them to the edge of their seats in breathless anticipation. Even the names of seemingly more esoterically-derived genres, such as fantasy and science fiction, reflect the tone of the films, where auteurs work to establish a mood that is either fantastical or, conversely, rooted in human visions, expectations, and anxieties over technology, exploration, and the future (i.e., fictions of science). Thus regardless of the nature and origin of each film genre, its appellation tends to develop from the particular tone or atmosphere the genre is most specifically connected to, is derived from and within, and/or works to re-craft, re-envision, and recreate.[1]

There are two significant exceptions to this rule.[2] The first is the Western, whose name is obviously derivative of the specific setting of these films. Though the setting is often less literal than it may seem (Westerns need not be set in the western portion of the United States, as Michael Mann's version of James Fenimore Cooper's *The Last of the Mohicans* [1992], for example, set in New York state during the French and Indian War, shows, and Westerns may not even be set in the United States at all, such as Ramesh Sippy's *Sholay* [1975], a Western set in India, or Tony Richardson's *Ned Kelly* [2003], an Australian interpretation of the genre, to name just two instances), and the classification of "Western" has come to be as evocative of tone and atmosphere as "fantasy" or "horror" is, it is certainly true that the genre's specific name-origin did not evolve from tone but rather place. Setting, then, becomes an essential characteristic in the crafting of a Western film itself; regardless of when the film is set, or what other liberties (of hundreds of possibilities) filmmakers may decide to take in creating the film, setting is essential to the Western movie; though not all Western films are specifically set in the southwestern United States, the landscape and place inherent to these films evokes that essential setting, replicating its bleak, panoramic rurality and often isolated, minimalist, "frontier" urbanity regardless of where or when a film is actually situated. Thus setting is, essentially, *the* definitive characteristic of the Western film, and the genre's name reflects this fundamentality; just as horror films must evoke horror, and fantasy films must evoke the fantastic (and romance films romance, etc.), so, too, must Western films evoke and conjure a strong sense of the American West to be classified as part of that particular genre.

The other exception from naming film genres based on tone, and perhaps the more interesting illustration, is the sword and sandal film. The sword and sandal film derives its common name from two objects, two aspects of a material culture that are recurrently utilized by the protagonists of the films themselves. It is the only genre of film thus named, and as such the premium placed on these objects, and other like representative aspects of the material continuum universally common to these films, insists that the discerning viewer question the relevance and significance of these objects to the overall genre itself. To put it plainly, the particular question this genre's name begs is, why swords? Why sandals? On the surface, the two objects appear to have little in common; indeed, they are almost diametrically opposed to the other in form, function, appearance, and significance. Swords, of course, are martial objects; they are distinctly masculine and often representative of the phallus. They can be viewed as objects of worship or great significance, especially in fantasy epics, such as John Boorman's *Excalibur* (1981) and other films based on the Arthurian tradition, but in sword and sandal movies swords tend to be more functional, a tool for the hero to use in hewing down enemies, fighting off mythological beasts, and in general saving the day. Swords in these films are made of metal, and often reflect the common Roman legion *gladius* style, though in some more fantasy-derived sword and sandal movies, such as John Milius' *Conan the Barbarian* (1982) and Don Cascarelli's *The Beastmaster* (1982), the hero's sword reflects contemporary re-envisionings of late medieval long sword design. In sword and sandal films, swords are almost always wielded by men, and are thus seen as distinct from objects that have a feminine or neutral sense of gender.[3] Yet they can be brandished by both hero and villain alike, whose swords are often indistinguishable from the other. Indeed, in the films' denouements, the sword is often lost or discarded, and the hero must look to his own strength, and his own hands, to save the day by crushing the monster, toppling the tower, or breaking the iron chains of bondage. Thus in sword and sandal films, swords are omnipresent, but usually in and of themselves not of utmost importance; largely they are an extension of the strongman hero himself, whose character and form acts cynosurally to the narrative.

Sandals, while also omnipresent in these films, are certainly much more unobtrusive to the eye. They are usually simple, pedestrian objects reflecting notions of pseudoclassical or premodern leathercraft, and very rarely do they take a position of import within the film itself.[4] Unlike swords, sandals reflect gender neutrality, as they are worn by men and women alike in the films. Symbolically speaking, footwear, according to Allison Protas, in its varying manifestations, denotes status: "Shoes might represent the lowly and the humble, or authority and power, depending upon the context." Bare feet, since they are associated with slavery and freedom from confinement, often reflect liberty, or the emancipation of the individual from some form of bondage. Thus in the films the sandal could be construed as symbolic of both freedom and a status that is, perhaps, neither high nor low. However, the symbolic value of the sandal is diminished by the fact that they tend to be found on the feet of all characters in the film. Indeed, they may perhaps be considered a distinguishing feature of these films less for their commonality within this species of movies and more for their general absence from other filmic genres. They neither aid the hero in any significant way nor play any role of general prominence, literally or symbolically, under the auspices of the movies themselves. They are there largely because they reflect what modern audiences would expect to see on the feet of individuals during the time periods in which these films are generally set. They are functional, yes, but hardly vital.

Thus while neither object can be deemed essential to the genre as a whole or to the heroes of these films, and while these objects seem enormously distinct from one another on the surface, they must be deemed important, and perhaps even essential, if for no other reason than that the film genre's name is derived from these two seemingly inconsequential objects. Yet what unites these two objects within the confines of these movies is what makes them essential to the sword and sandal genre overall: the sense of utility that connects them, one to the other, and to the sword and sandal hero himself. They are, in the end, both useful objects, sandals for motility and for establishing setting, and swords for violence, as a tool to aid the hero in his quest, and for further establishing the hyperdeveloped aura of masculinity that pervades these films. They are workmanlike matter; they *function* in particular ways for both the hero and the genre. It is no surprise that the other common names for sword and sandal movies likewise reflect this same sense of utility that distinguishes the nomenclature of this film genre. In Italy, these films are often referred to as peplum, a name first coined by French critics in the early 1960s that refers to the short "skirt" or "kilt" worn by the hero protagonists and other male characters in these films (after the Greek *peplos*, which began as a floor-length gown worn by Greek women and was eventually adapted by men into a garment that was shorter, more functional, and distinctly masculine in style and efficacy) (Günsberg 97–98). The peplum can trace its roots to Italian historical epics of the pre–World War I silent era, commencing with Luigi Maggi's *Gli ultimi giorni de Pompei* (*The Last Days of Pompeii*) (1908). The addition of the muscleman figure to these films, who first appeared in the guise of the character Ursus in Enrico Guazzoni's version of *Quo vadis?* (1913) but truly caught fire with the character of Maciste, a freed slave played by Bartolomeo Pagano in Giovanni Pastrone's *Cabiria* (1914, often considered the first true peplum film), aided in cementing the parameters and dynamics of the sword and sandal genre itself. Maggie Günsberg defines the peplum as "a fantasy genre celebrating musclebound masculinity in heroic action in the distant prehistorical, pre-industrialized past" (97). Peter Bondanella adds to this when he observes, "Peplum epics reject any neorealist interest in historical accuracy, or even any postrealist interest in psychological depth" (162). Instead, Bondanella labels the films "neomythological," reflecting both the scope and intent of the genre itself (159). Describing the neomythic aspects of the genre, Patrick Lucanio suggests that the films are

> highly stylized pictorialism, played out in panoramic widescreen and luscious color ... where polarized forces of good and evil vie for superiority over mortal (and immortal) souls: political and social behavior are reduced to manageable opposites—good and evil—where characters are clearly revealed as heroes and villains, and where notions of ideal moral behavior always triumph [2].

The peplum genre has been popular in Italy since *Cabiria*, though, like most film movements, its popularity has waxed and waned over the sprawl of the twentieth century. The growth of fascism in post–World War I Italy, culminating with the formation of the National Fascist Party in 1921, signaled a downturn in popularity for this First Wave of peplum heroes. Though individual peplum films were still made in Italy in the 1930s and 1940s, the genre did not return as a popular culture phenomenon until 1957, when Pietro Francisci directed a pair of low-budget Hercules films starring bodybuilder and former Mr. Universe Steve Reeves that became wildly popular not only in Italy but in the rest of Europe and North America as well. Both *Le fatiche di Ercole* (1958, released simply as *Hercules* in the United States in 1959) and *Ercole e la regina di Lidi* (released as *Hercules Unchained* in 1960) returned millions and millions of dollars in worldwide box office receipts. These successes prompted a slew of similar films, labeled the Second Wave of the peplum; Bondanella places the number of pepla made between 1957 and 1967 at 180 to 200 films, while Günsberg places the number closer to 300 (166, 97).[5] By the late 1960s the peplum had again receded in popularity, only to return magnificently with a Third Wave of films in the early 1980s, with the advent of such movies as the *Conan* series, the *Beastmaster* series, Luigi Cozzi's *Hercules* (1983) starring Lou Ferrigno, and the original *Clash of the Titans* (1981). The Third Wave lasted approximately seven years, but spawned numerous films, and, for the first time, popular (children's) television series including *Thundarr the Barbarian* (1980–1982); *He-Man and the Masters of the Universe* (first series, 1983–1985); and *She-Ra: Princess of Power* (1985–1987). The Fourth Wave of peplum film popularity commenced in 2000, when Ridley Scott's *Gladiator* grossed over $457 million worldwide and took home five Academy Awards, including Best Picture, Best Director, and Best Actor.[6] The genre has proven steadily if not spectacularly popular since, with such imitators as Wolfgang Petersen's *Troy* (2004), Oliver Stone's *Alexander* (2004), and Zack Snyder's *300* (2006), though current box office and critical reception suggests that the genre may again be moving into one of its periodic stages of decline.[7]

It is noteworthy that the Second, Third, and Fourth Waves of peplum or sword and sandal films have all become popular in the United States during periods of relative political conservatism, and in a way, sword and sandal movies are considered generically conservative, ideologically and politically speaking. The films are generally highly patriarchal, reinforcing traditional masculine and feminine societal roles, and espouse high moralistic standards (orgies, drug use, seduction, murder, and other such debaucheries are often depicted in these films, but those who partake tend to be on the villainous side and are usually destroyed by the film's end). From this perspective, the values these films espoused in the mid–1950s, 1980s, and 2000s reflect traditional, "American" political ideologies and ideals that were prevalent at those times: "righting wrongs, slaying enemies, and destroying marble palaces," as one critic puts it (Chapman 4). Nonetheless, in many ways, the movies are also subversively ideological as well. Governments often fall in these films, which was seen as a selling point of the genre, as graphic posters routinely promised and depicted the fall of tyrants or the toppling of empires. Religious institutions were likewise viewed as untrustworthy, as authoritative religious leaders and brutal, totalitarian cults were frequent antagonists in these films as well. The strongman hero often fought for those too weak, too poor, or too disenfranchised to fight for themselves against a strong, patriarchal, central government or religious authority; rarely, indeed, was the hero fighting for himself, his own cause, or his own people. Thus while many of the social mores of the patristic tradition were maintained by these films, those institutions that generally work to establish the patriarchy were often the antagonistic counter to the heroic strongman, a clashing dualistic ideology of masculinity that the films often both reveled in and, thematically speaking, largely ignored (at best, these films deliberated more on examining the nature and manifestations of patriarchy available to maintain order, and did not question whether the essence of patriarchy was in and of itself at issue here). Therefore, while it may be tempting to try and connote one particular political ideology to an entire corpus of films, it is hardly apt; while individual peplums or series of peplums often express political observations, the entire genre is generally, in and of itself, less than concerned with ideology.

Rather, the cynosure of the sword and sandal film is the form of the muscleman hero himself. As Bondanella notes, the "single most important feature of the Italian peplum is its typical protagonist: a strong man, usually a bodybuilder, whose muscular physique dominates the screen and defines the nature of the various plots" (163). Günsberg echoes this when she writes, "These films are particularly renowned for their depiction of mythical (Achilles, Ajax, Hercules, Theseus, Ulysses), invented (Maciste), literary (Saetta, Ursus), historical (Spartacus, Thaur) or biblical (Goliath, Samson) apotheoses of the heroic male body" (97). David Chapman takes this focus on masculinity one step further when he argues that "masculine torsos, nude and straining with effort, are at the heart of the message here" (19). Yet what is the message contained within these muscular forms? In presenting the male, in placing the male body at the forefront of the entire genre, the sword and sandal movie treats the male form as no other genre of films does. Generally speaking, in film, the male form is obtunded or, if celebrated, is done so in collusion with the female form, placing the two naked or nearly-naked forms side by side, suggesting both heteronormative eroticism and tantalizing the male gaze with thoughts of sexual and social dominance. Yet in the sword and sandal movie, the revealed male form is habitually presented on screen alone, continually exposed, and put on display for an audience Bondanella rightly describes as being "composed of men" (178). Günsberg reinforces the significance of highlighting the male form in the sword and sandal film when she writes, "In particular, consumption of the enlarged cinematic screen-as-surface also offers participation in a dynamic of desire set in motion by the various mechanisms of identification, voyeurism, fetishism, and scopophilia" (104–105). Normally, she argues, films generally—and generically—sexualize the female form:

> Fetishism of the female, rather than the male, body, then, dominates in cinema, resulting from anxieties concerning fragmentation and sexual difference rooted in basic fears of powerlessness. These fears are commonly relocated onto the female body, specifically the body of the m/other, separation of which is a vital part of individuation and recognition of a unified, independent self [107].

In the peplum, Günsberg contends, these fears are placed on to the *male* form:

> The excessive, overdetermined and parodic nature of the signifying properties of the heroic, built body, pulls away from the furthest opposite extremes of femininity.... This fetishistic display of the male body may be read as indicating anxieties about

both sexual difference and fragmentation of the body, under cover of excess and parody which function, like Freudian negation, to couch affirmation of an anxiety in denial [108–109].

Yet the hyperdeveloped male form in these movies does not act as a nexus of anxiety nor, indeed, is it treated in any parodic sense. If anything, the exaggerated muscularity of the sword and sandal strongman seems to unite the potentially fragmented form; just as the hero's muscles work to save the day and restore what was wrong, so, too, does his form come to represent that which unifies, restores, and recovers what had been lost. Chapman notes that, in both advertisements for these films and at numerous points during the movies themselves, "the hero's physique is usually shown ... performing some destructive feat of strength so that the musculature is displayed as it flexes, twists, and drips with perspiration" (26). Indeed, it is this *functionality* of the hero's body — its very utility — that is key to understanding how the male body should be read in the genre itself.

It is no accident that another name for this genre is the "strongman movie" (in Italian, the *fozuto*, derived from the word for a strongman, *forzuti*,) a name that would seem, at first, to go against the predominant material theme reflecting the other common generic names for these films. However, like the sword, the sandal, and the peplum, the hero's body exists as a tool, to serve a purpose, to *function*, in the larger schema of the film. Günsberg rightly notes that these movies "[allow] for little character development" (110). Rather, characterization in sword and sandal films is established by "what the hero does and how he does it" (Günsberg 110). Yet *what* the hero does (save the day) and *how* he does it (kill the monster, rescue the virgin, topple the tyrant, right the wrong) is all accomplished through his own singular muscularity. In fact, the hero's muscular development *is* his essential character development: "The hard musculature is key in differentiating the hero from other men, who either have less or no muscles, or whose bodies are not exposed to the camera eye" (Günsberg 116). The strongmen heroes of these films become different from other men, both within the confines of these movies and in the wider popular culture, through their forms, developing into "heroic protectors" whose existence is a combination of service and strength. "Heroic masculinity in the peplum also constantly defines itself through differentiation from other types of masculinity," Günsberg rightly argues, though not because of its parodic or excessive nature, but because of the functionality of the strongman's muscles themselves (115). Irmbert Schenk labels peplum heroes "saviors," but they are saviors not because of their innate, overdeveloped senses of right and wrong, but because their singular muscularity functions, in many ways, for no other real, distinct purpose. They must act when no one else can, not because it is the right thing to do (or, to be fair about this, not just because it is the right thing to do) but because they are the *only* individuals who possess the means to do so. When Conan destroys the evil cult leader Thulsa Doom, he acts not for any greater good, but out of revenge; when

Gladiator's Maximus kills Commodus, he, too, acts out of revenge. In the recent retelling of *Clash of the Titans* (2010), Perseus kills the Kraken to avenge the loss of his family at the hands of Hades. Spartacus, in the Starz television series *Spartacus: Blood and Sand*, likewise acts out of revenge for the death of his wife and his betrayal by the Roman *legatus* Gaius Claudius Glaber. None of these acts reflects noble intentions, and despite their well-deserved status as heroes, none of these men can rightly be labeled noble in intent. Yet each of them is viewed as a savior of an entire group or race of people. What they do—and *how* they do it—vociferates volumes more than *why* they do it. Schenk considers these figures "old-new heroes of individual and collective strength," and his description of their forms aptly encapsulates the dualistic nature of the sword and sandal hero; they are individual beings who possess a collective strength—i.e., the strength of ten, twenty, thirty men—and as such are called upon to act or to commit to action when others simply cannot, not because they lack the will to do so, but because, rather, they lack the *tools* to do so. All inhabitants of Argos would have longed to kill the Kraken and preserve their home, but only Perseus had the means to do so. His motivation for doing so—relatively futile attempts on the part of the filmmaker to craft some semblance of characterization—are largely irrelevant. He has the tools to do the deed, and thus by the dictates of the genre, act he must.

The other material aspects the genre's name manifests—the sword, the sandal, the peplum skirt—all work to enhance the essential muscularity of the central, strongman figure. The sword highlights the bicep and triceps, the power of the arms; the sandals and peplum enhance the muscularity of the thighs, calves, and legs. The lack of shirt—commonplace to the genre—emphasizes the torso in all its manly, thewy glory. Deborah E. McDowell suggests that "the peplum—film and kilt—cast the white [masculine] body as spectacle" (361). This is so, but the viewer gazes in awe upon these forms not for what they represent, but, rather, for what they are capable of accomplishing.

Each of the essays in this collection are concerned, in their own ways, with these questions of masculinity and utility, with examining a genre that so adroitly presents the male in ways that are continually heroic, violent, fleshy, and, ultimately, useful. To paraphrase Chapman, masculine forms, straining with effort, is what this collection is about, too. This is demonstrated in the first essay presented here, "Hercules, Politics, and Movies," by Maria Elena D'Amelio. D'Amelio examines the interrelations between the Italian Hercules movies of the Second Wave of peplum films and how the strongman hero reflects a pivotal historical era in modern Italian history. As a response to and redaction of Italy's recent Fascist history, Hercules represents both a path away from the past (and perhaps a fantasia on what might have been, had some representative strongman stepped forward for the collective will who lacked the tools to act) as well as a projection of forward-thinking values. Writing of these same films, Günsberg notes that pepla offer "validation of outdated traditional male muscle power in an era of economic boom and industrial advancement" (102). D'Amelio suggests that the depiction of the strongman, while representing perhaps old-fashioned or slightly outmoded manifestations of masculinity, nonetheless also rings forth with a strong sense of progression and promise for the future, a connection to both a dim past and hopeful outcomes for tomorrow.

Likewise, Kristi M. Wilson, in "Hero Trouble: Blood, Politics, and Kinship in Pasolini's *Medea*," observes the manner in which filmmakers—in this case, the famed auteur Pier Paolo Pasolini — use the figure of the muscleman and the sword and sandal genre as a means of crafting connections to a larger political society as a whole. However, in Pasolini's *Medea*, Wilson finds a specific critique at play, a sword and sandal film that rebukes the same past that D'Amelio argues the Hercules films both wrestle and reckon with. Thus the same filmmaking tradition both critiques and rehabilitates images and ideologies of the past, a difficult task requiring the strength of Hercules, indeed.

Sword and sandal films are not only concerned with what is past, of course; they are also very much critiques of present social conventions and gendered mores. Often, though, in connoting present to past, by examining contemporary ideas in a classical milieu, these films complicate the very social relationships they mean to examine or critique. In "'To do or die manfully': Performing Heteronormativity in Recent Epic Films," for example, Jerry B. Pierce demonstrates that Fourth Wave peplum films tend to exaggerate the presumed heterosexuality of the strongman hero in each film. Unlike earlier sword and sandal adventures, these films place the hero in a contemporary, patristic/paternal condition, going to great lengths to show heroes such as Maximus (*Gladiator*), Leonidas (*300*), and Hector (*Troy*) as husbands and fathers. Whereas the sword and sandal hero has often been played against submissive females who clearly represent the patriarchy's traditional view of the non-dominant role of women in society, in these more contemporary versions of the genre, the role of woman is to reassure the viewer of the heterosexual privilege and standing of the strongman hero; otherwise his oft bare body and masculine, homosocial company may suggest homoerotic underpinnings to an audience that has steadily become more savvy about sexual messaging in film. Chapman writes that "many secret sensations and unspoken desires washed up on the shores of modern masculinity itself" in peplum films, and that the thewy bodies on display in these movies may just be "tickling other deeper feelings in the movie-going public" (13). Concern over these "secret sensations" has caused contemporary creators of sword and sandal films to embellish the heterosexuality of their heroes, often by contrasting them with an exaggerated, non-normative sexuality, often exemplified by their male antagonists. Of course, this contemporary vision of "heroic" heterosexuality is at odds with the classical mores of these films' setting, creating a type of cultural impasse when old and new are thrust side-by-side in conflicting, and not conciliatory, ways.

Andrew B. R. Elliott also looks at the contemporary filmic strongman; in

"From Maciste to Maximus and Company: The Fragmented Hero in the New Epic," Elliott hypothesizes that the "old-fashioned" and outmoded forms of masculinity present in Second Wave peplum create a disparity with contemporary visions of masculinity and the masculine hero in the sword and sandal genre. Utility here is again at question: Elliott examines the function of the peplum hero in modern film, and suggests that the creation of a new, fragmented hero represents a modern perspective of hyperdeveloped masculinity. Thus how we view these heroes, how we use them, and what audiences expect from them, has changed. John Elia is likewise concerned with the functioning of the masculine, specifically with respect to violence. "Reverent and Irreverent Violence: In Defense of Spartacus, Conan, and Leonidas" suggests that the acts perpetrated by the heroes of sword and sandals film function as modern day parables about reverence and irreverence, much like the Homeric tales of ancient Greece. Elia observes that the deeds of these musclemen come with special moral challenges, since they are often called upon to act in accordance to sacred duties to protect humanity and yet to keep violence within reverent limits. Thus despite his otherworldly strength, limitations are placed upon the utility of the strongman's functioning; bounded by dictates of morality, the *forzuti* protagonist must conform to the heroic principles of the sword and sandal genre as well.

Kevin M. Flanagan's work is perhaps best to conclude this section of the collection, since he endeavors to consign the larger genre into a particular ideological niche, based largely on these films' understandings and representations of masculinity in its many and varied manifestations. In "'Civilization ... ancient and wicked': Historicizing the Ideological Field of 1980s Sword and Sandal Films," Flanagan uses *Conan the Barbarian* to demonstrate a conservative ideological bent—politically, socially, structurally—to Third Wave peplum and, by larger extension, explores the rudiments of ideology in other categorizations of sword and sandal films as well. In many ways, Flanagan argues that the holistic and whole-hearted embrace of masculinity in these films can only be read conservatively, that a chief function of the masculine is the preservation of dominant social structures that have served the capitalist patriarchy so well. Flanagan also notes that heroic masculinity is at work in these films as well; if, as he argues, these films uphold patriarchal readings of society and social mores, they also dictate that with such masculine powers (both in the collective and muscular senses of the word) comes a measurable and measured sense of accountability to act in accord to not only maintain the society but to uphold its (masculine) best as well. To paraphrase a recent popular superhero film (another type of film highly concerned with presenting the male), with great muscles, comes great responsibility.

The second half of this collection examines particular films located within the nexus of the sword and sandal genre, with each essayist adding to the arguments above by exploring specific examples in which masculinity engages form or function within the confines of one particular filmic expression. Robert C.

Pirro begins this section with "Homer's Lies, Brad Pitt's Thighs: Revisiting the Pre-Oedipal Mother and the German Wartime Father in Wolfgang Petersen's *Troy*." Using Petersen's 2004 interpretation of Homer's *Iliad* as a case study, Pirro provides a psychoanalytic and historically-informed reaction to a film that, perhaps more than any other sword and sandal movie, places the strongman hero into a larger familial as well as political context. *Troy* is a film rife with interrelated dependent relationships—parent to child, sibling to sibling, husband to wife, sovereign to subject—whose pre-oedipal valences are conditioned, Pirro argues, by Petersen's early childhood experiences of Germany's postwar devastation. According to Pirro, in presenting the male in *Troy*—in showing the function of what he describes as the masochistically-driven muscular male form, as encapsulated by the character of Achilles, played by Brad Pitt—Petersen demonstrates the pre-oedipal basis of male exhibitionism, transforming the usually opaque male form in these films into a source of sexual and social anxiety that must be symbolically resolved at the film's end with the death of the hero. Likewise, Larry T. Shillock draws inspiration from Homer and another film variation of his famous text, the 2003 USA Network miniseries *Helen of Troy*. In "An Enduring Logic: Homer, *Helen of Troy*, and Narrative Mobility," Shillock argues for the place of women in the larger context of these films, using the figure of Helen of Troy from both Homer's text and the varying film adaptations of Helen's tale to suggest that women's functioning in these films is not limited to the roles generally cast to them by the larger patriarchy. At issue here are the means through which Helen's characterization performs—with an emphasis on performativity—within the larger masculine sphere she inhabits; by achieving narrative and even ideological motility, Helen not only crafts a case for the larger functioning of women throughout a genre that either minimizes or sensationalizes them, but also demonstrates that the genre's fixation on the utility of being is not constrained to the male form, but may be placed on to the female form as well, creating new opportunities for other Helens and, consequently, new narratives that re-imagine women's social motility.

David Simmons, in "'By Jupiter's Cock!' *Spartacus: Blood and Sand*, Video Games, and Camp Excess," suggests that the popular 2010 Starz Network television series *Spartacus: Blood and Sand* derives its main narrative structures not from popular peplum films, but rather from contemporary video game forms. Using both camp aspects inherent to the series and the dialogue, structure, and artistic representation of violence in the show itself, Simmons creates a powerful argument that perhaps the next generation of sword and sandal filmmaking may owe as much to current obsessions over video games as it will to the previous waves of peplumic film. In *Spartacus: Blood and Sand*, Simmons traces the blankness of the main character (suggesting that Spartacus himself functions as a type of avatar, or player, for the viewer), the development of the plot (with its increasing "levels" of difficulty or difficulties needing to be overcome), the manner of the fighting, and the depiction of stylized violence directly back to video game culture. Crafting larger connections to both audience and reception, Simmons demonstrates that the sword and sandal genre's obsession with masculine utility may be taken quite literally, as a representation of the audience at "play," as well as symbolically.

My own contribution to the collection, "Beefy Guys and Brawny Dolls: He-Man, the Masters of the Universe, and Gay Clone Culture," explores the juvenilization of the sword and sandal film. In adolescent representations of the genre, including the 1980s Filmation studios syndicated thirty-minute action cartoon series *He-Man and the Masters of the Universe*, women are largely absent from the worlds of men, making an inherently homosocial and male-centric genre even more so. My essay compares the material culture of the He-Man action figure with the corresponding social movement of the gay clone, both of which emerged at roughly the same time, suggesting not a correlation of one to the other but reflections of social anxieties about the movement away from a male-constructed and dominated view of masculinity itself. By focusing on the hyperdeveloped male form, and then reproducing it ceaselessly, both *He-Man* and the gay clone draw attention to and simultaneously obtund the muscular male form; taking away the uniqueness of the strongman character results in the delineation of said figure's masculinity and the heroic form he generally represents. Chris Pallant also looks at a juvenile adaptation of a common peplum hero/myth. "Developments in Peplum Filmmaking: Disney's *Hercules*" explores the generic dynamics of the eponymous 1997 animated feature. Unlike *He-Man*, Disney's *Hercules* is a much more traditional take on the peplum, casting a classical, mythological hero in the role of *forzuti* who rights wrongs, defeats the bad guy, and generally saves the day. *Hercules* even shows its classical bent through highly stylized animation that reflects Grecian artistic forms. Yet even in such a faithful adaptation of the sword and sandal model Pallant demonstrates an anxiety in the inherent conflict between the originating genre and its juvenile facsimile. Pallant argues that the Disney animated feature, itself a distinct and nuanced genre of film, ultimately clashes in key ways against the peplum, creating a film that, in the end, cannot fulfill the dictates of either genre successfully.

Modern sensibilities and constructions of receptivity often conflict with filmic depictions of the ancient past, as filmmakers attempt to balance the dictates of history and/or genres based in ancient times versus the expectations and mores of contemporary audiences. Sometimes, however, this inherent tension can be utilized by the filmmaker to create an interesting commentary on both ancient and contemporary social structures and strictures. In the concluding essay in this collection, Daniel O'Brien demonstrates this in "Hercules Diminished? Parody, Differentiation, and Emulation in *The Three Stooges Meet Hercules*." A peplumic parody, *The Three Stooges Meet Hercules* mocks the sword and sandal genre's fascination with and depiction of hyperconstructed muscular masculinity, arguing that such overdeveloped male forms do not connote heroism but rather violence, thuggishness, and simplicity. Yet, at the same time, the film cannot hide the desirability of such forms as well, ultimately recrafting the peplum hero into a more modern man, one who is still singularly developed but who, nonetheless, possesses modern social mores regarding intelligence, women, governance, and justice, suggesting, perhaps, that the ideal man is both contemporary and old-fashioned, with one muscular leg in the past and one stepping towards the future.

McDowell concludes that "the whys and wherefores of masculinity are far-flung and often mutually contradictory" (363). It is true that the sword and sandal genre can never hope to present every aspect of masculinity that continually complicates and obfuscates representations of the male in both high and popular culture. Yet peplumic tradition does insist on the utility of what is male, on creating masculine figures that are overly developed but that, through this exaggerated muscularity, reflect a sense of usefulness as well. Ultimately, we admire the sword and sandal strongman not because of how he looks or how bulging his biceps are but, rather, because of what he has done or, to be more precise, because of the inherent possibilities of what he can do with his oversized, overdeveloped physique. Like the objects that give the genre its two most common names, heroic men in these films are extraordinary in their sense of functionality; useful not as objects of a representative gaze but rather as tools perfectly appointed for the completion of impossible tasks—slaying monsters, toppling towers, ending the reigns of tyrants—that no mere mortal would be capable of implementing. Ultimately, sword and sandal films remind us that masculinity is perhaps best admired when it is constructive, protective, and obliging. In the end, the hero's muscles are like his peplum, his sword, or his sandals—not necessarily unique unto themselves, but dead useful all the same.

Notes

1. I am, of course, not the first critic to make this distinction. Kevin M. Flanagan, in his essay in this collection, "'Civilization ... ancient and wicked': Historicizing the Ideological Field of 1980s Sword and Sandal Films," makes a similar, if briefer, observation.

2. It should be noted that there are subgenres within larger generic fields—such as the martial arts movie, a subgenre of the action film, or the "torture porn" film, a recent addition to the horror genre—whose names are not derivative of the tone or atmosphere of the movie itself, though that descriptive aspect is covered by the larger genre the subgenre is housed within.

3. There are rare sword and sandal films that feature female heroic protagonists, such as *Red Sonja* (1985), directed by Richard Fleischer. Such instances, however, are exceedingly rare. Predictably, the common movie poster for the film features actor Arnold Schwarzenegger (famous for the *Conan* series) more prominently displayed than the heroine played by Brigitte Nielsen, with a larger profile and, also tellingly, a much larger sword.

4. Perhaps the only exception to this rule is when the sandals belong to Hermes/Mercury, and thus have the power of flight. These specific footwear make highly infrequent appearances in sword and sandal films, and most recently appeared in Chris Columbus'

adaptation of Rick Riordan's popular juvenile novel, *Percy Jackson and the Olympians: The Lightning Thief* (2010), where Percy, the titular hero and son of Poseidon, borrows a pair of the winged sandals from the son of Hermes. Interestingly, this film is more a pastiche of sword and sandal movies than a traditional take on the genre itself, which can best be viewed by the fact that Hermes' sandals are depicted as a pair of high-top sneakers. It is perhaps significant that in the re-telling of such Greek myths as the tale of Perseus, where the sandals of Hermes play a prominent role, the footwear is often written out of the film. For example, in both the original and re-make of *Clash of the Titans*, Perseus' sandals are replaced by Bellerophon's winged horse Pegasus, a more striking means of flight for the hero in these versions of the Perseid legend.

5. The discrepancy here is caused, at least in part, by each researcher's shifting means of precisely defining a peplum film, and by imprecise record-keeping on the part of filmmakers and distributors, since so many of these films were made on tiny, shoestring budgets and had their names frequently changed as they moved from one country, or one part of a country, to another.

6. All box office data used in this chapter is obtained from www.boxofficemojo.com.

7. Critics often disagree on the appropriate categorization of peplum films; some critics argue that the First Wave identified here do not represent true sword and sandal movies, while others fail to recognize the Fourth Wave as commanding enough significance to be constituted as such. Still, for the purposes of this essay, the First Wave of the peplum runs roughly from 1914 to 1924/5; the Second Wave from 1957 to 1966/7; the Third Wave from 1981 to 1987/8; and the Fourth Wave from 2000 to the present day, though this wave, distinct from the others, seems more representative of a slow and steady progression of sword and sandal films as opposed to the popular gluts viewed in the other waves. For more on the history of the sword and sandal/peplum film, see Günsberg 97–100; Bondanella 159–179. Irmbert Schenk provides a brief but detailed history of the First Wave of peplum films in his work "The Cinematic Support to National(istic) Mythology: The Italian Peplum 1910–1930" (see Works Cited). It is interesting to observe that other scholars represented in this text codify the peplum/sword and sandal genre differently; rather than impose my own particular classification onto the various authors herein, I decided to let their own systems of classification stand, to more accurately demonstrate the inherent tension regarding the codification of these films into particular "Waves" or groupings by date.

WORKS CITED

Bondanella, Peter. *A History of Italian Cinema*. New York: Continuum, 2009.
Chapman, David. *Retro Stud: Muscle Movie Posters from Around the World*. Portland, OR: Collectors Press, 2002.
Günsberg, Maggie. *Italian Cinema: Gender and Genre*. New York: Palgrave McMillan, 2005.
Lucanio, Patrick. *With Fire and Sword: Italian Spectacles on American Screens 1958–1968*. Metuchen, NJ: Scarecrow Press, 1994.
McDowell, Deborah E. "Pecs and Reps: Muscling in on Race and the Subject of Masculinities." In *Race and the Subject of Masculinities*. Eds. Harry Stecopolous and Michael Uebel. Durham: Duke University Press, 1997. 361–386.
Protas, Allison, ed. *Dictionary of Symbolism*. University of Michigan Symbolism Project. Web. 28 Jan 11.
Schenk, Irmbert. "The Cinematic Support to National(istic) Mythology: The Italian Peplum 1910–1930." In *Globalization, Cultural Identities, and Media Representations*. Eds. Natascha Gentz and Stefan Kramer. Albany: State University of New York Press, 2006. 153–168.

Hercules, Politics, and Movies

Maria Elena D'Amelio

The legend of Hercules finds its apogee in the Italian mythological movies of the Sixties, commonly called peplum or the sword and sandal genre. The Hercules series were low-budget productions made to exploit the international success of the Italian movie *Hercules* (*Le fatiche di ercole*, 1958), for in this film Italian producers thought they had found the "magic recipe" to make low-cost movies with a high commercial success that could successfully compete with Hollywood epics. Generally the peplum revolved around a Herculean-type character played by an American bodybuilder performing feats of bravery in order to restore a legitimate sovereign against an evil dictator. The strongman character who starred in the Hercules movies was not only the semi-god Hercules, with more than twenty films between 1957 and 1965, but also Maciste, a Herculean character who had his cinematic origins in the 1914 silent film *Cabiria* and was resuscitated for this series.

My purpose here is to investigate the connections between the Hercules myth, the peplum genre, and contemporary Italy. The strong, moral righteous hero of the Italian peplum flourished during a crucial turning point in Italy's history, during the so-called "Italian economic miracle," which catapulted Italy into a new era of economic, social, political, and cultural changes dominated by an industrial economy and mass culture. This study takes what can be described as a contextualist approach to these movies, analyzing the way the filmic texts engage with particular historical and social issues, such as the representation of the tyrant and the "repressed" memory of the past fascist regime, the relation with the Italian politics of the time, and the influence of American culture in shaping the social and intertextual representation of Hercules.

This essay examines how and why the character of Hercules became so popular in the Italian movies of late Fifties and early Sixties, and how Hercules represents and negotiates some of the Italian political issues of the time. While the Herculean strongman's goal is to rid society of the evil ruler, the hero always refuses the political power for himself; he'd rather leave the power in the hands of the legitimate heir to the throne. I show that this is the way in which the peplum genre deals with the "repressed memory" of the fascist regime: how the danger of a popular leader turning into a fascist dictator is exorcised through the narrative of a strongman hero who saves the country but refuses to be in charge of any political mandate. Finally, I show that the Herculean upper-body of the American bodybuilders playing Hercules symbolizes an idea of "American-ness" that relates to the Italian perception of the United States in the aftermath of the war. Ultimately the American Hercules in the Italian peplum genre represents the America of Truman and the Marshall Plan, and the lure of the American consumerist way of life that the Marshall Plan intended to establish in the postwar Italian society.

Echoes of Fascist Memory

As stated by Italian film historian Vittorio Spinazzola, the post–World War II period brought a surge of interest in the first experiences of democratic life — after the fascist dictatorship — that could not be totally ignored by the popular movies of the time, such as the *film d'appendice* and the peplum (61). The *film d'appendice*, coming out a decade before the movie *Hercules*, was significantly affected by the influence of a Dumas-style hero, such as the Count of Monte Cristo, a hero who struggles for revenge. Restoring order and hierarchy after the removal of a cruel usurper is natural to him, though not his main aim.

Conversely, the peplum genre creates a mythical hero who fights for a higher purpose, such as the salvation of an entire community, rather than the emptiness of personal revenge. For instance, in the movie *The Two Gladiators* (*I Due Gladiatori*, 1964), the brave legionnaire Crassus turns out to be the twin brother of the cruel Emperor Commodus, leading some Roman senators to plot to unseat the cruel brother in favor of the good one. Reluctant at first, Crassus eventually overthrows Commodus in an effort to save the people from Commodus' barbaric methods of governance. A sequence in the movie depicted through intercutting shows the starving people of Rome pleading for bread being ridiculed by guards, while a feasting Commodus wastes large quantities of food on himself and his dog. In response, Crassus leads the people's revolt against the emperor and is successful. However, when the same people, led by the Senators, want to crown him Emperor, the Legionnaire refuses, stating that "power is an inebriating drink, and I might get drunk" (*The Two Gladiators*).

The strongman hero in the sword and sandal genre would always rather leave the power in the hands of his sidekick, usually a young prince who is the rightful heir to the throne, than hold on to it himself. According to Luciano Canfora, the Greek word *Demokratia* was often used in Roman times to indicate the "dominion over the people," and that the term *demokràtor* was often used when referring to a dictator (9). Hence, Canfora implies that being a leader of the people might result—in extreme cases—in a conversion to a popular dictator. Canfora also states:

> It appears so, in all its certainty, the extreme closeness of embarrassing and perhaps different forms classified by the doctrine as distant or opposed. It seems undeniable that the political experiment, or political "remedy," that has helped better to create this feeling of closeness, and to confuse the ideas of not only the masses, but also of the political theorists, is the Caesarism-Bonapartism-fascism [10].

Yet the danger of a popular leader turning into a fascist dictator, and the memory that this danger could trigger in the minds of the Italian audience after World War II, are exorcised through the narrative and the iconography of the peplum. In a sequence in *Hercules Against the Tyrants of Babylon* (*Ercole Contro I Tiranni di Babilonia*, 1964), for instance, Hercules fights alone, bare-handed, against the well-equipped Babylonian army. Babylon—in the fictional world of this movie—is a vast empire that has conquered Greece and made its inhabitants slaves, with the exception of Hercules, who arrives in the heart of the empire to free the queen Esperia. Hercules is represented as the hero of the people, using only his bare hands and superhuman strength to defeat the Babylonian army and free the masses from slavery. In terms of film language, Hercules is often shown in medium shot, with the horizon at his back. Also, he is often shot from a low angle, standing above his enemies or overlooking the masses. Similarly, the same type of shots and plot may be seen in *Son of Samson* (*Maciste nella Valle dei Re*, 1960). Here, it is Egypt that is oppressed by the evil kingdom of Persia. Again, the strongman character Maciste (who is the alter ego of Hercules in many peplum movies, as well as Goliath or Samson) arrives to head the revolt and free the masses from the evil oppressor.

Therefore the recent and yet promptly removed memory of the fascist regime in Italy is sublimated through the representation of the tyrant, while the strongman hero is purged of his potential dictatorial element inherent to the role of popular leader. Richard Dyer, talking about the Hercules series in his book *White: Essays in Race and Culture*, rightly points out that "it is usual for the hero to restore traditional authority. Significantly, unlike Mussolini, he is never himself ruler, nor explicitly identified with leadership" (174). In the Hercules series the main protagonists never seek power for themselves. Rather, they refuse to take any political office, and always reject the throne offered to them by the people they saved. Instead, at the end of the film the strongman hero is ready to ride out for a new adventure or, conversely, decides to settle down in the tranquility of the Arcadian countryside. In the movie *Hercules Unchained* (*Ercole e la Regina di Lidia*, 1959), for instance, Hercules must save his wife Iole from the clutches of the Argive army chief, who also wants to take over the vacant throne of Thebes. Yet after saving Thebes from the foreign usurper, Hercules leaves the throne of Thebes to Creon, the legitimate heir, to go away with the faithful Iole.

Hercules and Maciste fight against tyranny and, at times, against the danger of tyranny. In the movie *Hercules in the Haunted World* (*Ercole al Centro della Terra*, 1961), the hero must save the princess Deianira from Lico, the king's advisor who aspires to take over the throne. In the first frame we see Lico in medium shot, completely dressed in black, against a red and black background, calling for "the evil that will dominate the world" (*Hercules in the Haunted World*). Colors in the peplum genre are crucial semiotic signs that help indicate the characters' moral identity. Director Duccio Tessari, in his *Ten Tips for Those Who Want to Make a Historical Film*, states, "The colors of the costumes are well differentiated: white or yellow ones for the good, the bad in black or red ones. The public should immediately recognize the characters of each side" (qtd. in Locatelli 14).

That notwithstanding, the all-black raiment of a sorcerer who aspires to become a dictator may remind the Italian audience of the fascist uniform that had recently dominated Italian politics and society. The memory of this recent past is also present in the scenes of violence, war, and oppression against villages and towns. In the final sequence of *Hercules Against the Tyrants of Babylon*, for example, the film depicts the people moving, tired and wounded, toward their houses. This sequence recalls images of the devastation that Italy endured during the War, images that were already sadly familiar to Italians and had been displayed by the neo-realist cinema without the "filter" of the peplum's imaginary, mythical past.

In addition, the memory of foreign occupation and the conflict between republicans of Salò and partisans that followed the armistice of September 8, 1943, are recalled in the movie *The Loves of Hercules* (*Gli Amori di Ercole*, 1960) through the words of the tyrant Licos. Licos has imprisoned Deianira, Queen of Ecalia, and has taken over the throne. Hercules then urges the people in the surrounding countryside to march on the king's palace, in order to rescue Deianira. In the meantime, a messenger tells Licos that the citizens have joined Hercules and the peasants in their uprising:

> Licos: Our soldiers are stronger than this rabble.
> Messenger: Many soldiers will throw down their weapons; they won't fight against their brothers.
> Licos: So let's kill these deserters to set an example.
> Messenger: But it's a big risk!
> Licos: We have no choice! It's the only way to quell the revolt [*The Loves of Hercules*].

Although this dialogue may seem standardized and typical of the epic genre, the images evoking brothers to slaughter each other, and the use of words such as "fight against their brothers" and "deserters," actually recall the collective memory of the civil war after the fall of Fascism. At a time when the Italians were widely discredited for their acceptance of Mussolini's regime, the sacrifice of the Italian Resistance did much to salvage Italy's tarnished image, and succeeded in creating a lasting tradition of anti–Fascism. The long term objective of the Resistance was to rouse the ordinary Italian by settling scores with the past and by acknowledging the complicity of the masses under Fascism. However, this long term objective was never reached, because, as Carlo Pavone states, "paradoxically, the Resistance has partially hidden in the Italian conscience the collective responsibility toward Fascism. For the Resistance, which was the work of a minority, has been used by the majority of Italians to exonerate themselves from their fascist past" (190). The peplum genre, in evoking images of foreign occupations, war, and heroic resistance, negotiates the complex and controversial memory of this past, and the difficult transition from fascism to democracy that the Italian society faced after the war.

The Tyrant

A stout man with a receding hairline and a deep scar on his face sits at a lavishly set table. While eating with pleasure, he tells his companions his good news. Hercules is dead, and tomorrow he will have the hero's son Illus executed. Then he summons a slave girl and introduces her to his guests as Alcinoe, the daughter of the king he had killed and whose throne he usurped. This is how the despot plotting to destroy Thebes is introduced, in the film *Goliath and the Dragon* (*La Vendetta di Ercole*, 1960).

Through the character and the death of the tyrant, the peplum genre negotiates the controversial and repressed memory of the death of Mussolini. Ultimately, the death of the tyrant is always cathartic, coming at the climax of the diegetic plot, and is commonly depicted as a horrifying death. This brutality recalls the exemplary punishment of Mussolini, who was executed by the partisans along with his mistress Claretta Petacci. Mussolini's execution is still a subject of controversy in Italy: in killing the dictator and being ready to move on, the Italian society failed to question itself about its specific and collective responsibilities during the fascist regime (Luzzatto 61).

In *Hercules Unchained*, the head of the Argive army, who attempted to seize the throne of Thebes by trickery and force, is crushed on the battlefield by a wooden tower that Hercules himself topples. The sequence shows the king of Argos being crushed by the tower. While his helmet falls to the side revealing his bald head, the wicked antagonist dies in agony. In *Hercules in the Haunted World*, the sorcerer Licos is burned alive by the light of the sun, while in *The Loves of Hercules* the tyrant who had seized Deianira's throne is killed by a humanoid beast, which is then slain by Hercules. In these examples, it is almost never the hero, and much less the people, who executes the tyrant. On the contrary, the masses in the sword and sandal genre are usually depicted as incompetent, frightened, or simply immobile victims. They are ready to become supplicants of the "strong man" and liberator Hercules, but not to actively oppose the dictatorship, much less commit tyrannicide. Moreover, the hero generally does not kill the antagonist by his own hand. The villain dies by his own doing (*Hercules in the Haunted World*), by some natural or extraordinary calamity (*The Loves of Hercules*), or amidst the "natural" violence of the battlefield (*Hercules Unchained*). His death is always "just" and "dutiful," but no one takes the credit or responsibility.

In fact, in the peplum movies, it is the villain who pays on behalf of everyone. The only responsibility for the villain's death lies in the innate wickedness of the antagonist himself. I would posit that this narrative repression is not very far from the interpretation of Fascism as a "digression" and the essential blamelessness of Italians during the twenty years of dictatorship. This attitude led to the notorious "continuity" of the postwar period, when the desire for social security produced a "collective purification" in the name of the unitarian experience of the Resistance. As Paul Ginsborg affirms:

> The entire issue of the purge proved to be one of the most delicate problems of the time. Those who had fought in the Resistance or had suffered under Fascism demanded, with some justification, that the members of the Fascist regime not escape some form of punishment. On the other hand, purging the administration of registered Fascists meant more or less closing it down, given that membership in the Fascist Party had been obligatory for all civil servants. The activity of the purge committees succeeded in combining the worst aspects of this state of affairs. It left some of the most important directors of Fascism free, while it incriminated staff at the lowest levels. In 1960 it was calculated that 62 of the 64 serving prefects had been civil servants under Fascism. The same was true of all 135 police commissioners and their 139 deputies [120].

Between the postwar years and the economic boom, Italians wanted to forget their recent, unflattering past as soon as possible. The big screen yet again assimilated and negotiated the desire for peace and the distancing of the tragedies of war, even in memory. In *Goliath and the Dragon*, the final sequence concludes with all the citizens rebuilding Hercules's house, which had been destroyed by the tyrant Euritus's army. Furthermore, in the last sequence of *The Giant of Marathon* (1959), Phillipides (played by the "herculean" Steve Reeves), who has returned to his home in the countryside, lays down his sword by sticking it into the plowed land and walks off toward the horizon with his wife Andromeda. On the right of the screen, a pair of oxen is depicted in long shot, which symbolize the "healthy" toils of farmers and the peaceful life of the fields. These images contribute to feeding the view of Fascism as a "digression" in Italian history, which only momentarily veiled the true, fundamentally positive character of Italians, an interpretation which was commonplace throughout Italy in the 1950s and 1960s. Thus, the peplum highlights the difficult negotiation that Italy continued to face, by interpreting its history and addressing its repressed memory.

It is essential to consider that in the period from 1957 through 1965 (when these movies were produced) the country was ruled by the Christian Democrats

(DC), a center-right party based on Christian values, with strong opposition to the Italian Communist Party (PCI). Given the economic support that the peplums received from the Italian government at the time (unlike other films such as Mauro Bolognini's *La Viaccia* and Pier Paolo Pasolini's *Accattone,* considered too leftist), Hercules does not simply represent anti–Fascism; he evokes a concept of "freedom" used in the ideological terms of the Cold War between the United States and the Soviet Union, for which Italy became one of the most heated battlefields. As we have seen, Hercules, Maciste, and Goliath are strong men, saviors of an oppressed people who avoid the danger of dictatorship by being ontological incarnations of absolute good. The peplum genre is linked to the portrayal of "traditional" tyrannical powers. There are clear references to Nazi-like regimes (*Hercules and the Captive Women*, 1961), general references to subjugated peoples (*Hercules Against the Tyrants of Babylon*), and to advisers who aspire to usurp the throne (*Maciste, Gladiator of Sparta*, 1964). However, the emphasis on a poor people exploited by the rich and powerful has no "revolutionary" intent, since the framework of these films is clearly conservative at a narrative and semiotic level. For instance, in *The Loves of Hercules*, the people rise up against the tyrant Licos on Hercules's instigation. Hercules, however, is not fighting for the people's social demands, but rather fights to restore the legitimate sovereign to the throne. The revolt of the people in the movie is not linked to a socialist and/or communist ideal, nor is it a cinematic representation of the Pelizza da Volpedo painting *Fourth Estate* (1901). Rather, it is a defense of the legitimate monarchy, which is threatened by a foreign usurper. The same mechanism works in the movie *Son of Samson*, which opens with a massacre sequence. Persian soldiers attack an Egyptian village, slaughter the men, and take the women as slaves. While in the background the caravan of slaves is presumably headed to Persia, in the foreground a horrible death is in store for the survivors. They are buried alive up to their necks in the desert sand and left to die. The image of the heads of the dying sticking out of the sand was rather strong with respect to the traditional canons of the peplum. The succeeding sequence depicted a group of poor Egyptians in an audience with the Pharaoh, explaining what the Persians are doing in his name: "We are poor people, but we can not lie. We have come to reveal to you the great injustices that are being carried out in your name, because we know that you are just and good and that you love your people" (*Son of Samson*). In fact, the Pharaoh is portrayed as a "great elder," who is wise and paternal toward his suffering people. However, because of his old age, he is virtually powerless to oppose the maneuvers of his consort, who is betraying him with the Great Vizier, an ally of the Persian enemies. Suddenly, the hero Maciste appears to help the Egyptian people restore power to the legitimate heir, the Pharaoh's young, "progressive" son.

Thus Hercules is not Spartacus. He isn't the revolutionary leader who aims to subvert an existing social order, but a defender of democracy who tries to re-establish a usurped government. In an Italy that preferred "continuity between fascist fascism and democratic fascism," rather than the radical change dreamed of and hoped for during the Resistance, Hercules and Maciste are conservative heroes who offer simple dreams of justice and social equity to an audience eager for peace and stability (Pasolini 129).

What I assert here is that the peplum puts a negotiatory strategy into action, which placates the audience's anxieties—particularly those of the lower classes—through a powerful superman who is able to re-establish a principle of justice and social equity. At the same time, however, he is respectful of the legitimate and socially accepted authority and thus avoids both the absolutist trap of the Fascist past and the highly feared drift toward Italy's first experiments with a center-left, communist government.

America

> *In trying to express Hercules' impact on the twentieth and twenty-first centuries, we will find that "the children of Hercules" still live and walk among us. They have merely left the rugged Peloponnese for the more hospitable climes of Malibu and Venice Beach.*
> — Alastair Blanshard

Although the peplum is an autochthonous genre, born in Italy and using characters from classical literature, the actors were often American. The most famous was Steve Reeves, a Mr. Universe discovered by Pietro Francisci in his adolescent son's bodybuilding magazine. There was also Gordon Mitchell, a high school science teacher and bodybuilding enthusiast; Gordon Scott, an ex–Marine; Reg Park, an Englishman who won Mr. Universe in 1951, 1958, and 1965; Mark Forest, an Italian-American from Brooklyn, New York; and Mickey Hargitay, more prominent for his marriage with Jayne Mansfield (with whom he filmed *The Loves of Hercules*) than for his athletic and bodybuilding talent. This selection of actors, together with the portrayal of Hercules as liberator of a people oppressed by a despot and/or foreign occupation, has led some scholars to identify Hercules with the United States during the Liberation of Europe (Günsberg; Abruzzese). For my argument, Hercules does not symbolize America the Liberator, but depicts the America of Truman and the Marshall Plan. As Alberto Savinio observes, it portrays the America of consumerism and social well-being, the America "of liberalism and democracy" (92).

The identification of Hercules with the United States did not originate with the peplum. Before cinema, there was theater. In 1950 Savinio, an Italian writer, painter, playwright, and the younger brother of the painter Giorgio De Chirico, wrote the play *Alcesti di Samuele*, adapting Euripides's tragedy *Alcestis*. Savinio transported the drama from ancient Greece to World War II, making Alcestis a Jewish woman. Savinio chose Hercules to be portrayed by Franklin

Delano Roosevelt, the thirty-second President of the United States. In the play, one of the characters on stage is the Author, who exclaims:

> Mr. Franklin Delano Roosevelt! I salute you as the last in a series of Hercules who, from time to time, have raised their clubs, brandished their swords, and directed their minds—no less strong than the club and no less sharp than the sword—in defense of good against evil, light against darkness, freedom against slavery, and the dignity of man against subjugation and humiliation. You have carried out the greatest of Hercules's labors. Now the lesser of those labors await you. Are you familiar with the play *Alcestis*? [96–97].

Savinio thus identified Hercules with the United States in the 1950s, calling the mythical hero "the purest expression of democracy and liberalism" (95). Moreover, he affirmed that *l'ercolismo* (the quality of being Hercules) is "closely connected to the liberal and democratic concept, and Hercules, being of a political mind, is liberal and democratic" (92). The tone of Savinio's work, particularly in the dialogue between Roosevelt and the Author, straddles the line between serious and grotesque. The two characters converse about postwar international politics, the western and eastern blocs, and the role of the United States. The Author strongly insists on calling Roosevelt "the champion of 19th century herculism," as if America's role as a land of freedom ended with World War II (93). Finally, Roosevelt, the symbol of a Herculean America, descends into the underworld like Hercules in the myth. Unlike Hercules, however, the President dies along with Alcestis. For Savinio, the war marked the end of the nineteenth-century and its ideals of liberalism and democracy.

Ten years later, in Italian sword and sandal cinema, Hercules is no longer Roosevelt, the heroic President of World War II, but Truman, the controversial "hero" of Italy's postwar reconstruction, which began with the European Recovery Program (ERP), the official name of the Marshall Plan, "the largest international propaganda campaign ever seen in times of peace" (Ellwood 87). For its specific geo-political and historical conditions, the Americans chose Italy as the focal point of the information campaign that accompanied the delivery of food aid, although not without some dissent. The Marshall Plan was a means of projecting American hegemony into Europe and exporting their economic policies.

Most important is the extent to which the Marshall Plan's reconstruction of Italian identity influenced the images of the sword and sandal movies. There are, in fact, various analogies between the vision of Italy assembled by ERP officials and the one constructed by the peplum genre. As David Ellwood affirms, the majority of ERP documentaries portray Italy as a small and simple country, mostly agricultural and oppressed by the weight of its history. This is contrasted with America's dynamism and power to help, a notion which is predicated on the myth of ships arriving with loads of primary goods (Ellwood 100). For instance, in *Goliath and the Dragon,* Hercules returns home, where his wife and son are waiting for him. Along the way the hero visits his farm properties and is greeted by his subjects, farmers, and shepherds, who are struggling with the hard work of the fields. A few sequences show Hercules intent on helping them. In one scene, Hercules helps some shepherds repair a beam that had fallen from the roof of their hut. In the next sequence, the hero uproots a tree with his bare hands, a tree that the farmers had been trying to remove in vain with oxen pulling ropes. Everywhere he goes, Hercules is always greeted and acclaimed by the people, who recognize him for alleviating their daily toils. Just as the Marshall Plan was presented as the only way to liberate Italy from poverty and backwardness, Hercules frees his subjects from the hardest physical labors and helps them rebuild their country.

Hercules is the flaunted prosperity of the Marshall Plan, the attraction to new forms of consumption, the promise that one day Italians will all be strong and powerful like him, and like America. "You can be like us," said the ERP (Elwood 113). It wasn't so much actual prosperity as it was potential prosperity that was depicted in cinemas and contributed to shaping the American dream in Italy. Various studies have brought the Marshall Plan into question and put its economic significance into perspective, for it did not achieve all its aims, precisely due to a lack of analysis of the European context (Ellwood 100–101). However, historians still concur on the political and psychological impact of this American influence in Italy, particularly at the level of popular imagination and mass culture. Among all European countries, Italy has been the leader in importing the greatest number of American films each year. In the postwar period, they were the principal means through which the American way of life penetrated the Italian imagination and dreams (Brunetta 9). With the economic miracle close at hand, it was precisely cinema that created a hybrid character of Italian origin with an American body, used American funds for Italian production, and depicted industrial ambitions against the backdrop of a rural landscape. For these reasons, the hybrid character of Hercules was able to negotiate for his audience Italy's complex transformation during the boom.

Hercules and Maciste appear in an environmental context that seems to belong, by right, to Italy's cultural substratum and even to its landscape. However, the heroes are industrial products imported from a foreign and more developed civilization, beginning with their bodies, where artificiality substitutes nature. Rational muscle building, a high protein diet, and the new bodybuilding craze symbolize the prosperity imported from a society of mass culture and consumption (Salotti 151). The fact that the sculpted body became a "myth" is also proven by its depiction in the artistic trend which reflects and revises mass culture the most, Pop Art, which was born and developed roughly at the same time as the peplum genre. In fact, among the new myths of consumerism that Pop Art artists chose to represent, one that is depicted symbolically most often is the "new" body of the 1960s "modern" man and woman. Thus the body itself becomes a form of consumption, as evidenced by pin-ups and their male counterparts. Examples of the latter include the bodybuilder in Richard Hamilton's famous collage *Just What Was It That Made Yesterday's Home So Different, So Appealing* (1956) and Italian artist Mario Ceroli's *Mr. Muscolo*, a wooden sculpture of a man flexing his muscles in the classic bodybuilder pose, presented for the first time in 1964.

The Herculean hero of the peplum is therefore a hybrid creation, born in the Italian film genre system from classical parentage, but with a body that belongs to the American bodybuilding culture. As with the cinematic Hercules, the peplum genre itself is a hybrid, situated between Italy and the United States. It is characterized by a double dialectic of a "meager" budget and production, on the one hand, and "noble" intentions on the other. For Italian producers, directors, and scriptwriters, producing peplum movies meant spending an "Italian" low budget, while trying to convince the audience that they were watching an expensive American epic. As Stefano Della Casa explains in *Una postilla sul cinema mitologico*, the peplum genre's main characteristic is indeed "the will to be something it's not" (163).

Is Hercules, thus, America? He is, yet more. The superheroes of Technicolor cinema embody the memories of silent film's athletes and acrobats, a manager's bourgeois desires, the heroic dimension of American comics, memories past, and the present desire for release. The American dream is literally materialized in the artificial, health fanatic, and consumerist physicality of the bodybuilder starring in Italian films. In the peplum, fantasy prevails over realism, and the desires imported from another culture are embodied by a hero from Italy's literary and cinematic past. Perhaps this is why the mythical hero has traveled from Italy to the United States, from the wonderful Cinecittà of the 1960s to the frenetic Hollywood of today. A guiding thread composed of "Classicism, Californianism, barbarianism and crucifixionism" ties the Mediterranean Sea with the shores of the Pacific, transporting the heroes of the Italian sword and sandal genre into the cavern of wonders of contemporary Hollywood, a Vulcan's forge of new deities and new universal mythologies (Dyer 150). Cinema has the technical capacity to either resuscitate a world that no longer exists, or to imagine one that never existed. As memories can be real, so, too, can an audience reinvent themselves and their past.

The Hercules series helped to negotiate the difficult transition from the fascist dictatorship to democracy in Italy after the war, and the relations with the American lifestyle and the upcoming economic and cultural changes of the Sixties. It accomplished this task in three distinct ways. Firstly, its main hero is a fearless strongman who—although devoted to restore a peaceful and rightful government threatened by tyrants—never identifies himself with any political leadership, as this would be a painful and disturbing reminder of Mussolini, the "strongman" of the past fascist regime. Secondly, although the hero does defeat the tyrant, he generally does not kill the antagonist by his own hands. It is the villain who pays on behalf of everyone, symbolizing the Italians' common view of Fascism as a "digression" in Italian history, and the essential blamelessness of Italians during the twenty years of dictatorship. The Herculean character embodies a concept of conservative democratic "freedom," which is able to avoid both the absolutist trap of the Fascist past and the highly feared drift toward a communist government. Lastly, the American body of Hercules is the semantic sign that negotiates the contradiction between Italian national identity and desire of the Other. It relates to the new myth of American mass culture and consumerism, which Italy eagerly embraced after the war and, in turn, helped shape cultural changes during the Italian economic boom. Thus, by shifting the emphasis from national cultural matters to industrial and sociological issues, the peplum opens up the possibility of further exploration of the connections between Hollywood and Cinecittà regarding genre, masculinity, and the transnational — a possibility bound together by the brawny, muscular form of Hercules himself.

WORKS CITED

Abruzzese, Alberto. "Mito della violenza e pistole scariche." *Cinema 60* 54 (1985): 2–10.
Blanshard, Alastair. *Hercules: A Heroic Life*. London: Granta, 2007.
Boschi, Alessandro, ed. *I Greci al Cinema* (The Ancient Greeks at the Theater). Bologna: Digital University Press, 2005.
Brunetta, Gian Piero. *Storia del Cinema Italiano* (History of Italian Cinema). Vol. III. Rome: Editori Riuniti, 2001.
Canfora, Luciano. *La Democrazia. Storia di una Ideologia* (Democracy: History of an Ideology). Bari-Rome: Laterza, 2006.
Della Casa, Stefano. "Una postilla sul genere mitologico." *Sull'industria cinematografica italiana*. Ed. Enrico Magrelli. Venice: Marsilio, 1986. 171–179.
Dyer, Richard. *White: Essays in Race and Culture*. London: Routledge, 1997.
Ellwood, David W. "L'Impatto del Piano Marshall sull'Italia, l'impatto dell'Italia sul piano Marshall." *Identita' italiana e identita' europea nel cinema italiano*. Ed. Gian Piero Brunetta. Turin: Agnelli, 1996. 87–110.
The Giant of Marathon [*La Battaglia di Maratona*]. Dir. Jacques Tourneur and Mario Bava, 1959.
Ginsborg, Paul. *Storia dell'Italia dal dopoguerra a oggi* (A History of Contemporary Italy: Society and Politics, 1943–1988). Turin: Einaudi, 1989.
Goliath and the Dragon [*La vendetta di Ercole*]. Dir. Vittorio Cottafavi, 1960.
Günsberg, Maggie. *Italian Cinema: Genre and Gender*. London: Palgrave Macmillan, 2005.
Hercules [*Le Fatiche di Ercole*]. Dir. Pietro Francisci, 1958.
Hercules and the Captive Women [*Ercole alla conquista di Atlantide*]. Dir Vittorio Cottafavi, 1961.
Hercules and the Tyrants of Babylon [*Ercole Contro i Tiranni di Babilonia*]. Dir. Domenico Paolella, 1964.
Hercules in the Haunted World [*Ercole al Centro della Terra*]. Dir. Mario Bava, 1961.
Hercules Unchained [*Ercole e la Regina di Lidia*]. Dir. Pietro Francisci, 1959.
The Loves of Hercules [*Gli Amori di Ercole*]. Dir. Carlo Ludovico Bragaglia, 1960.
Locatelli, Ludovico. "Come ai tempi di Cabiria" (As at Cabiria's Time). *La Fiera del Cinema* 2.2 (1960): 12–15.
Luzzatto, Sergio. *Il corpo del Duce* (The Body of the Dux). Turin: Einaudi, 1998.

Maciste, Gladiator of Sparta [*Maciste, Gladiatore di Sparta*]. Dir. Mario Caiano, 1964.
Pasolini, Pier Paolo. *Scritti Corsari*. Milan: Garzanti, 2001.
Pavone, Carlo. *Alle origini della Repubblica* (At the Origins of the Republic). Turin: Bollati Bordighieri, 1995.
Salotti, Marco. "1957–1964: L'industria cinematografica italiana gonfia i muscoli."
Sull'industria cinematografica italiana. Ed. Enrico Magrelli. Venice: Marsilio, 1986. 149–156.
Savinio, Alberto. *Alcesti di Samuele* (Samuel's Alcestis). 1949. Milan: Adelphi, 1991.
Son of Samson [*Maciste nella Valle dei Re*]. Dir. Carlo Campogalliani, 1960.
Spinazzola, Vittorio. *Cinema e Pubblico* (Cinema and the Audience). Rome: Bulzoni, 1985.
The Two Gladiators [*I Due Gladiatori*]. Dir. Mario Caiano, 1964.

Hero Trouble
Blood, Politics, and Kinship in Pasolini's Medea

Kristi M. Wilson

Following upon a tradition that began in the 1920s in Italy, American producers became interested in the revival of mythological epics in the 1950s and saw Italy as an appropriate venue for the production of these films. Pietro Francisci's *The Labors of Hercules*, the first in a series of high-grossing mythological films, made an unheard of 900 million *lire* in Italy, a huge profit in the United States, and brought the Italian film studio Cinecittà to the forefront of the international film scene.[1] In the years 1957 to 1964, 170 mythological films were made with stories drawn from the ancient Greek, Roman, Christian, Incan, Egyptian, Hungarian, Arabic, and Amazonian (among others) traditions. Vittorio Spinazzola suggests that the social impact of these mythological "blockbusters" is one of spectator identification with and desire for an altruistic, protective, larger-than-life force:

> Hercules invites the spectator to abandon completely the world of reality and human logic. On the other hand, he is not inaccessible, like a divinity, nor is he, like prophets, a mere reflection of divinity. In spite of his superhuman qualities, he remains an earthly hero and as such demands from the spectator not a passive adoration but an active process of identification. This duality is quite important for a sociological identification of the character. Hercules is the incarnation of a noble hero who does not come from the people but who is ready to fight for them, to protect the poor, and to restore order and social peace. He brought back to the screen the eternal tale of the knight errant, challenging his own class in the name of justice [qtd. in Liehm 184].

Although the genre of the mythological epic died out in 1965, desire on the part of spectators for formulaic narratives about omnipotent heroes did not. Mythological films were quickly replaced with a new tradition of Italo-American co-productions about superman-like cultural heroes. As film historian and critic Toby Miller argues, such thematic transference—from mythological heroes to superheroes—is made seamless with the financial and distribution support of the Hollywood studio system. The blockbuster, thus, lends itself to the cultural colonization and domination of smaller national industries because of the familiarity of the stories and easy transferability of themes onto diverse cultural topoi.

Pier Paolo Pasolini followed the mythological film genre in Italy with his own set of classically-themed films that resisted easy, "for export" escapism and critiqued, in part, the monolithic Italo-American cinematic powers that repeatedly portrayed absolute, mythological heroes. Pasolini's 1969 adaptation of Euripides' *Medea* deflates the heroic epic of Jason (itself part of an ancient Greek epic cycle that included the adventures of Hercules) and his 1967 postmodern version of Sophocles' *Oedipus Rex* refuses to separate the legacy of Oedipus' hubris from Italy's Fascist past. His anti-heroes (Medea, Jason, Jocasta, and Oedipus) scramble heroic ideals and complicate spectator identification. They unveil a powerful critique of European colonialism and its lasting impact on popular, local, and sometimes subaltern cultural histories.[2]

The story of Medea and Jason has long been a popular topic in feminist circles. A foreigner, part-witch, guilty of fratricide and infanticide, Medea has been described by feminist scholars as a heroine for standing up to infidelity, misogyny, and abandonment; as a criminal for murdering her children in a horrific act of revenge; and as the ultimate victim of western (Greek) colonialism. In his film adaptation of this tragic tale of blood vengeance, Pasolini articulates Medea's potential as a queer rupturer of values in the context of western, normative kinship structures. His decision to cast Maria Callas as Medea bore particular relevance for queer culture as well as high culture. Following his principle of capturing "reality" on camera by filming people as they are, Pasolini cast Olympic athlete Giuseppe Gentile as Jason, making the character's ultimate failure as a hero more noticeable and disconcerting.[3] By casting opera diva Callas in a role already immortalized by her concert performances (Medea was her comeback role in January 1964), Pasolini contaminates his own depiction of Medea's "barbarity" and alludes to her mythological history as a partial divinity. Callas' status as a high-culture icon and her operatic legacy permeate the primitive theme music that underscores Medea's scenes, just as visions of adoring fans (who, in some cases, traveled the world to hear her sing) provide a mythical subtext for the action of the film. Pasolini refers indirectly to Callas' fame as a soprano during an early scene in the film in which Medea's village prepares to sacrifice a young man. A close-up of the victim's face as he is led to the slaughter shows him transfixed, gazing at Medea as if he is starstruck with happiness. In a different scene which occurs later in the film, Callas is depicted in a long, tightly framed shot underscored by the sound of women from her village singing about Jason's invasion. The awkward quality of Medea's silence during this scene draws attention to the actress's alter ego as a soprano— as if she waits, in anticipation, for a cue to sing.

In "Callas and Her Fans," Wayne Koestenbaum draws attention to the importance of Maria Callas to gay opera fans and addresses the historical links between opera and homosexuality. Koestenbaum argues that Callas' vocal range (which includes sparingly applied vibrato) was at times "dangerously schizoid," suggesting a wavering between one value and another: "much as the third sex, a fin-de-siècle image of the homosexual, was thought to hesitate, with an indecisive and uncanny shudder, between the two legitimate genders" (9). This inconsistency in Callas' voice provoked a skepticism and curiosity about her womanliness, according to Koestenbaum, which carried over into speculation about her private life; she was perceived in the public eye as aristocratic and sexually troubled. He describes Callas as a queer icon, arguing that "the forces that shaped 'Callas' as a charged intersection of secret sadness and publicized splendor are the same currents that created the closet and its spectacular opposite, the scene of coming out; Callas and gayness are both symptoms of modern society's pervasive split between silence and speech, secrecy and disclosure" (12). Similarly, Pasolini's *Medea* is permeated with silences, queer moments of wavering inconsistency and troubled subjectivity.

Such temporal, cultural, and gendered moments of non-correspondence in the film, invoked in part by Callas' fame and reputation, add weight to Silvestra Mariniello's argument that Pasolini was trying to create a poetic sense of rupture or a gap in the notion of dialectical synthesis in his work. Mariniello calls attention to a newspaper article Pasolini wrote the year of his death in 1975, in which he stresses the failure of the concept of evolution or progression to hold any further meaning in Italian politics:

> In this article, published in the Italian newspaper *Il Corriere della Sera*, Pasolini sketches an analysis of the Italian social-political situation that is brimming with consequences implied by the concept of evolution: the gap between, on the one hand, a rural paleo-industrial society and, on the other, a consumer society, the reality of multinational corporations, and the end of the state. *We are able to act, to intervene, only if we understand the links between old Fascism and the state and between new Fascism and the new economic-political structure. Political parties are finished, and "it is no longer a question of ruling,"* Pasolini remarks, inviting the Italian Left to rethink its political role [113, emphasis in original].

By connecting popular political pronouncements of economic progress to Italy's fascist past in this way (in fact, Pasolini called for several politicians in the Christian Democratic party to stand trial as traitors), Pasolini proposes a gap in the Italian historical narrative of cultural and economic progress since World War II. He sees, rather, a negative dialectic which only produces more fascism under the guise of political and cultural evolution and neo-capitalism. The conundrum of what Pasolini believed to be Italy's fascist past coexisting with its neo-fascist present in 1960s politics took the aesthetic form of dual-temporality in both *Oedipus Rex* and *Medea*. Thus, Maurizio Viano's suggestion that Pasolini failed in his efforts to use the past as a metaphor for the present is unconvincing, especially since he so succinctly draws attention to the role of the centaur in *Medea* as a bridge between species, the divine and secular realms, and historical periods (242). The centaur, Chiron, serves as Jason's guardian at the beginning of the film when he appears as a baby. The centaur evolves into a man as Jason becomes an adult and reappears mystically as both centaur and man later in the film (standing next to his own image in a split screen shot). Accordingly, mythical thinking (represented by the centaur) is effaced but not completely eclipsed by enlightened rationality (represented by the man). Chrion's dual appearance illustrates Pasolini's conviction that man has failed to evolve from one (historical) moment to the next.[4]

My emphasis on the politics of kinship in Pasolini's *Medea* stems largely from the material he added to the myth, like the expanded role of the centaur. Marianne McDonald points out that Pasolini also alters Medea's image in Euripides' play as a woman with particularly "modern" ideas about women's equality by omitting her address to the women of Corinth (19). However, the amount of time he devotes in depicting Medea helping Jason steal the golden fleece and murdering her own brother, Apsyrtus, suggests that Medea's agency, particularly in the context of marriage and kinship, is a central theme in the film. The scenes in Medea's village begin with a fertility ritual underway. A young victim is sacrificed and the community spreads his blood and body parts all over the land and crops. In the process of the ritual the royal family is ridiculed by their subjects but soon thereafter reinscribed in their positions of power. The fertility ritual is followed by Medea's visit to the shrine which houses the golden fleece, where she encounters Jason. The theme of heterosexual desire becomes explicit at this point, whereas the theme of homosexuality has already been introduced by Apsyrtus' desirous gaze at the sacrifice victim at the beginning of the film.

The organization of these first scenes suggests that Pasolini was conscious of the differences between the relations of sexuality and the means of production, an awareness that resonates with Gayle Rubin's concept of sex/gender or kinship systems. Rubin identifies this key difference in Frederick Engels' *The Origin of the Family, Private Property, and the State* in her pathbreaking 1975 essay "The Traffic in Women: Notes on the 'Political Economy' of Sex." She cites the following passage from Engels as crucial to understanding his notion of the twofold nature of social production:

> According to the materialist conception, the determining factor in history is, in the final instance, the production and reproduction of immediate life. This, again, is of a twofold character: on the one hand, the production of the means of existence, of food, clothing, and shelter and the tools necessary for that production; on the other side, the production of human beings themselves, the propagation of the species. The social organization under which the people of a particular historical epoch and a particular country live is determined by both kinds of production: by the stage of development of labor on the one hand, and of the family on the other ... [qtd. in Rubin 165].

For Rubin, this passage provides evidence for a sex/gender system and suggests that both types of production (the production of the means of existence and that of human beings) are subject to control and organization. The control of sexuality in the guise of kinship is nowhere better illustrated in Pasolini's *Medea* than in the scenes depicting Medea breaking tradition and offering herself as an object of marital exchange to Jason, rather than remaining a passive object of exchange between men. Following upon shots of the villagers harvesting crops (ensuring the material means of existence), Medea arrives with her brother to Jason's camp in a horse-drawn cart. The golden fleece is draped over the back of the cart, implying that she is offering the mystical treasure as her dowry.[5] Medea and Jason exchange desirous glances, as do Medea's brother and Jason, and Jason gazes victoriously at the golden fleece. This triangle of desire between Jason, Medea, and Apsyrtus is thus contaminated by Jason's parallel desire for the golden fleece.

The realm of mobile sexuality (in the movement of desire between the three characters) is juxtaposed with the realm of power and organized heterosexuality. Medea's decision to offer herself to Jason involves a sacrifice and underscores the violent repercussions of acting outside of prescribed roles in the sex/gender system. After enlisting Apsyrtus to help her obtain the golden fleece for Jason, Medea murders him. During the long, drawn-out murder scene, Pasolini registers the shock of her actions on the faces of Jason and his men. Medea is shown repeatedly hacking her brother to bits (mimicking the manner in which the sacrificial victim was dismembered in the fertility ritual) and throwing pieces of his body out of the getaway cart to ward off her father's army. Medea's violent departure from Colchis emphasizes the complete annihilation of her previous kinship structure and the repression of homosexual desire as a component of her pending roles as wife and mother. Apsyrtus' desirous glances at Jason mirror the manner in which he looked at the young sacrificial victim minutes before his death during the fertility ritual, a scene that suggests for Viano an allegory of contemporary, legally sanctioned violence against homosexuals (245–246).

Medea, however, is not the only female character in the film who ruptures the sex/gender system. Pasolini refers to two versions of the story of Medea's rivals Creon and the princess Glauce; Euripides' version, which appears as a dream sequence, and the director's own version. In Euripides' version, Glauce and Creon die as a result of Medea's poisonous gifts. In Pasolini's version, their deaths are depicted as Medea's fantasies about her own abilities as a sorceress, a vision, perhaps, of what is supposed to happen as a result of the gifts but does not come to pass due to a diminishment of her power. Instead, when Glauce receives Medea's gifts (this time supposedly for real), Glauce decides that she will not become Jason's bride, thus removing herself as an object of exchange between her father and her would-be husband. Once again, this decision comes with violent consequences and sacrifice. Murder in Euripides' version of the myth is reinterpreted by Pasolini as a dual suicide. Glauce jumps to her death from a cliff after trying on Medea's garments, followed by her despairing father. Pasolini makes explicit the connection between Medea and Glauce as rupterers of kinship organization by superimposing their images during Glauce's suicide. When she jumps to her death, Glauce wears the very garments that Medea wore in her native village. The suicide scene depicts the possibility of an alternative form of kinship between the two women, one that exists nowhere in Euripides' tragedy.

Pasolini's *Medea* deviates conspicuously from the original tragedy in other ways as well, most overtly in its use of a non–Western setting in the first half of the film to indicate Medea's foreign place of origin. Filmed on location in Turkey and then in a castle in Pisa, the cultural and geographical juxtaposition in the film embodies Medea's cultural and ethnic difference from Jason and Greek society in general.[6] In the first half of the film, Pasolini establishes Medea's royal status in her native village and her close relationship with Apsyrtus. The first two thirds of the film reflect his poetic vision of the myth, while the last third is modeled on Euripides' play. Pasolini employed Turkish locals as extras in the scenes that depict a human sacrifice and fertility ritual on the outskirts of Medea's village. The extras wear traditional clothing and are shot against a stark landscape of rustic dwellings built into steep cliffs. Pasolini has been criticized on many fronts for what some call cinematic tourism or orientalism. In a scathing critique that indulges in homophobic language, William Van Watson refers to Pasolini as the "creampuff of the Italian left," and suggests that many of his films are "retreats and excursions into the undeveloped third world," characterized by a "constructed subproletariat innocence" (389; see also Viano 4). Elsewhere, Van Watson calls these "retreats" examples of Pasolini's personal "transgressive consumption" (389). By contrast, Mariniello suggests that Van Watson's type of "rhetoric of nostalgia," frequently associated with critical work on Pasolini, is often brought into academic analyses of the filmmaker's work in order to neutralize, cover up, or misread his critique of the dialectic.[7] In fact, she highlights Pasolini's continual insistence, both in his writings and in his cinematography, on the inadequacy of materialist dialects through the continual juxtapositions of opposing models of history in his work. She suggests that the way in which a non-correspondence between diverse models of history and temporalities is created is more significant than Pasolini's use of the third world as a discursive element in his films:

> In *La Divina Mimesis*, for example, written between 1963 and 1965, he creates the prosopopoeia of the old inspiration coming to terms with the new reality: a totalizing, panoramic, ordering vision stands counter to the new that resists narration. As in this interview, the emphasis was on the dynamics between the old and the new, a dynamics that does not correspond to a materialist dialects leading to an ideal synthesis. The emphasis is on the contrast, on the abyss between the two moments rather than on the fullness of a solution. The concept of the dialectic gives way to other concepts—those of contamination and mediation. The gap between past and present,

history and prehistory, exists, but it is unbridgeable.... The awareness of such a historical gap makes it necessary to rethink modes of intervention ... [112].

Based upon this idea of a reality that resists narration, scholars might begin to rethink the substance behind the obvious juxtaposition between the first and the third world, and East and West, in Pasolini's *Medea* by looking at the way he defines the third world and the role of classical mythology in his work.

In a series of interviews in which he claims to "tell the story of my own Oedipus complex," Pasolini points out the link between a type of highly personal autodescription and his first classical film, *Oedipus Rex*: "I narrate my life — mythified, of course — made epic by the legend of Oedipus" (Liehm 244). According to Viano, with *Medea*, Pasolini plunged into the realm of mythology to such an extent that he abandoned his capacity to evoke contemporary reality as he had in *Oedipus Rex* and *Teorema* (237). However, as I have pointed out, Viano's take on the film is conspicuously at odds with Pasolini's own description of his intentions in his historical films. In an article written for *Cinema Nuovo* in 1970, Pasolini wrote, "By its nature film cannot represent the past.... Therefore in my historical films I never had the ambition of representing a time that is no longer: if I tried to do it, I did it by analogy: that is, by representing a modern time somehow analogous to the past" (qtd. in Mariniello 132).[8] Mariniello adds that Pasolini's *Medea* is informed by an urgency to rewrite history and reject the categories that made it possible.

Pasolini's depiction of the third world, so important in his adaptation of *Medea*, was to a great degree infiltrated with his views of the Italian peasantry (largely from the south of Italy):

> You must remember that Italy was and still is in a fairly unusual position in western Europe. While the peasant world has completely disappeared in the major industrialized countries like France and England (you can't talk about peasantry in the classic sense of the word there) in Italy it still survives, although there has been a decline in recent years.... My relationship with the peasantry is very direct, as it is in most Italians — almost all of us have at least one peasant grandfather, in the classical sense. Now the communists in Friuli were peasants, and this is very important. Perhaps if they had been urban working-class communists the class factor would have been too strong for me and I would have resisted; but I couldn't hold out against peasant communists, who are the ones who make revolutions, in Russia, in Cuba, in Algeria — although they make them in a pre-class way ... this is perhaps why there is such a strangely ambiguous symbiosis, which is also a valid one, as well as being poetic, between the peasantry of the third world and the students here [Pasolini qtd. in Stack 21–22].

Clearly, when Pasolini refers to the third world in his writings or film, he both performs an act of autodescription and refers to an almost mythical, geographical site that incorporates Italian peasantry (or those Italians outside of industrialization and thus, outside of history) with perhaps more remote, foreign communities that fit into his vision of locations that do not correspond to ideas of Western progress. Seen in this light, the Turkish peasant setting used to depict Medea's role as a community leader before meeting Jason takes on the appearance of a particularly colonized space when Jason and his band of men enter the village temple to steal the sacred golden fleece (the object of their travels). Pasolini emphasizes the importance of this encounter by characterizing the arrival of Jason's men with sadistic violence and carelessness. The men steal the first objects they come upon (horses and jewelry) from nearby farmers. When they reach the village, they dislodge the treasury guard with ease, steal the treasury, and mock the villagers by tossing a single coin to the guard who has been thrown to the ground. There is no resistance to Jason and his men from Medea's people. In fact, it seems as if an invasion is the last thing they suspected. Jason succeeds in infiltrating the sacred temple alone where he comes face to face for the first time with Medea. Accordingly, Pasolini's depiction of Jason and his men pillaging Medea's village could refer to colonial violence inflicted by Italians in foreign lands, to violence committed by neo-capitalist Italians on Italian peasants and foreigners within Italy, or both.

Pasolini was concerned with particular forms of colonialism and exploitation inside and outside of Italy up until his death. Days before he died, Pasolini gave a lecture on Antonio Gramsci in which he attempted to distance himself from charges of traditionalism, idealism, and reactionary tendencies whenever he spoke of subaltern cultures:

> For Gramsci, it was legitimate to talk about emancipation because he worked, forty years ago, in an archaic world that we cannot even imagine. [...] It was right then ... because Sardinian shepherds lived in a very particular manner. The difference is inconceivable. So you cannot quote Gramsci as an example of emancipation; you can recall Gramsci as a link in a historic chain that leads us to new questions today. To propose a new way of being progressive, a new way of being Gramscians. [...] when Gramsci says genocide ... he takes a position in favor of the victims and against those who victimize them; he takes a position in favor of particularistic cultures that were being destroyed and against the centralist culture that destroyed them [qtd. in Verdicchio 173].

If one follows the logic of the above quote, which refers to recent and ongoing cultural genocides in Italy, it seems more likely that Pasolini is making reference to his contemporary political and cultural milieu in *Medea* than simply creating an aesthetically pleasing portrait of ancient Asia. In the film, he represents Medea and her ancient homeland as existing in a completely different time period than Jason's through the use of ancient Turkish cliff dwellings to represent Medea's village, and Italian medieval dress and architecture to characterize Corinth. Thus, Medea's village stands in for "particularist" cultures destroyed by "centralist" culture.

In keeping with Pasolini's criticism of centralist culture and its victims, his queer intervention into the heteronormative qualities of the mythological film genre should not be overlooked. Although it is no longer taboo in film theory to discuss the homosexual aspects of many of Pasolini's films, explicit links between Pasolini and queer theory are nevertheless uncommon. Viano suggests that we should not ignore ways in which homosexuality appears in Pasolini's films, as many Italian critics have done over the years in order to avoid tarnishing his status as a producer of high culture. Yet simply embracing Pasolini's homosexuality does not bring us any closer to understanding the degree to which Pasolini's work troubled and threatened the Italian state: while he was alive, he was dragged into court thirty-one times on charges ranging from obscenity to blasphemy to corruption of minors. He was tried once posthumously, and immortalized by the Italian police as a desecrated corpse in a series of photos they published after his murder. While there may be valid reasons to rescue the homosexual over- or under-tones in Pasolini's film adaptations of the ancient past, a deeper exploration of the stigma of deviance that marked his own body and body of work is in order if scholars wish to understand how Pasolini can be seen as a precursor to fields such as queer theory. Michael Warner stresses the fact that sexual deviance has historically been deemed non–normative to the body politic, and suggests that a queer politics around sex does not have to constitute a form of simple libertarian indulgence (Warner). He proposes instead that we look toward the kind of politics that can be articulated by those who refuse to behave properly.

In an article entitled "Picturing Pasolini," John Di Stefano discusses Pasolini's life in the Italian tabloids, including photos taken at the controversial opening of *Accatone*, at which the filmmaker was physically assaulted. Di Stefano suggests that Pasolini's status as a sexual deviant was always emphasized in photos at the expense of his intellectual attributes: "Photographs portrayed him as a subversive, a troublemaker, a pervert, a corrupter, a homosexual, all words that overshadowed other terms like poet, filmmaker, critic, novelist, screenwriter, intellectual" (19).[9] The absence of discussion of Pasolini's queer forms of political resistance from interpretations of his life's work can only point, as some have suggested, to homophobia on the part of some of his most renowned critics. Viano suggests that the homosexual "discourse" in Pasolini's work complicates the oppressor/oppressed dialectic in such a way as to expose Marxism's inadequacies in confronting sexual oppression. This idea is especially relevant to Rubin's argument about kinship systems. Pasolini depicts Medea as a radical agent who implodes her own kinship system. In the process, discourses of homosexuality and colonialism appear necessarily intertwined. Shots of Medea's escape with Jason are cross-cut with the discovery of Apsyrtus' body parts strewn along their path, calling to mind the aforementioned triangle of desire. Meanwhile, Medea's father and his men recover and grieve for each separate body part ceremoniously, as if it were a whole soldier cut down in battle.

In the introduction to his interviews with Pasolini Oswald, Stack suggests that with Pasolini's turn toward classical mythology he intended to restore a mythological or epic dimension to life. Stack argues that Pasolini saw the Italian peasantry as still sustaining "a sense of awe and reverence to the world" even though it was up against the destructive power of the bourgeoisie (9). He suggests that Pasolini's view of the peasantry is difficult to reconcile with a Marxist political analysis. Stack is particularly interested in the fact that with his classical films, Pasolini seems to make a sudden shift toward sex as the main threat to the bourgeoisie, thus reconciling "the idea of sexual liberation with his attachment to the peasantry" (10).[10] In a response to one of Stack's questions about his political attitudes toward the various classes in Italy, Pasolini discusses the difference that the Friulan peasantry posed to his own class and culture; a difference that was, among other characteristics, a sexual difference:

> As for the other popular class—the working class—I've had a very difficult relationship with them, which was initially romantic, populist and humanitarian. When you are born in a petit bourgeois milieu, you think the whole world is the same as the environment you live in. As soon as I got to see another kind of world, naturally, my own was thrown into crisis. When I realized that the Friulan *braccianti* [day laborers] existed, and that their psychology, their education, their mentality, their soul, their sexuality were all different, my world broke down [qtd. in Stack 26].

Pasolini's notion of a "world" in this non-theoretical context is equivalent to the raw materials that become the relations of sexuality (concerning the production of human beings) and the relations of production (concerning the means of existence), both of which are organized socially in any given historical epoch. Thus, in the above comments, Pasolini refrains from making a liberationist political statement about the sexuality of the Friulan peasants. Rather, he alludes to a different type of sex/gender systemic organization that stands in contrast to the hegemony of bourgeois heterosexuality, and intersects with several other characteristics of the Friulans' marginalization, such as cultural and ethnic difference.

Pasolini's Medea is radically Other, deviant, and unwilling to behave. Nowhere in the landscape of his adaptation of Euripides' play will one find an absolute hero. In fact, Pasolini's heroes fail in a conventional sense, calling to mind his anti–Enlightenment, anti-humanist, queer political stance. His films about the ancient world prompt spectators to rethink political action, masculinity and femininity, culture and history. Time wavers between two parallel yet irreconcilable periods rather than move forward. As such, spectator identification is "dangerously schizoid," at best. Not only does Pasolini's *Medea* offer a critique of enlightened notions of a universal, absolute hero (such as Hercules), but it also interrogates capitalistic notions of progress, not least of which are embraced by the global Hollywood studio system.

Notes

1. Some of the names of these mythological blockbusters include *The Vengeance of Hercules, The Love of Hercules, Hercules Challenges Samson, The Challenge of the Giants, The Triumph of Maciste, Maciste in Hell, Maciste Against the Vampires, Maciste Against the Monsters, The Titans Are Coming, Samson Against the Pirates, The Heroes of Babylon,* and *Goliath and the Rebellious Slave* (see Liehm 348).

2. The bulk of this essay is focused on Pasolini's adaptation of Euripides' *Medea*. For more on his film version of Sophocles' *Oedipus Rex*, see Foley's "Bad Women" (in Hall, Macintosh, and Wrigley).

3. Maurizio Viano suggests that Pasolini's choice of Gentile to play Jason reflects his desire to have the character represent Italy's "new bourgeoisie, the contemporary spirit of the Enlightenment" (241). He refers to Jason as an iconic translation of the "fitness is fun" hedonistic ideology so frequently attacked in Pasolini's criticism.

4. See Viano, *A Certain Realism*, 237, and Mariniello, 114.

5. See McDonald (19) for the earliest references to the story of Jason. McDonald points out that Jason's image as an epic hero is comically shattered in Pasolini's film by his own arrival on a raft as opposed to a "lavish ship" (9). I would add that the men are shown sleeping on the raft, making their arrival even less heroic as they seem to expend little or no effort on rowing.

6. Although, as McDonald points out, the ancient scene of Medea's homeland is infused with Renaissance aesthetics, further confusing the time and space divisions in the film. In a scene which depicts the royal family standing in front of their subjects in Medea's village, the family is shot standing still framed by an archway, a composition that suggest a Renaissance painting (*Euripides in Cinema* 9). In her analysis of the musical themes in the film, McDonald points out that the different cultural and temporal spaces in which the action takes place are represented aurally by a violent percussive music, associated in the film with Medea, and a form of ancient Japanese music that suggests (bourgeois) refinement and is associated with Jason (5). Jason's soundtrack is perhaps an ironic comment on the terror that his men have reaped on Medea's village.

7. Mariniello points out that "even Pasolini refers to himself as nostalgic, often with the rhetorical awareness of one who assumes the opponent's position in order to dismantle their discourse from within" (112). Pasquale Verdicchio also suggests that due to Pasolini's pessimistic vision of the state of Italian diversity, which he compares to a genocide brought about in part by the Italian educational system and consumerism, his critics accuse him of being romantically enamored with the past. Verdicchio argues that such a "reduced version of his work earned Pasolini the unjustified label of reactionary, idealist, and even fascist" (69).

8. Pasolini's earliest film, *Accatone*, was the first film in Italy ever to be restricted to viewers over the age of eighteen due to its "vulgar" depiction of the Roman subproletariat. Its 1961 debut immediately launched the director into what some critics refer to as the "New Italian Cinema" movement, a heterogeneous, rageful response to the "well-being" of consumer society.

9. Two weeks before his death, Pasolini satirized the notion that his stigmatized gay body was separable from his intellect by commissioning nude photos of himself posing with a book by photographer Dino Pedriali. See Di Stefano, 22.

10. Stack cites Pasolini's film and novel *Teorema* as an example of a depiction of the destruction of a bourgeois family via sex. Although I will not argue it here, I will suggest that *Teorema* has many structural similarities in common with Euripides' *Bacchae* and may have been influenced by it, even though Pasolini claims to have invented the mythological character of the Guest himself.

Works Cited

Di Stefano, John. "Picturing Pasolini: Notes from a Filmmaker's Scrapbook." *Art Journal* 56.2 (1997): 18–22. Print.

Edipo Re. Dir. Pier Paolo Pasolini. Arno Films, 1967.

Hall, Edith, Fiona Macintosh, and Amanda Wrigley. *Dionysus Since 69: Greek Tragedy at the Dawn of the Third Millennium*. New York: Oxford University Press, 2004. Print.

Koestenbaum, Wayne. "Callas and Her Fans." *Yale Review* 79.1 (1990): 1–20. Print.
Liehm, Mira. *Passion and Defiance: Film in Italy from 1942 to the Present*. Berkeley: University of California Press, 1986. Print.
Mariniello, Silvestra. "Temporality and the Culture of Invention." *Boundary 2* 22.3 (1995): 111–139. Print.
McDonald, Marianne. *Euripides in Cinema: The Heart Made Visible*. Philadelphia: Centrum, 1983. Print.
Medea. Dir. Pier Paolo Pasolini. Perf. Maria Callas, Giuseppe Gentile. San Marco, 1969.
Rubin, Gayle. "The Traffic in Women: Notes on the 'Political Economy' of Sex." *Feminist Anthropology: A Reader*. Ed. Ellen Lewin. Boston: Blackwell, 2006. Print.
Stack, Oswald, and Pier Paolo Pasolini. *Pasolini on Pasolini: Interviews with Oswald Stack*. Bloomington: Indiana University Press, 1969. Print.
Van Watson, William. "(B)Oinking with Pier Paolo: Pasolini's Pigsty and the Death of Dialectic." *Romance Languages Annual* 9 (1998): 383–89. Print.
Verdicchio, Pasquale. "Reclaiming Gramsci: A Brief Survey of Current and Potential Uses of the Work of Antonio Gramsci." *Symposium* 49.2 (1995): 169–176. Print.
Viano, Maurizio. S. *A Certain Realism: Making Use of Pasolini's Film Theory and Practice*. Berkeley: University of California Press, 1993. Print.
Warner, Michael. "The Politics of Sexual Shame." *University of California Summer Research Institute with Judith Butler*. Berkeley: University of California, 1999.

"To do or die manfully"
Performing Heteronormativity in Recent Epic Films

JERRY B. PIERCE

After obliterating the first attack of mighty Xerxes' army, the Spartan king Leonidas stood defiantly before the Persian ruler as Xerxes encouraged him to surrender in the face of certain death. The two men were clearly the antithesis of the other: bearded, strong and sporting a battle-hardened physique, Leonidas arrived alone and unarmed while Xerxes, pierced and bejeweled, his smooth, hairless body covered in gold makeup and heavy eyeliner, literally arrived on the backs of his slaves. "Consider your women," he suggests. "You don't know our women," Leonidas retorts. "I might as well have marched them here, judging by what I've seen today. You have many men, Xerxes—but few soldiers. And it won't be long before they fear my spears more than your whips" (*300*). This brief exchange from Zack Snyder's *300* (2006) offers the clearest representation of positive and negative masculinity found in recent epic movies about the ancient world. Leonidas (stern, toned, and manly) is a solider ready, as the Greek historian Herodotus noted, "to do or die manfully," fighting to save Sparta and the rest of Greece from Persian tyranny, while Xerxes (arrogant, decadent, and femininized) wishes to see the world kneel in submission before his whip (Herodotus 7.209). Ironically, Herodotus' assessment of Spartan manliness comes from Xerxes' supposed misunderstanding of a scene at Thermopylae where the Persians witnessed the Spartans grooming and otherwise pampering their bodies. Xerxes interpreted these actions as frivolous, when in fact, according to Herodotus, the Spartans apparently engaged in such actions as they prepared "to do or die manfully" in battle. In the modern cinematic interpretation, however, it is Xerxes who appears to be pampered and frivolous.

Leonidas' suggestion that Spartan women could just as easily defeat the Persian soldiers further reinforces the notion that the tyrannical Persians are not "real" men, Xerxes above all. In short, this movie continues a long tradition of pairing "proper," heterosexual, masculine, and just heroes with "improper," homosexual or otherwise "deviant" and tyrannical antagonists. In doing so, *300*, as well as two other recent epic motion pictures about the Greek and Roman worlds, *Gladiator* (dir. Ridley Scott, 2000) and *Troy* (dir. Wolfgang Petersen, 2004), promotes a heteronormative masculinity by linking heterosexuality with heroism and democracy. These three epic movies each present their male heroes as strong, determined warriors who are ready to safeguard their people (whether Romans, Trojans, or Greeks) from a menacing despot.[1] In all three of these movies, the heroism of the male protagonists is made apparent to the viewer though the use of standard tropes of "positive" masculinity demonstrated by the "safe" display of the male body, a physically active struggle against tyrants, a strong moral compass and, perhaps most importantly, a seemingly unambiguous affirmation of his heterosexuality.

Each movie goes to great lengths to make their depictions of ancient masculinity safe and heteronormative by emphasizing the heterosexual performance of the leading men. For example, Maximus (Russell Crowe, *Gladiator*), Hector (Eric Bana, *Troy*) and Leonidas (Gerard Butler, *300*) all are identified, in part, by their role as husbands and fathers. These three, as well as Achilles (Brad Pitt), are also equally adept as warriors, and frequently are seen in little-to-no clothing in carefully constructed heterosexual settings. The masculinity of these heroes is further reinforced by the representation of other males in the movies, predominantly their antagonists, who appear as the opposite of these strong males in every way: physically weaker, less active, morally degenerate, or feminized. These antagonists are also depicted as engaging in (or at least plotting) some form of "deviant" sexual behavior that ranges from incestuous desire, to adultery, to cross-dressing, to (implied) homosexuality which, by relying on age-old cinematic stereotypes, are designed to reinforce their role as the antithesis to the positive masculinity of the hero.[2] Ultimately, by presenting the masculinity and heterosexuality of the heroes as normative, the narrative arc of these movies also implies that it is this very type of masculinity that will save their families and their societies from the threat posed by unmanly men.[3]

The tropes of masculinity in these recent motion pictures about the classical era depend on a presentation of male identity that is heteronormative in nature, or based on the notion that heterosexuality is the default orientation of individuals. These movies enhance the concept of heteronormativity by implying that heterosexuality is also the only acceptable identification and, as Chrys Ingraham notes, is considered "natural, universal, and monolithic" (207).[4] Anything that deviates from this "straight" norm, as Wheeler Winston Dixon points out, "is seen as something that is not part of the supposedly normative system of values, something that is a potential threat to the family, to the dominant social system, something that needs to be erased" (2). By holding heterosexuality as the norm, and thus as positive, anything that transgresses those rigid lines of sexuality is therefore "suspect" (Dixon 1–2). Moreover, as Dixon argues, "being straight is, as in the dictionary, equated with decency" (6). As such, many villains in movies tend to be portrayed as openly homosexual or, if they are not, often exhibit characteristics stereotypically associated with stereotypes of on-screen homosexuality, such as an effeminate demeanor, excessive emotionality, or even weak or thin body types. The threat posed by these antagonists (even if "straight") is thus augmented by a reliance on visual tropes indicating deviance and rejection of heteronormative society. This threat of transgression also manifests itself in the roles ascribed to non-straight characters: "violent serial killers, drug dealers, hit men, sadistic siblings or parents, traitors—in other words, every form of human wreckage" (Dixon 12). Significantly, Vito Russo, in his work on the portrayal of gays and lesbians in film as negative and villainous, notes that "symbols for a decadent destruction of moral values become homosexual in nature," part of a "decision to link the destructive characters with homosexual iconography" (252).[5]

To counter this challenge, and to provide a clear example of proper masculine heterosexuality, the male heroes engage in heteroperformance. These examples can occur through direct action taken by a character (wedding ceremony or consensual sexual encounter), via appropriately masculine attire (rugged clothing), or even indirectly, through the staging of certain scenes (the display of a baby's crib next to the matrimonial bed).[6] The most common demonstration of male heteroperformativity involves the use of the male figure as a literal embodiment of normative masculinity. Typically, the heroic male body has physically conformed to certain oft-repeated standards termed "performative body tropes" because they evoke both strength and heterosexuality (Dixon 20, 49). Thus, male protagonists are physically fit and toned, indicating their bodies' preparedness for immediate action. The power of the hero's body is then demonstrated through some form of violence, either as his body endures punishment (usually instigated/ordered at the behest of his less masculine rival), allowing for the gratuitous display of the male form, or exhibited by physical prowess as he defeats his feminized adversary. These examples of heteroperformance then become linked with the movie's narrative regarding positive displays of proper masculinity and power, all of which are portrayed as supportive of traditionally patriarchal roles with the male father/protector providing security and stability as a direct result of these heteroperformative acts.

Ridley Scott's *Gladiator* provides an example of the use of male body as indicative of traditional heterosexual masculinity. The first visual introduction to the Roman general Maximus actually displays only a small, but very representative, part of his body as a whole. Gliding across a robust field of grain is a weathered, callused, yet strong male hand. The subsequent cut introduces the lined and bearded face of Maximus himself, the presumptive "owner" of the hand, looking wistfully at a small colorful bird in the midst of a landscape made barren by both winter and the destructively efficient Roman army. The scene ends with the heavily armored Maximus grimly returning to the bleak and colorless present, dutiful yet reluctant. These few seconds of screen-time immediately identify Maximus as strong, determined, and grounded. The hand passing over grain signifies not only strength, but also a power that is tied to the land and manual (agricultural) labor, a trope indicating Maximus' simple and uncomplicated nature. His grizzled features reinforce his agrarian hardiness and are augmented by his soldier's attire. As Monica S. Cyrino explains, the character of Maximus is thus appealing to viewers because he "reaches back to an idea of masculine bravery and goodness that is old-fashioned by both modern and ancient standards" (131).

All subsequent physical depictions of Maximus reinforce his strong (and thus normative) masculinity. First, as a general personally leading his troops to battle against Germanic barbarians, Maximus actively engages in brutal hand-to-hand combat, ultimately conquering this last stronghold of resistance. This show of masculine force and aggression is repeated several more times, from his fight with and escape from the Praetorian Guard, to his swift killing of opponents as a gladiator, to his final duel with the emperor Commodus (Joaquin Phoenix) where he gruesomely dispatches his nemesis, despite being mortally wounded.[7] Another demonstration of Maximus' physical prowess is the stripping and display of his toned and muscular body, alongside those of all the newly acquired slaves, at Proximo's (Oliver Reed) gladiator training facility in North Africa. As Lynne Segal has argued, "The contemporary guardians of true manhood still believe that living one's life as a man involves toughness, struggle and conquest" and an "increasing glorification of a more muscular, militaristic masculinity," creating "a new ideal of manhood based on physical fitness, courage and audacity" (89, 91, 92).[8]

The display of Maximus' body, along with those of the other gladiators, is safely heterosexualized in part because these scenes never allude to any potentially homosexual or even homoerotic activities. This safely heterosexual zone of display is crucial because, as John M. Clum explains, "the point at which intense male-male relationships become a threat to that homo-hetero boundary becomes a place of extreme anxiety" for the viewer (xix). Therefore, the slaves are almost universally shown in sleeveless, knee-length tunics or smocks, and there is nary even a bare chest to be seen. *Gladiator* has no bathing scenes, no partially clothed gladiators sleeping in the same cell, and only a select few references or connections linking gladiators and sex. These few exceptions occur with Maximus, and are all safely heterosexual.

Gladiator and the other films discussed here purposefully avoid potentially homoerotic scenes in part because of the tendency or the expectation of earlier sword and sandal epics to be viewed as homoerotic because of their very physical display of the male body. This expectation of homoeroticism stems in part from the common motif associating the antagonists (predominantly Roman) with "degenerate" sexual tastes, such as homosexuality or bisexuality, as in the infamous "oysters and snails" scene where the Roman general, Crassus (Lawrence Olivier), attempts to seduce his slave, Antoninus (Tony Curtis), while bathing in Stanley Kubrick's *Spartacus*.[9] Audiences thus expect some expression of sexual deviance when watching these films and are primed to look for it. Another reason is that toga films, especially those of the 1950s and 1960s, prominently featured male bodybuilders, glorified for their well-oiled physiques (not their acting skills), as the main objects of the audience's gaze. According to Susanne Turner, this "celebration of the bare flesh it puts on display encodes both empowered masculinity and eroticized spectacle" (131). Many elements work together to enhance this homoerotic spectacle, not least of which are the ubiquitous scenes of semi-nude males interacting with other equally disrobed males in bath houses or grappling with each other in little more than loincloths, often with nary a female in sight. Moreover, as Turner notes, the formerly typical objectification of the female body on screen is here replaced, or at least marginalized, "in favour of *male* spectacle and *male* bodies" (144, emphasis original; see also Fitzgerald 36). As stressed by Clum above, this erotic objectification becomes problematic when it creates a tension or anxiety on the part of the (presumably) heterosexual male viewers and how they are to identify with these bodies on display (Fitzgerald 37). Thus, in an attempt to straighten the homoerotic gaze, these elements are often repressed or displaced with scenes of violence by or against the very bodies on display (Turner 144, Fitzgerald 37). In terms of *Gladiator*, *Troy*, and *300*, each film utilizes this approach of violent displacement but also subtly acknowledges the audience's potential anxiety by overtly countering any hints of homoeroticism with unambiguous displays of heterosexuality.

In *Gladiator*, the first link between gladiators and sexuality occurs after Maximus demonstrates his swift and ruthless efficiency in dispatching opponents in the Zucchabar arena, to the dismay of Proximo, who wants these matches to be more entertainment than hasty execution. Hoping to assuage Maximus' restless anger, Proximo asks what he wants and, assuming his needs are sexual, suggests "Girl? Boy?" (*Gladiator*). Tellingly, Maximus does not respond to the sexual offer, instead informing Proximo that he desires to be the best gladiator so that he can stand before the emperor Commodus (presumably to kill him in order to avenge his family's deaths). Aside from the rejection of sexual desire in general on the part of Maximus, this exchange also illustrates the default assumption of heteronormative behavior ("Girl?"), with the remote, "other" possibility of homosexual desire ("Boy?") introduced as an afterthought. The second exception takes place in the dungeon scene where Lucilla (Connie Nielsen), the emperor's sister (and former love interest of Maximus prior to their respective marriages) speaks to a chained Maximus, telling him that wealthy Roman matrons are wont to pay large amounts of money "to be pleasured by the bravest champions" (*Gladiator*). Though no sexual union takes place, Lucilla's statement constructs their potential sexual encounter in clearly heterosexual terms.

The final instance overtly connecting gladiators and sexual activity in *Gladiator* occurs when Juba (Djimon Hounsou), observing Maximus praying to figurines of his wife and child, asks what he says to them. After relating horse-riding advice that he gives his son, Maximus tells Juba, "To my wife ... that is not your business" (*Gladiator*). The sly look and laugh shared by the two gladiators alludes to not just a private exchange between husband and wife, but a *sexual* exchange shared only by the couple. This scene, like the previous ones, does not just link this sexuality to Maximus, but binds it specifically to his heterosexual nature, making it a heteroperformative act. Taken together, these scenes with Maximus and the modest clothing of all the gladiators preclude any hint of non-normative sexuality on their part, thus making their all-male interactions safely heterosexual.[10]

Gladiator provides numerous other examples of heteroperformativity, most of them centered on establishing or reinforcing the traditional masculinity of the hero. The most obvious reinforcement comes in the form of the near-constant references to Maximus' nuclear family, as Martin Fradley has noted (245). Prior to their murder, Maximus desires an end to the war so that he may return home to his family. When asked whether he will go to the barracks or perhaps Rome, now that the battle is over, Maximus responds with a third alternative: "Home. To my wife, my son, the harvest" (*Gladiator*). He is intent on returning from the all-male surroundings of the militarized frontier to his simple home in Spain to be husband to his wife and father to his son. Maximus' longing to return home, to reestablish his patriarchal position within the household, remains constant until he learns of the murder of his family and the destruction of his home. Despite a momentary period of apathy, once Maximus realizes that his new status of gladiatorial slave will allow him to confront his family's murderer, he becomes bent on revenge.

This traditional representation and spectacle of the male body, masculine virility, and heterosexual activities are likewise displayed in Petersen's *Troy*, primarily through the bodies and actions of the two male leads, Achilles and Hector. Unlike that of Maximus, the introduction of Achilles highlights his naked, tanned, and muscular body. It is subsequently and frequently presented throughout the movie in various stages of undress (often after competing with and killing an opponent), such as when he washes himself before his captive Briseis (Rose Byrne) or bathes after defeating and slaying Hector. When Achilles is dressed, or even armored, his clothing is much more revealing than that worn by Maximus. Unlike the knee-length tunics of *Gladiator*, Achilles' leather skirt, and those of most of the male actors in *Troy*, barely reaches mid-thigh, revealing and eroticizing much more of the male body. Yet despite the increase in exposed male flesh, these presentations, like those in *Gladiator*, are displayed safely in a heterosexual context.

From his very first appearance onscreen, Achilles' body is meant to epitomize male heterosexual physical perfection and virility. Indeed, the audience witnesses a starkly naked Achilles in the post-coital company of not one, but two women. This not-so-subtle scene indicates that these two women are simply the latest in a string of heterosexual conquests. Achilles himself has no emotional (read as "weak") attachment to these women, nor any use for them other than sexual, which he demonstrates by annoyingly throwing one of their arms off of him so he can go into battle. This callous disregard for women and their treatment as sex objects clearly identifies Achilles as a traditionally chauvinistic, and thus demonstrably heterosexual, male.

Like Maximus, Achilles constructs his heteronormative traits through brave and dangerous feats of heroism. His first violent encounter, with the muscled giant Boagrius (Nathan Jones), appears at first to be set up as a protracted duel, but the battle is swiftly and efficiently ended by a single lunge and sword-thrust by Achilles. Facing the large army of Thessaly, Achilles challenges the soldiers by yelling, "Is there no one else?" (*Troy*). When no one steps forward, Triopas (Julian Glover), king of Thessaly, asks for Achilles' name. He offers, "Achilles, son of Peleus," emphasizing his own masculinity via the paternal link to Peleus, himself a hero who adventured with Heracles and Jason of Argos (*Troy*). Interestingly, when Triopas offers Achilles the royal scepter of Thessaly to give to Agamemnon (Brian Cox), Achilles refuses to be the bearer of this phallic representation of royal power from one man to another.

Despite Achilles' initial portrayal as chauvinistic, or at the very least indifferent to female needs, the mutual taming and domestication that occurs between him and his war-prize, the virgin priestess Briseis, allows Achilles to (temporarily) function in a domestic, heteronormative space. Though not officially husband and wife, Achilles performs many of the domestic activities expected of a male head of household, from deflowering his virgin "bride" to establishing a protective and secure home environment by his decision to remove himself from Agamemnon's war and return to Greece. In attempting to leave the battle of Troy, Achilles recalls Maximus' initial desire to return to his home in Spain, the key difference of course being that whereas Maximus planned to return home *after* fulfilling his military duties, Achilles opts to return *during* the battle inside Troy. Another important distinction between Achilles and Maximus in terms of domestic heteroperformativity is Achilles' lack of progeny, that classic indicator of a properly consummated heterosexual union. Yet despite the absence of offspring, Achilles nevertheless demonstrates paternalism (or at the very least fraternalism) with respect to his Myrmidons, especially Eudorus (Vincent Regan), who he sends home to safety prior to the final, deadly assault on Troy, and most importantly with Patroclus (Garrett Hedlund), conveniently changed from the possible homosexual love interest of the *Iliad* and re-imagined onscreen as his cousin.[11] The refiguring of the connection between Achilles and Patroclus from homosexual to heterosexual and paternal (a brief bit of dialogue early in the movie between Odysseus [Sean Bean] and Achilles establishes that Patroclus' parents have died and that he is now under the care of Achilles) normalizes their relationship by unquestionably asserting that Achilles' actions and desires are firmly heterosexual.

In fact, *Troy* goes to great lengths to completely disassociate all of its characters from any hint of non-normative sexuality, especially homosexuality. Numerous scenes constantly reinforce the rigid heterosexuality of all the male characters, even the vast cast of extras. For example, when trying to convince Achilles to fight Boagrius in the opening scene, Nestor tells Achilles that he can swiftly end the war (with Thessaly) with a single swing of his blade, allowing the Greek soldiers "to go home to their wives" (*Troy*). Likewise, in an attempt to persuade Achilles to do battle with the Trojans, Odysseus asserts his own heterosexuality by telling Achilles, "My wife will feel much better if she knows you're by my side" (*Troy*). This insistence on heterosexuality extends to the Trojans as well when, after the first battle between Greeks and Trojans, Hector asks Achilles, "How many wives wait at Troy's gates for husbands they will never see again?" (*Troy*).

As representative of the Trojans, Hector complements the heteronormative ideal exhibited by Achilles. Hector's body is also on display, though it occupies fewer scenes than Achilles' does. Like Achilles, Hector's masculine form is displayed in various scenes of heteroperformativity, so that when he appears barechested, for example, it is always in relation to the private bedchamber he shares with his wife and infant son. In keeping with the displays of masculine prowess exhibited by Maximus and Achilles, Hector demonstrates his strength through both physical exertion and leadership over other males, in this case the entire Trojan army. In terms of fighting, Hector duels one-on-one with a series of Greek champions, including Menelaus (Brendan Gleeson), who he kills with a single sword thrust; the much larger Ajax (Tyler Mane), who he vanquishes after a protracted and grueling struggle; Patroclus, who he mistakes for Achilles; and finally Achilles himself. Considering how quickly Achilles dispatched all his previous opponents, even those much larger than him like Boagrius, the drawn-out nature of the Achilles/Hector duel is indeed a testament to the masculine worthiness of Hector, despite the fact that he is ultimately slain.

Hector's masculinity is also reinforced by his paternalism. Hector is very protective of his brother Paris (Orlando Bloom), especially when he refuses to hand Paris over to the Spartans (and certain death) for stealing Menelaus' wife. Likewise, when Paris foolishly decides to duel with Menelaus, Hector attempts to instill in his brother his own skills as a warrior, telling him how to avoid Menelaus' sword and exhaust his opponent. Interestingly, when Paris tries to ensure that his brother will protect Helen, Hector commands Paris to forget about such sentiments and to focus "on his sword and your sword" (*Troy*). Hector's manly advice is simple: in battle, there is no time for feminine, and thus "weak," expressions of emotion; victory is assured through focused aggression and superior swordsmanship. Of course, Paris is bested almost immediately, but when Menelaus moves in for the kill, Hector steps into the duel and slays Menelaus instead, justifying this interference by claiming, "He's my brother!" (*Troy*).

Coupled with his paternalistic relationship with his brother, Hector also demonstrates his heteroperformative nature in scenes with his wife, Andromache (Saffron Burrows), and infant son. Indeed, their first scene together reinforces Hector's virility, as his wife presents their son to him (and to the audience) after his absence in Sparta. In their bedchamber, the child's bassinet is also prominently displayed in close proximity to their bed, further connecting their sexual activity with proper heterosexual performance: the production of a suitable (male) heir. Even the couple's final scene together, just before Hector engages in the fatal duel with Achilles, emphasizes Hector's role as husband and father, as Andromache tearfully presents him with his son in the hope of thwarting his inevitable death. Bound by his masculine duty for his city, which in martyr-like fashion supersedes his familial obligations, Hector attempts to ease the tears of both wife and son, but nevertheless continues determinedly toward his fate. In fact, Hector foreshadowed this devotion to country just prior to the first Greek assault on Troy, telling his fellow soldiers that they would fulfill their heterosexual, masculine obligations if they remembered to simply "honor the gods, love your woman and defend your country" (*Troy*). Thus, Hector's selfless sacrifice, like those of his fellow soldiers, operates as yet another proof of his normative masculinity.

Unlike *Gladiator* and *Troy*, where issues of masculinity have to be teased from bits of dialogue or the staging of scenes, Snyder's *300* allows for little ambiguity in its attempt to depict the Spartan warriors as rigidly heterosexual and indeed the epitome of manliness. *300* presents King Leonidas and his faithful warriors as sculpted spectacles of male physical perfection and the embodiment (quite literally) of archetypes of male heteroperformativity. In fact, the Spartans are an example of hypermasculinity, a (hetero) masculinity that far exceeds that exhibited by Maximus, Hector, or even Achilles.

The importance and centrality of the body to the movie's definition of masculinity is made apparent in the opening sequence, where the narrator details the harsh upbringing of Spartan boys, from being inspected at birth for physical worthiness, to having to fight one another for scraps of food, to incredible feats of perseverance and survival in the wilderness. The message is clear: anyone who cannot endure such physical hardship is not fit to be a man in Spartan society. Throughout the entire movie, the exquisitely toned bodies of Leonidas and his Spartans are on constant display, often absurdly so. Marching into battle (and there is nothing if not an abundance of battle scenes in *300*), the warriors wear little more than their red cloaks and tight leather briefs. Other than their shields and helmets, there is not a glint of body armor in sight. Unlike the man-made muscled chest armor worn by Maximus or Achilles, the Spartans have only their own chiseled pecs and abs on display. In this movie, it is not hard to find scenes where Leonidas and his men are virtually naked; indeed, the difficulty comes in finding scenes where they are even modestly dressed. This blatant spectacle of the male form highlights a progression from a modest display of the male body (one bare-chested scene of Maximus), to somewhat risqué (brief glimpses of Achilles' naked backside), to the fetishized quasi-nudes of Sparta.[12]

Considering the historically homosexual "baggage" associated with Spartan warriors, *300* goes to great lengths to present these exceptionally virile specimens of masculinity as unequivocally heterosexual, and their interactions as simply homosocial.[13] The movie attempts to "straighten" the Spartans in two ways: directly, through dialogue, and indirectly, through scenes of heteroperformativity. The first example occurs at the beginning of the movie when Leonidas is confronted by the first Persian messenger demanding Sparta's submission. The king's response is that since the Athenians, "philosophers and boy-lovers," have decided to resist the Persians, the Spartans can do no less (*300*). By deriding the Athenians as soft intellectuals and pederasts, Leonidas asserts that the Spartans, by way of contrast, properly exemplify heterosexual masculinity. A similar situation occurs later between two of Leonidas' soldiers who constantly try to outperform one another in battle. Revealingly, their method of asserting their own virility and worth is to jokingly imply that the other is in some way less of a man. One jab is rendered as a warning to not "offer your backside to the Thespians," a doubly homoerotic challenge playing off both the implication of homosexual anal sex and the audience's inclination to understand "Thespian" not as a regional identifier (like Arcadian), but as code for "actor," especially a homosexual actor (*300*). A later retort, seemingly couched as a compliment after a hard-fought battle, claims, "You fought well today ... for a woman" (*300*). Ironically, although intended to assert the heterosexuality of the Spartans, both of these jokes instead draw the audience's attention to the ponderingly obvious displays of homoeroticism, in part because they can also be seen as flirtatious teasing.

Perhaps hoping (in vain) to nullify any hint of homoeroticism, *300* also contains scene after scene of Spartan heteroperformativity. One example is the first scene of Leonidas as an adult, which finds him, bare-chested, wrestling with his young son while his wife, Queen Gorgo (Lena Headey), looks on. This scene thus exhibits Leonidas' masculine strength, his heterosexuality, as well as the product of his heterosexual union. Leonidas' heteroperformativity is also quite literally expressed through a subsequent lovemaking scene with his wife, the only extensive and actively sexual encounter between male and female in all three of these films. Like Leonidas, the Spartan warriors themselves are also depicted as safely heterosexual, as witnessed in the scene where the captain tells Leonidas that all the men preparing to march to Thermopylae "have born sons to carry on their names" (*300*). This detail implies that, just like their king, all the warriors come from clearly heterosexual, child-bearing unions. Moreover, to solidify the impression of Spartan heterosexuality even further, the film stresses that the bond between these men is simply homosocial and that, "A Spartan's true friend is the warrior next to him" (*300*). The implication is that this bond is clearly based on asexual, or, at the very most, homosocial friendship.

All three films, *Gladiator*, *Troy*, and *300*, share a commonality in their presentation of heteronormative tropes of masculinity. Just as compelling is their method of reinforcing this type of manliness by juxtaposing it with non-normative masculinity, which is often literally embodied by the various antagonists. Typically, these male antagonists are portrayed as feminized, overly emotional, or of questionable sexual orientation (and in some cases, all of the above.) In all instances these antagonists are nowhere near as manly as their heroic opponents. This contest between the heteronormative male and his non-normative foe is common to all three movies.

The struggle even manifests itself politically, as another common motif in these movies is that the antagonists have not only transgressed their proper masculine roles, but in so doing they have also disturbed the (imagined) democratic, albeit patriarchal, political order. Ina Rae Hark has noted that, as a general rule in ancient epics, "the rightful exercise of masculine power has been perverted by unmanly tyrants" (145). In order to underscore the severity of this usurpation as the antithesis of appropriate patriarchal authority, Hark argues that the antagonists "often display characteristics not marked as signifiers of masculinity," such as effeminacy or non-normative body types (152). In each of the three movies, these markers are often various components of the stereotyped homosexual villain, yet they appear to be used not so much to overtly identify the antagonists as homosexual, but more to associate them with those negative tropes and suggestively undermine their masculinity and thus their moral character. According to Dixon, the "villains" in these films are identified through a combination of their bodies, their sexuality, and their socially immoral acts (45). Their feminization, indeed emasculation, is then both the cause and indicator of their "perverse" identity and tyrannical rule.

Maximus' nemesis, Commodus, is a primary example of a non-normative male antagonist. From his first scene, riding in a heavily armored wagon while lounging in ornate robes and furs, Commodus is depicted almost exclusively as decadently soft, which is in keeping with the consistent portrayal of antagonistic Roman emperors as "effeminate and extravagant" (Fredrick 215–215). Accordingly, as Cyrino explains, *Gladiator* "employs the image of transgressive sexuality to suggest moral depravity and the abuse of tyrannical power" (142). This depiction is reinforced immediately by his late arrival to, not just a single battle, but his father's entire war in Germania. It should be noted that the only other occupant of the protected wagon, Commodus' sister, Lucilla, wears similar attire. Commodus' effeminate character likewise is reinforced by his whining protests and his excessively emotional (and thus non-normative) outbursts: "They [the crowd] love Maximus more than they love me!" (*Gladiator*). Even when Commodus wears armor, as when he addresses the Senate, watches the gladiatorial games, or fights in the arena with Maximus, his attire is uncannily clean, implying ceremonial, rather than active, use. In the case of his final battle, Commodus is clothed in brilliantly white armor, a stark contrast to the earth-toned and dirtied attire of the hero, Maximus. Moreover, Commodus' failure to perform and fight as a proper masculine warrior is underscored by his underhanded attempts to ensure that Maximus dies in the arena by bringing Rome's best gladiator out of retirement (as well as several vicious tigers), and when that fails, to literally stab Maximus in the back prior to their final duel. In fact, according to Fradley, Commodus' anti-masculine qualities, "sexually ambiguous, cowardly, narcissistic, morally corrupt, effeminate, affluent, decadent ... incestuous and patricidal," help define Maximus' masculinity precisely because they are so antithetical to it (246).

Physically, Commodus' boyishly smooth face and body represent a pampered and spoiled lifestyle, markedly different from the rugged masculinity of Maximus. In fact, Commodus' only physically revealing scene presents a shirtless, smooth-chested (perhaps oiled?) figure engaging in some highly choreographed swordplay with his similarly shirtless and smooth Praetorian Guard. The staged nature of the swordfight belies Commodus' poor fighting skills, while this solitary glimpse of him partially undressed suggests a homoerotic relationship between the prince and his men. Unlike training scenes with Maximus, or swordplay between Achilles and Patroclus, or even the semi-nude (but ponderously heterosexual) camaraderie of Leonidas and his Spartans, this scene is a conscious effort on the part of the director to play off of these culturally charged signifiers of homoeroticism to undermine Commodus' sexuality, his morality and, by extension, his leadership. As the story progresses, Commodus' lack of normative sexual desires is in fact reinforced through his repeated, yet constantly thwarted, incestuous attempts to sleep with his sister. He even goes so far as to demand late in the story (by threatening to kill Lucilla's son, Lucius) that she love him and provide him with an heir. In so doing, Commodus disrupts the heteronormative stability of the family unit by threatening both the murder of a rightful (male) heir and forced, non-normative sex, in this case incestuous rape. Commodus' sexual inadequacy, his inability to consummate his relationship with his sister, is yet another characteristic typical of corrupt emperors in film. This inadequacy is usually accentuated by the emperor's "submission" to a woman, often the empress (Fredrick 215–216). In the case of Commodus, Lucilla does indeed hold power over him, as it is she who facilitates the plot against her brother and appears to possess far more agency than he does.

Commodus' depiction as an unmarried male, with no love interest outside his sister, in part mirrors the status of the other Roman males, all of whom are (presumably) single and never shown with a female companion. Only senator Gaius is mentioned as having mistresses (note the plural, indicating excess and a lack of masculine reserve and temperance), while senators Falco and Gracchus are apparently bachelors, although Gracchus' sexuality is called into question when he is warned of his impending arrest by his heavily made-up and scantily clad boy slave. In keeping with stereotypical depictions of Rome, these unmarried Romans, possibly adulterous (Gaius), possibly homosexual (Gracchus), are indicative of the moral decadence of the Empire, evidenced by their failure to engage in the heteroperformative display of procreative marriage.[14]

In *Troy*, the audience is not presented with a singular feminized antagonist. Rather, the challenges to normative masculinity and especially legitimate patriarchal rule are split between the characters of Paris and Agamemnon. Technically, as brother to one of the film's two heroes, Paris is not an antagonist in the same sense as Commodus nor, indeed, is he presented as an adversary. He does, however, provide a counterpoint to the performative masculinity of Achilles and Hector, and he is also partly the cause of the outbreak of Greek and Trojan hostilities. In terms of masculinity, Paris is physically depicted in a more feminine fashion than his other male counterparts. Compared to both his brother and Achilles, Paris has a much more slender body and appears significantly less muscular than the other males. Even when armored, his small frame seems to provide an uncomfortable fit, as if his body barely fills the armor. Paris' smooth and virtually hairless chest seems rather adolescent and, especially when compared to Hector, his sparse, nearly invisible goatee gives the impression of one who is trying (yet failing) to appear more masculine.

Paris' physical inadequacy is also heightened by his inexperience in warfare, a telltale performative indicator of classical masculinity. Upon hearing that the Greeks will be coming to retrieve Helen, Paris suggests that they flee into the backcountry rather than fight. As if this abrogation of his manly duties was not enough, Paris' foolish (and cowardly) solution is challenged not by another male, but by Helen, his lover. This cowardice and inexperience are again on display, this time for all of Troy and the Greek army to see, when Paris clumsily challenges Menelaus to a duel; when he is obviously losing, he literally crawls back to certain protection behind his brother. However, this feminization of Paris stops short of challenging his heterosexuality. After all, the root cause of the Trojan War was his sexual conquest of Helen. Confirming his brother's heterosexual exploits, Hector recalled that Paris would "roam from town to town, bedding merchants' wives and temple maids," while his father, Priam (Peter O'Toole), claimed that "women have always loved Paris and he has loved them back" (*Troy*). Interestingly, it is not just heterosexual promiscuity in general which Paris engages in, but specifically adulterous liaisons and the deflowering (presumably) of virgin priestesses which, although nominally heteroperformative, nonetheless threatens the patriarchal authority of other men, both husbands and fathers.

Unlike *Troy*, *300* goes to great lengths to both feminize and homosexualize the enemy. Just as *300* hyper-masculinizes Leonidas and the Spartans, it also hyper-feminizes Xerxes and the Persians, without much subtlety. The first introduction of the Persians confirms their status as markedly "other" than the light-skinned Spartans, with the arrival of a dark-skinned African messenger (Peter Mensah) who wears elaborate "Eastern" robes and sports numerous facial piercings. The messenger's entourage is likewise foreign, wearing Bedouin-styled clothes with their faces wrapped in scarves and only their heavily made-up eyes exposed. This feminization by way of clothing and especially accessories becomes more elaborate as the Spartans encounter more Persians. After arriving at Thermopylae, Xerxes sends another messenger who is decadent, arrogant, and feminized. Bejeweled, pierced, and sporting significant eyeliner, this corpulent emissary is carried by slaves, further feminization that neatly contrasts with the Spartans, who have journeyed the entire route on foot.

Yet nowhere is this non-normative masculinity on better display than with the Persian god-king Xerxes (Rodrigo Santoro) himself. Whereas the emissary was carried by a handful of attendants, Xerxes, seated atop an impossibly large and elaborate golden throne, is carried by dozens of faceless slaves. As he confronts Leonidas, Xerxes descends to the earth via a staircase made of the backs of his slaves. Physically, Xerxes is a monstrously exaggerated display of a feminized male. Although his body is toned, spectacularly muscled, and unrealistically tall, his accessories and body language imply that Xerxes is, in fact, a decadent parody of Leonidas' masculinity. Xerxes' body is conspicuously clean-shaven; there is not a hair to be seen, a stark contrast to the virile locks and beards of the Spartans. Xerxes does not even have eyebrows, which are instead replicated with more makeup. In fact, in close-ups, his entire body appears covered with a golden, shimmering foundation. This feminization by way of cosmetics is even more exaggerated by his abundance of jewelry (necklaces, bracelets, rings, armbands, even a shawl of golden beads and rings) and piercings (nose, eyebrows, ears, cheeks, jaw). Taken together, these details (plus his long, manicured nails) clearly mark Xerxes as hyper-feminized, and thus an unquestionably non-normative male. Moreover, Xerxes' extreme feminization, unlike that of Paris, is not tempered in any way with markers of heterosexuality or even anything marginally heteroperformative, thus allowing the audience to easily read Xerxes' femininity as suggestive of homosexuality. In fact, the suggestive scenes of bizarre sexual decadence in Xerxes' tent, with disfigured, mutilated, and bound lesbian slave women, as well as transsexuals, merely reinforce the film's message that non-normative sexuality is somehow depraved and in marked contrast to that "proper" display of heteroperformativity, the heterosexual, heir-producing marriage.

Though not overtly feminized like Commodus or even Paris, as the main antagonist of *Troy*, Agamemnon exhibits non-normative behavior by acting like a tyrant, and therefore abusing patriarchal authority.[15] Like Commodus, Agamemnon is motivated by his own personal desires and arrogance. His earlier conquest of Greece, and soon Troy, is the result of his selfish desire for power, wealth, and control. Yet Agamemnon's conquests are not of his own personal doing, and are instead accomplished through the masculine skill and prowess of soldiers like Achilles and Odysseus. This passive means of conquest entails others doing the hard labor of fighting for him, and it is through his abrogation of direct, heteroperformative combat that Agamemnon is feminized. Desiring to sack the city of Troy, Agamemnon declares that he will tear down the city's walls, "even if it costs me 10,000 Greeks," proving that the lives of his loyal soldiers are of no consequence in the pursuit of his own agenda (*Troy*). Indeed, not only does he typically stop short of leading his men directly into battle, but when Agamemnon finally does kill someone personally, it is the aged and feeble King Priam, who he quite literally stabs in the back. This passive/aggressive portrayal marks Agamemnon as less active in the manly pursuits of war. Like Paris, Agamemnon is feminized through his lack of display of masculine prowess in battle yet, also like Paris, there is no indication that he is anything other than heterosexual. Indeed, the main conflict between Agamemnon and Achilles is the former's abduction of the latter's war prize, Briseis, as a domestic (heterosexual) sex slave.

The common thread that ties Agamemnon to the more feminized antagonists is that their aberrant, and especially selfish, masculinity has far-reaching consequences, resulting in acts of tyranny and despotism. Their desire for personal power and gain thus comes at the expense of the collective, and inherently democratic, good, requiring a man exhibiting proper masculinity to restore the political and social balance.[16] According to these movies, it is not inherently wrong for a man to strive for power and glory, so long as his goals fall within the proscribed realm of appropriate, consensual leadership. Violations of this masculine code abound in terms of both deeds and goals. Commodus usurps his father's authority and plans for succession by murdering the emperor and ordering the death of Maximus, the proper and more suitable heir, thereby inaugurating a hedonistic reign supported by the murderous consumption of real men in the arena. Agamemnon similarly wastes the lives of countless good men, and causes the complete destruction of one of the greatest kingdoms of the Aegean through his selfish quest for land and power. Paris' self-centered desires clearly resist the will of his father, who had sought peace between Greece and Troy, threatening not only his own family members, but also his country as a whole. Finally, Xerxes' desire to dominate the ancient world is clearly presented as despotic, not only because his empire is built on the backs of slaves, which apparently are expendable by the tens of thousands, but also because his tyranny threatens the democratic republics of Greece, cast as the hope for a free world and the bastion of liberty, justice, and the benevolent rule of law and reason.

Resistance to this tyranny is expected on the part of the true representatives of masculinity. For example, even though Commodus is emperor, he does not hold the position of rightful ruler, and thus Maximus' resistance, originally nothing more than vengeance, is transformed into a struggle for political freedom and the restoration of the power of the republican Senate.[17] Even as he is dying, Maximus resists the temptation to enter Elysium and rejoin his family so that he can first see that his men are freed, the Senate restored, the last wishes of Marcus Aurelius fulfilled, and that Lucilla's heir, Lucius, is safe. He has thus reaffirmed "the ideals of family and simplicity" (Cyrino 142). Likewise, Achilles' resistance to Agamemnon's rule, seemingly self-interested, is permissible precisely because of Agamemnon's characterization as a tyrant. Despite his initial feminization, Paris' nature is actually redeemed through a process of re-masculinization, by fighting for Troy during its final moments and "rescuing" Briseis when he kills the great Achilles (something his masculine brother Hector could not accomplish). He also helps Trojan citizens escape, including Aeneas, to whom he gives the phallic sword of Troy and thus ensures a Trojan future. Finally, Leonidas declines Xerxes' offer of peace that would allow him to be warlord of all Greece because such a settlement would entail Spartan subjugation to the effeminate Persians, with their anti–Western mysticism and tyranny. Ultimately, these masculine and often fatal struggles for freedom successfully eliminate the threat posed by the feminized imposters, restoring and reaffirming democratic (or at least consensual) rule and by extension both proper patriarchal authority and traditional gender roles. Although referring to the Spartans under Leonidas, Gideon Nisbet's observation that such determined resistance to despotism creates "icons of democratic machismo" is in fact applicable to all these male heroes (77).

Gladiator, *Troy*, and *300* each display remarkably similar constructions of proper, heterosexual masculinity. Their heroic protagonists exhibit common traits such as physical strength and prowess, a paternal concern for the security of their families and countrymen, and an unstoppable desire to thwart tyranny. They are, in short, both martial and marital. By contrast, their antagonists are presented as the antithesis of appropriate masculinity in every way: physically, sexually, morally, and especially in terms of their improper exercise of authority. These feminized, degenerate usurpers help to define heteroperformative masculinity by exemplifying everything that it is not. Therefore, in opposing them, men like Maximus, Hector, and Leonidas prove that they themselves are the true embodiment of masculinity, and that they are willing to die "manfully" to prove it.

Notes

1. Due to its significant departure from the tropes of masculinity discussed here, my analysis of sexuality and masculinity in Oliver Stone's *Alexander* (2004) can be found in a separate work, "Great Ambiguity: How Oliver Stone's *Alexander* was Defeated by its More Masculine Cinematic Rivals," *Journal of the Indiana Academy of Social Sciences* 12 (2008): 46–65.

2. See Dixon's argument that normative heterosexuality is often defined through contrast with homosexual "deviance" (100).

3. See Joshel for a brief discussion of the standard cinematic tropes of masculinity and effeminacy in Roman-themed films (16–18).

4. The following discussion of heteroperformance is based, in part, on my earlier work on Alexander the Great. See Pierce, "Great Ambiguity."

5. For further discussion of the negative portrayal of homosexuals, see Russo (122–23, 178).

6. For the connection between masculine identity and performance, see Chopra-Gant (96).

7. See Neale for a discussion of the "pleasure" derived from viewing this type of masculine violence (13).

8. For a discussion of the fawning and at times homoerotic press surrounding Maximus/Crowe's body, see Fradley (243–244).

9. See Wyke (70) and Fitzgerald (38).

10. For the homosocial relationship of the gladiators, see Fradley (246).

11. Though some scholars of the *Iliad* contend that the epic itself lacks a conclusive statement of the Achilles/Patroclus relationship as homosexual, many of the ancient traditions surrounding the epic, as well as many modern scholars, contend that the relationship was more than simply Platonically heterosexual. An in-depth discussion of the history of the relationship between Achilles and Patroclus can be found in Crompton (3–6). See also Nisbet (78).

12. See Nisbet for a discussion of the "fetishistic leather gear" worn by the Spartans and the unabashed homoeroticism evident in Frank Miller's graphic novel, *300*, the basis of Snyder's film (73).

13. For a survey of Greek/Spartan homosexuality, see Crompton (6–10).

14. See also Clum, who notes that "one of Hollywood's most important functions has been to market conventional patriarchal heterosexuality expressed through marriage as the only means to true happiness" (23).

15. The political context of Agamemnon's lust for power is discussed in more detail by Rabel (186–201).

16. As Hark explains, "The narrative trajectory in such films most often traces the male star-protagonist's liberation from his subjugated position to effect the restoration of appropriate patriarchal authority and the removal of the male-impersonator from power" (152).

17. Winkler explains that in films about ancient Rome, the protagonists' struggle against oppressive emperors "become quests for political independence and spiritual freedom or both" styled on "Americans' perception of themselves as champions of liberty" (53–54). Maximus can then be seen as a classical version and a predecessor of male American freedom fighters in the Revolutionary War. For a discussion of Maximus' farmer-hero persona and its resonance with American audiences, see Cyrino (140–144). In the same vein, in a bit of fanciful reinterpretation, *Gladiator* presents the Roman Senate in its opposition to Commodus as the democratic voice of the Roman "people," despite its oligarchic and aristocratic nature.

Works Cited

Chopra-Gant, Mike. *Hollywood Genres and Postwar America: Masculinity, Family and Nation in Popular Movies and Film Noir*. New York: I.B. Tauris, 2006.

Clum, John M. *"He's All Man": Learning Masculinity, Gayness, and Love from American Movies*. New York: Palgrave Macmillan, 2002.

Crompton, Louis. *Homosexuality and Civilization*. Cambridge: Harvard University Press, 2006.

Cyrino, Monica S. "*Gladiator* and Contemporary American Society." *Gladiator: Film and History*. Ed. Martin M. Winkler. Malden, MA: Blackwell, 2005. 124–129.
Dixon, Wheeler Winston. *Straight: Constructions of Heterosexuality in the Cinema*. Albany: State University of New York Press, 2003.
Fitzgerald, William. "Oppositions, Anxieties, and Ambiguities in the Toga Movie." *Imperial Projections: Ancient Rome in Modern Popular Culture*. Eds. Sandra R. Joshel, Margaret Malamund, and Donald T. McGuire, Jr. Baltimore: Johns Hopkins University Press, 2001. 23–49.
Fradley, Martin. "Maximus Melodramaticus: Masculinity, Masochism and White Male Paranoia in Contemporary Hollywood Cinema." *Action and Adventure Cinema*. Ed. Yvonne Tasker. New York: Routledge, 2004. 235–251.
Fredrick, David. "Titus Androgynous: Foul Mouths and Troubled Masculinity." *Arethusa* 41 (2008): 205–233.
Gladiator. Dir. Ridley Scott. Dreamworks, 2000.
Hark, Ina Rae. "Animals or Romans: Looking at Masculinity in *Spartacus*." In *Screening the Male*. Eds. Steve Cohan and Ina Rae Hark. New York: Routledge, 1993. 151–172.
Herodotus. *Histories*. Trans. George Rawlinson. New York: D. Appleton, 1875.
Ingraham, Chrys. "The Heterosexual Imaginary: Feminist Sociology and Theories of Gender." *Sociological Theory* 12.2 (1994): 203–219.
Joshel, Sandra R., Margaret Malamund, and Maria Wyke. "Introduction." *Imperial Projections: Ancient Rome in Modern Popular Culture*. Eds. Sandra R. Joshel, Margaret Malamund, and Donald T. McGuire, Jr. Baltimore: Johns Hopkins University Press, 2001. 1–22.
Neale, Steve. "Masculinity as Spectacle: Reflections on Men and Mainstream Cinema." *Screening the Male*. Eds. Steve Cohan and Ina Rae Hark. New York: Routledge, 1993. 9–19.
Nisbet, Gideon. *Ancient Greece in Film and Popular Culture*. Exeter, UK: Bristol Phoenix Press, 2006.
Rabel, Robert J. "The Realist Politics of Troy." *Troy: From Homer's Iliad to Hollywood Epic*. Ed. Martin M. Winkler. Malden, MA: Blackwell, 2007. 186–201.
Russo, Vito. *The Celluloid Closet: Homosexuality in the Movies*. Rev. ed. New York: Harper and Row, 1987.
Segal, Lynne. *Slow Motion: Changing Masculinities, Changing Men*. 3d ed. New York: Palgrave Macmillan, 2007.
300. Dir. Zach Snyder. Warner Bros. Pictures, 2006.
Troy. Dir. Wolfgang Petersen. Warner Bros. Pictures, 2004.
Turner, Susanne. "'Only Spartan Women Give Birth to Real Men': Zach Snyder's *300* and the Male Nude." *Classics for All: Reworking Antiquity in Mass Culture*. Eds. Dunstan Lowe and Kim Shahabudin. Newcastle Upon Tyne, UK: Cambridge Scholars, 2009. 128–149.
Winkler, Martin M. "The Roman Empire in American Cinema After 1945." *Imperial Projections: Ancient Rome in Modern Popular Culture*. Eds. Sandra R. Joshel, Margaret Malamund, and Donald T. McGuire, Jr. Baltimore: Johns Hopkins University Press, 2001. 50–76.
Wyke, Mariae. *Projecting the Past: Ancient Rome, Cinema and History*. New York: Routledge, 1997.

From Maciste to Maximus and Company
The Fragmented Hero in the New Epic

ANDREW B.R. ELLIOTT

There is an old and well-worn adage that a given society will get the heroes it deserves. A society based on a culture of violence and iniquity, it suggests, will in turn see the rise to power of appropriately violent and iniquitous heroes; conversely, a culture based on fairness and justice will produce heroes of valor, righteousness, and what T. H. White famously refers to as "might for right." Though — as with many such adages— there is undoubtedly a great deal of simplification, assumption, and normalization at work here, the recent spate of sword and sandal epics seem to confirm the rule far more regularly than they refute it. Despite the truisms on which the adage relies, an interesting further proposition presents itself, that reading backwards, "getting the hero we deserve" means that an examination of the heroes of a given culture ought to reveal some of the ideological constructs at work in the background. Over the course of the last decade epic heroes have been placed (with varying degrees of success) into an often vague, loosely-defined or wholly mythical Classical Antiquity, but this essay will argue that from *Gladiator* to *Centurion* one trend seems to hold true: among the heroes represented, the kind of hero which the New Epic presents to us is one which embodies a complex range of traits. The heroes provided for a twenty-first century audience must balance and assuage complicated gender debates, while simultaneously reconciling a fundamentally ambivalent attitude to violence and combining an uneasy sense of spectacle with a level of agency unknown to many of cinema's earliest epic heroes.

I will begin this chapter by examining the role and function of the Italian *forzuto*, or muscleman, arguing that his representation in Italian pepla of the late 1950s (itself a reworking of earlier, often silent, epics from the 1914 version of *Cabiria* onwards) was dependent on his physical strength which asserted his authority on the level of the body and which overtly rejected any wider political and ideological influence. This will lead in the second section of the paper to a consideration of the more complex range of heroic attributes on offer in the Hollywood epics of the same decade, which seek to present a sort of "tamed" *forzuto* figure, and one whose power lies not in his purely physical strength (though cases can of course be found which draw influence from these muscular *forzuti*) but on their authority and capacity to wield power on the politico-ideological level. Drawing these two disparate trends together, in my final section I propose that these various (and often mutually exclusive) demands have brought about a renegotiation of the nature and value of the epic hero, one who—rather than embodying all of these heroic virtues—has become fragmented into a heroic group.

Given the enormous scope which this hypothesis represents, however, this chapter will focus on one or two cases in particular—deemed symptomatic of the wider trends at work in each "genre cycle"—in order to bring to the surface a more general pattern in the construction of heroes in the New Epic.[1] This will lead me to propose a new understanding of the function of the hero which is drawn as much from reception theory and contemporary thought about gender and masculinity as it is from genre theory proper. While such an essay can only ever scratch the surface of what is patently a complex and multifaceted issue, my main hope is to at least open this area up to the sort of measured debate which recent scholarship in hero culture and reception theory has inaugurated.

The Forzuto in Italian Pepla

The first hurdle, perhaps, in understanding the role of the peplum hero, is to understand what precisely is meant by the term peplum (and its plural pepla), since over time the terms have acquired a range of possible meanings, and even within single works it is possible to see it used in very different ways. Though a great deal of scholarship has rendered this term in and of itself problematic, the most precise and succinct definition for my purposes here is one which "restrict[s] the use of peplum to the group of films depicting the ancient world made in Italy by Italian directors in the period 1958–65" (Pomeroy 48).[2] Given that I am relying on the reception of a specific body of films rather than a genre, the benefit of this definition is that (in contrast to many other definitions which are reliant on costuming, time-frame, or even narrative intent) Pomeroy's classification uses a specific time and place of production, allowing us to treat them relatively unproblematically as a *filone*, a loose strand of films made consciously and deliberately according to a common pattern.

Throughout this cycle of pepla, one of the most dominant features is the evolution of a stock character in the muscular hero, a character type which is drawn whole-cloth from the earlier epics of the silent era. Despite a range of appearances and settings, from *Le Fatiche di Ercole / Hercules* (1958) through to the later *Ercole, Sansone, Maciste e Ursus gli invincibili / Samson and the Mighty Challenge* (1964), it is fair to say that the *forzuto* hero varies very little other than in name. The ubiquity of the hero as a character type rather than an individual is demonstrated *ab initio* by the lack of distinction between individual heroes both within the *filone* and in their translation to other cultures. For example, what begins as a Maciste film to an Italian audience (such as *Maciste, l'eroe più grande del mondo*, 1964) might end up as a film about Goliath for an American audience (*Goliath and the Sins of Babylon*). Similarly, where Maciste becomes Hercules in *Maciste e la regina di Samar* (U.S. title: *Hercules against the Moon Men*, 1964), in the same year Hercules in *Ercole l'invincibile* (1964) becomes his own son in the translated title (*Son of Hercules in the Land of Darkness*). Countless other examples could easily be adduced here, but suffice to say that this interchangeability indicates perhaps more than anything else that the only stable element underpinning the peplum films of this period was the space which the ubiquitous hero filled in the cultural imagination: "Whether he was called Goliath, Ursus, Samson, Hercules or even Maciste, the hero is the same beefy warrior who fights injustice, villains and gruesome monsters" (Chapman 16).

Equally importantly, a part of this re-negotiation of cultural ideals was deeply concerned with the masculinity of the *forzuto*, since "the most striking recurring feature is the way the male body is valorized" (Lagny 170). Whatever the hero's name, one prerequisite which the films demanded was an extraordinarily built body that would be on permanent display throughout the film. The hero's musculature extended far beyond the capacity for power through violence, but became a defining characteristic of the films themselves, meaning that "the peplum can take place almost anywhere, but one ingredient of the formula is immutable: the film must have a shirtless, muscular hero" (Chapman 34). The exposed male body works as a perfect example of masculinity as spectacle not action, which explains in part the prevalence of the short skirts which were to give the peplum its name (from the Greek *peplos*) and ultimately which were to characterize their approach to the body, since they expose the most, or cover the least, amount of flesh on both men and women.

What is particularly striking about these exposed bodies is how little they were eroticized. Despite the vast array of nubile, scantily-clad, lithe bodies of both sexes put on display, and despite the endless series of dancing girls, attempted seductions, and the tendency to clasp the vulnerable young heroine to the hero's oversized chest, there is almost no overt sexuality — and certainly nothing that would worry an age-advisory board. The same, broadly speaking, can be said for the films' approach to violence, both explicit and implicit within the films. In general, scant examples exist of either the objective "systemic" violence which for Slavoj Žižek sustains "relations of domination and exploitation," or the more direct, "subjective" battles and confrontations which pervade the pepla (8–10). For a series of films which promise so much sex and violence in their manly men and delicate nymphs, there is a curious absence of both, an absence which leads Domenico Paoella to term the pepla as "a poor man's psycho-analysis," owing to the level to which the violence is only suggested and vicariously purged (qtd. Lagny 172).

Given such restrictions in formula, narrative, and the narrow characterization of gender roles in the persistent appeal to imagined expectations of audiences, it becomes clear that very little variation can be established within the peplum framework, engendering a great deal of resemblance from one film to another. As the peplum phenomenon grew towards the late 1950s, and despite minor variations in location and incidental detail, the limited number of situations which demanded such superhuman strength (coupled with the inexhaustible flow coming from Cinecittà) meant that this simple resemblance began to descend into outright repetition. Nervous producers whose fortunes rode on the success or failure of the latest feature began to fear any divergences from the stock characters and plots, to the extent that, by the early 1960s, the peplum film in many cases became simple variations on a well-worn theme:

> A majority of these films follow the same basic pattern. Set during some generic period of ancient Roman or Greek history, our hero discovers a "wrong" (usually an evil dictator who has usurped the throne of a kingdom) and in setting out to right it will upset the villain who will sent [sic] waves of cannon fodder soldiers at the hero, all building up to a climactic confrontation with a nice happy ending [Young].

What emerges from this repetition, then, is that regardless of the name, or even the narrative situation, the pattern of the pepla produces an archetypal Maciste, who represents a man of the people, and one who is able to use his strength to right wrongs, fight injustice, and overpower all threats to the law (which in Steve Neale's terms is largely synonymous with the ruling ideology). It quickly becomes apparent that despite the avowedly "lowbrow" quality of the films, an ideological dimension is added to the light tone of the piece which

> is most notable when comparing the Pepla to many of the later Euro-cult genres, from the Western to the Giallo, in which nihilism and tragic endings were all too common — the Traditional Peplums [sic] were almost invariably light in tone and although rarely resorting to all-out comedy, comic relief characters were often a feature of the genre ... [Young].

While representing a cheery affront to all enemies of freedom, the ur-Maciste nevertheless takes it upon himself, however unwittingly, to uphold the law, which requires a clear conception of right and wrong, and an unblinking acceptance of the prevalent ruling ideology. Simultaneously, and more problematically, the violence of the films begins to adopt a more sinister dimension in order to avoid becoming pure spectacle with no meaning. Given that "violence becomes spectacle when there is no narrative function," the films' insistence on Maciste's physical strength condemns them to concoct plot points which *require* a highly visual display of power while avoiding violence wherever possible, because "a display of the male body needs to be compensated for by the suggestion of action" (Hark 154–5, Tasker 75). As Claude Aziza comments, "These exposed bodies, in order to be valued, must deliver tours-de-force which the actors struggle to achieve: to lift up blocks of stone, break down doors or walls" (39). Consequently, while the hero's muscles are there to be admired as synonymous with "real" masculinity, they must not be simply ornamental: they must instead be put to work to avoid becoming pure spectacle. Fusing these two strands together, we see that the *forzuto* is required to use his muscles to fight against "enemies of freedom" and uphold the law, precisely to avoid spectacle, and to show that his strength is being placed in the service of a higher power.

Underpinning the heroic redemption narrative, then, the *forzuto*'s heroics come to represent a confluence of two distinct trends; on the one hand, his muscles and intertextual reputation reinforce his unique position as one who is able to uphold the law, while on the other his support of the law constructs him as an ideologically charged hero (but one without political agency)—what Louis Althusser might otherwise term a function of the Ideological State Apparatus. In other words, because he is in a position to subjugate others with violence, yet he only uses that violence in the service of the status quo without actually playing a part in the political process of governance, the muscleman hero is liable to be harnessed as an agent of the ruling state ideology.

A useful example of this seeming paradox occurs in one of the more able offerings from the peplum cycle, *La Battaglia di Maratona* (directed by Jacques Tourneur and an uncredited Mario Bava, 1959). The opening credits use a montage of various well-built, male athletes engaged in suitably ancient Greek sports to introduce our hero, Philippides (played by Steve Reeves, the Hercules *per antonomasia* of the peplum cycle), as a muscular, dashing, and powerful hero of the Olympic Games (it is no coincidence that the film was made the year before the Olympic Games were to be held in Rome) who is offered as a prize the position of Commander of the Sacred Guard of Athens. Thus, within only a few minutes of the film's opening, and with a bare minimum of dialogue, a democratic drive is put in place; the winner of the games (that is, the strongest) becomes in turn the visible symbol of state strength. His role as Commander, however, is somewhat paradoxically not a political one, but rather reflects a desire by the Athenian Senate to harness the power of the "strongest man in the world" in support of the political elite—despite his elevation, the film takes great pains to stress his roots as a man of the people, showing him working in the fields as the archetypal hero of popular extraction.

With Philippides safely bound to the soil, the politico-ideological level of the film is confined wholly to the Senate, a world deprived of the exposed male body (wrapped in the ubiquitous—and, in the world of Hollywood, androgynous—toga). The politico-ideological sphere is a world characterized by a power struggle between Callimaco and Teocrito (Philippe Hersent and Sergio Fantoni), representing the *weakness of* the law and *traitor to* the law respectively. Callimaco embodies the familiar trope of a weak figure of authority being led astray by an ambitious and ruthless villain (Teocrito), placing him in direct opposition to Philippides, who emerges as an unequivocal hero and whose strength and unshakable moral compass align the fortune of the state with the strength of the common man. Having thus polarized the characters along two axes (defined unambiguously as hero and villain), the remaining chips are left to fall as they may, with the various plot twists and complications serving only to underscore this central opposition. Philippides meets and falls in love with Callimaco's beautiful daughter Andromeda (Mylène Demongeot), who fills the stock role of the meek, innocent love interest (the pure), and who is in turn contrasted with "the seemingly perverse yet maternal seductiveness of the courtesan Charis [Daniela Rocca], who has been told by the evil Theocritus to betray Philippides" (Lagny 165). By the end of the first act of the film, the principal characters have been reduced to players along two groups arranged around the central figure of Callimaco, with those seeking to pervert the law on one side, and those seeking to uphold it on the other.

The Hollywood Epic Hero

On a purely narrative level, the above outline of *La Battaglia di Maratona* may sound suspiciously familiar to viewers of *The Fall of the Roman Empire*, made five years later in 1964. In the absence of a just and wise representative of the Law (here Marcus Aurelius), a treacherous and power-hungry young usurper (Commodus) tries to seize control of the state. The only barrier to his ambitions comes in the form of a Commander of his army (Livius), whose official function draws him, albeit reluctantly, into the political and dynastic power-struggle, and whose involvement with the innocent daughter of the ruler (Lucilla) unites his desires—both on the political and the emotional level—to create one single objective: to use his power to overthrow the usurper and restore the Law.

This is not to say that they are essentially the same film, of course; far from it. Nor does it imply that there is a level of influence, intertextuality, or borrowing from one film to another, since it is clear that there is a great deal more to a film than can be gleamed from the reduction of its plot to a series of key structures, and in any case there is no evidence to suggest that the makers of the later film had ever even heard of *Battaglia*. Rather, my point here is that, for one reason or another, *The Fall of the Roman Empire* expounds a very similar narrative situation which calls for a very similar kind of hero; one who would— in Neale's terms—negotiate the contradiction "between narcissism and the Law, between an image of *narcissistic* authority on the one hand and an image of *social* authority on the other" (9). This is achieved, according to Ina Rae Hark, through a process as a result of which "the narcissistic ego-ideal, given more to action than words, undermines the tyrant's hold on political power through physical rebellion until a proper enunciator of the law of the father can replace him" (163).

Nevertheless, despite the various plot similarities, even a cursory glance at the film in relation to the Hollywood epics which dominated the 1950s and early 1960s is sufficient to demonstrate that the heroes on display differ markedly from those of the Italian pepla. In *The Fall of the Roman Empire*, for example, the hero Livius is played neither by Victor Mature nor Kirk Douglas, two of the most prominent muscular heroes, nor even by Richard Egan, whose earlier *The 300 Spartans* had demonstrated a grandeur and leadership which went far beyond his shirtless role in *Demetrius and the Gladiators* (discussed below); instead the role went to Stephen Boyd, the powerful (but neither muscular nor exposed) Marcellus of *Ben-Hur*, just as the role of Judah Ben-Hur had itself gone to Charlton Heston, a chiseled and imposing — but not overly burly — leading man. What this suggests, then, is that even in a similar narrative situation to that of *La Battaglia di Maratona*, it was no longer sufficient for a hero of the Hollywood epic to wield a purely physical power, but that he must also play an active role on the politico-ideological level, too. Boyd, then, must possess not simply muscular power to confront an oppressive regime, but the sort of dignity and rectitude of characters like Ben-Hur, Spartacus, and his Biblico-Greco-Roman forebears. A similar case occurs in a film made two years earlier, Rudolph Maté's 1962 *The 300 Spartans*, in which the characterization of King Leonidas must negotiate this fine balance between power and spectacle, all the while satisfying stringent censorship requirements. Like Stephen Boyd in his role as Livius, *The 300 Spartans* conceives of the epic hero as a similarly powerful hero, but one which is conceived as a man of valor, not of brawn. Egan's heroic exploits as King Leonidas place him in direct contrast to his role in *Demetrius and the Gladiators*, in which he is exposed as pure spectacle, driving the plot along — as so many later pepla would do — by simply lifting, carrying, and throwing things while flexing his pectorals in a display of to-be-looked-at-ness.[4]

Taking two revealing scenes from Maté's film in particular, the implications of this form of heroic representation become clear: where Egan's power is foregrounded in his initial construction as a beefy warrior in *Demetrius and the Gladiators*, his transmutation into epic hero in *The 300 Spartans* adds a second ideological layer to the characterization. In the first film, Egan appears as the ruthless gladiator Dardanius who, in an effort to provoke Demetrius, seizes the latter's beloved Lucia and tries to force himself on her in full view of our hero. Holding her aloft in his arms, a low camera angle coupled with harsh key lighting paints Dardanius in a strikingly similar pose to that of the peplum heroes discussed above. His exposed, muscular torso, coupled with the submissive position of the female lead, serves to underscore the simplified gender roles characteristic of the peplum, transforming the scene into an archetypal snapshot which could just as easily be taken from a Sergio Corbucci film as from Hollywood's pageantry. What is particularly interesting about Egan's role in *Demetrius and the Gladiators* is that the shot which would later be synonymous with buff heroism in the peplum genre is in fact designed to show the polar opposite: that Dardanius is a barely civilized bully whose overly masculine display of power is symptomatic of precisely the kind of barbarism which the state sought to contain, as his later violence both in and out of the arena would reveal.

On the surface, however, Egan's later characterization in *The 300 Spartans* works hard to reverse the outward signs so as to remove any question of legitimacy or unchecked power. As the noble King Leonidas, he must be seen to embody the nobility and civilization of an urbane, restrained, and ideologically-neutral hero. Accordingly, he is loaded with the outward signs which would come to be familiar to all fans of the sword and sandal genre; gone is the exposed, muscular torso and bare-chested aggression of Dardanius. Instead Leonidas becomes a dignified soldier, decked in the "the red war cloaks [which] are so becoming to men," as one character defines the Spartan uniform (*The 300 Spartans*). Clad in the helmet and breastplate which belong to Hollywood's ancient worlds (if not the historical Sparta), Egan as Leonidas, through a direct reversal of his earlier characterization, comes to represent the sort of ideologically-approved, just warrior who would be infinitely more palatable to a middle–American audience in the wake of a series of external threats. It is of course not enough simply to deck the warrior in the signs and regalia of state-sanctioned violence; yet the visual construction of the character clearly speaks volumes about what kind of hero is being imagined here. Equally at home on the senate floor as on the battlefield, both Egan and Boyd embody a wholly new kind of hero who reflects— in terms of both narrative construction and of visual attributes— the kind of righteousness and legitimacy which the peplum hero's spectacular masculinity never quite managed to attain. Nevertheless, even this construction of heroism is subject to a range of audience expectations which are tied far more to the period of production than to the period being represented.

The New Epic Hero

So far, then, what emerges is that the typology of the epic hero is not developed necessarily as a response to narrative requirements, nor even according to the socio-demographic gradations of the audiences sought, but according to *perceived* audience expectations. On the one hand, the sculpted muscle of the peplum's *forzuto* courted a gaze which celebrated the male body's potential as a means of upholding the law but without interference in the political sphere, serving as a vindication of manual labor in the face of rapid industrialization in post-war Italy. On the other hand, the Hollywood epics of the 1950s saw the evolution of a very different kind of hero, one whose strength was more ideologically rooted in his moral courage and integrity, feeding audiences' preoccupations with freedom and the extirpation of the "enemy within."[5] In the latter group of films, far more important than the physical strength of the hero was his political power, which demanded the courage to stand up and fight against a corrupt state, against the threat of hostile regimes (be they Communist infiltrations in *The Robe* or a denunciation of McCarthyite witch hunts in *Spartacus*). In this regard, a greater importance comes to be attached to the mastery of the weapon rather than to physical, muscular force, a borrowing from the Western genre (see Cawelti 58–60) which functions both as a visual demonstration of controlled, "pure" violence as well as an exculpation of the hero's moral guilt by placing him at a distance from the villain. Where both use their power to protect against clear, identifiable threats (gender equality and industrialization, political enemies/Cold War), it was the nature of those threats which dictated to some extent what kind of hero was required.

As a result of this, in the New Epic subgenre (characterized—if not inaugurated—by Ridley Scott's *Gladiator*) the muscular epic hero stands at the end of a complex evolution of the hero and his relationship through violence. Filtered through an entire generation's ambivalent (and sometimes contradictory) attitudes towards violence, political hostilities, and an increasingly complex relationship with masculinity, the New Epic hero found himself instantly on difficult grounds. Throughout the 1980s and early 1990s, as the muscular hero became hijacked by the action genre (with box-office stars like Stallone and Schwarzenegger epitomizing the shirtless muscleman), the body became harnessed once again as an ideological construct, who is in equal parts passive spectacle and active aggressor against corrupt regimes (see Arroyo and Takser, *Bodies*). In an article discussing the shift in representations of the action body over two decades, Christina Lee observes that "in the 1970s and 1980s the residual after-shocks of the Cold War and Vietnam paved the way for a generation of hulking heroes whose bodies seemed as indomitable as their spirits" (560). This emphasis on spectacular bodies and their political significance was to lead to films like *Rocky* and *The Terminator*, which proposed an ideal body "iconic of brute strength, industrialisation and the colonisation of public space" (Lee 560). In the wake of these films, and along with the long-overdue backlash against male domination of the genre, Lee notes that "within the last decade, there has been a shift away from the bulky towards the lithe and compact action figure," which places *Gladiator*'s Maximus, like Livius of the *Fall of the Roman Empire*, at a critical point in the evolution of the hero figure (560).

Taking into account the general dissatisfaction with overly and overtly masculine heroes through the action genre, it became clear that the New Epic must turn its attention elsewhere for a new heroic ideal. Harking back to the historical epics of the 1950s and 1960s was no longer an option, since the centrality of the political concerns of the 1950s which infused these earlier epics led eventually to an ideological overdetermination of the hero; placing too much emphasis on the prevailing ideology had (somewhat paradoxically) fixed the hero not in Ancient Rome or Greece, but firmly within the confines of the mid-twentieth century and its political concerns. Nevertheless, to claim that the New Epic hero was to be free from ideology altogether would be a naïve — if not outright misleading — proposition, since the parallels which director Ridley Scott would later draw between the Crusades and the Gulf War (in *Kingdom of Heaven*), along with the clear influence of modern ideals of freedom incorporated into the apolitical hero, set Maximus firmly into the same mold as his Hollywood forebears.

Re-framing the issue in the terms of ego-ideals and narcissism outlined above, the problem emerges more clearly. With the demise of the muscular hero and audiences' general ambivalence toward unchecked aggression, Scott was no longer able to rely on an automatic narcissistic identification with the *forzuto*, since the kind of innocent, apolitical strongman so popular in the peplum was no longer the ideal to which a given spectator would aspire. In fact, over-emphasizing the hero's musculature or physical power would risk a return to the increasingly niche subgenres of violent 1990s action films of sculpted martial artists like Jean-Claude Van Damme, or else recall certain ultra-violent cult films like *Chopper* (2000) or Crowe's former skinhead in *Romper Stomper* (1992). This was precisely the kind of characterization Scott was obliged to avoid if he was to court sufficient audience numbers to recoup the huge production budget. The narrative necessity for action rather than spectacle (exemplified by Maximus' intra-diegetic rejection of his role as pure spectacle in his famous cry of "Are you not entertained?") equally precludes the use of built body as spectacle, obliging the hero instead to earn his place as a hero by his moral leadership (*Gladiator*). This leadership, however, must not be so prominent as to make of him an ideal ruler, since it embodies precisely the kind of narcissistic ego-ideal which, to repeat Hark, "undermines the tyrant's hold on political power through physical rebellion until a proper enunciator of the law of the father can replace him" (163). This dual evolution means that Maximus emerges as a new kind of epic hero at a critical juncture in which he must embody a wide range of *contradictory* values: he must be hard but forgiving, built but agile, exposed but impermeably armored, sensitive but hard-hearted, violent but not aggressive.

Given this exhaustive, and at times mutually exclusive, laundry list of conflicting values required from the New Epic hero in order to appeal to a wide audience base, these fissiparous demands have led, I argue, to a fundamental fragmentation of the heroic role. Rather than attempt to make one hero demonstrate this impossible mix in its entirety, my argument here is that the hero tends to be judged less by his ability to conform to such (contradictory) values, and more by the company he keeps, forging new character types into a loose-knit group designed to appeal to this broad spectrum of audience expectations. To some extent, this fragmentation is already visible in the characterization of *Spartacus*, in which Spartacus' role as rebel is supported by the traditional musclemen of the gladiator school; yet in Kubrick's film the protagonist nevertheless bears a clear resemblance to the muscular hero in his exposed torso and visualized capacity for violence, as Hark has demonstrated. What is interesting about a film like *Gladiator*, then, is the extent to which these supporting character typologies assume many of the characteristics traditionally expected of the *forzuto* (if not his Hollywood equivalent). The secondary roles of Draba and Crixus (Woody Strode and John Ireland) in *Spartacus* contribute to generic convention by providing a loose framework for Scott's film in which Maximus' "heavies," Juba and Hagen (Djimon Hounsou and Ralf Moeller), rework the legacy of the exposed male body so prominent in the peplum. Traces of the muscular *forzuto* can, in fact, be discerned in the characterization of the "gentle giant" Hagen. His function within the narrative of the film seems predominantly to provide heavyweight back-up to Maximus and foreground his leadership skills (the insinuation here is that if a captured Teutonic warrior can become a devoted follower of Maximus, anyone can).

By invoking a split in the characterization of the epic hero, Scott is able to have his cake and eat it, too: with subsidiary characters absorbing the spectacle which is "required" of the genre, Maximus is free to play a more active role in fighting tyranny on the politico-ideological level. *Gladiator*'s hero accordingly embodies the requisite elements of leadership and the promulgation of the law in the absence of an ideal ruler, yet without the fundamentally violent aspect which mars the action hero to such a great extent. Since he is clearly no weakling, the covered-up body raises new questions for masculinity, since it represents the *potential* for violent action without necessarily foregrounding those capabilities (in some respects it is a visual representation of the "kind words and a gun" diplomacy). Such a conception of the New Epic hero, alongside new masculine ideals which call into question the reign of the musclebound heroes of the previous decade, inaugurates a new kind of hero, one who is no longer the lone warrior of *Conan the Barbarian*, *Rambo*, or *Terminator*, but is instead the head of a heroic unit, assembled ad-hoc to depose tyrannous regimes. As a whole, the team comes to embody an ideal balance of qualities which negotiates the disparate and conflicting requirements of the New Epic hero.

A more obvious instance of this fragmentation occurs in the recent adaptation to the screen of *The Last Legion* (2007), based on Valerio Massimo Manfredi's novel *L'Ultima Legione*. With the accession and immediate downfall of the emperor Romulus in the late fifth century A.D., the remnants of the destroyed

Ninth Legion, led by deposed general Aurelius, must shepherd the young emperor to safety in Britain.[6] The "army," therefore, rather than embodying the State with its concomitant legitimacy, is instead relegated to the status of outsider, placing the hero into the position of narcissistic ego-ideal. Yet the film takes a rather different turn, combining a group of disparate character types (drawn, like the Alamo-style plot itself, from the Western and Vietnam War film genres) into the collective hero. The various issues facing the New Epic outlined above—gender theory, the politico-ideological framework, and the civilization of the violent *forzuto*—are resolved by precisely this fragmentation in which a range of perceived audience expectations are met by a variety of character types. Gender debates and the problems of occidental bias are met by the inclusion of exotic Other in the form of an Indian princess, Mira; the exposed male body comes in the form of Nonso Anozie's Batiatus, a heavily-built warrior who fulfills a remarkably similar role to *Gladiator*'s Hagen; the problem of politico-ideological legitimacy is countered by the druid/priest Ambrosinus, who lends the team the otherworldly wisdom and counsel which, as a representative of a venerable and "worthy" institution, replaces the questionable legitimacy of the state. As a result, the heroic group is able to uphold the law of the father (by protecting the boy-emperor Romulus) and defending against the tyrant's hold on power by physical rebellion without seizing power itself.

In one particularly revealing scene, the spatial compositions of the frame reflect precisely this loss of legitimacy, when Aurelius (Colin Firth) shields the young emperor from the attacking "barbarians" who are, quite literally, at the gate. Standing in the foreground of the shot, Aurelius stands in front of a wall of shields formed by the emperor's guard with only his sword to protect himself; the defenseless Romulus stands behind the row of shields, in the doorway of the palace. Such an arrangement places both Romulus and Aurelius outside of the security of the imperial guard (state protection), recreating precisely the narrative situation seen in *Battaglia di Maratona* and *The Fall of the Roman Empire*, in which the weakened state (Callimaco, Lucilla, Romulus) is defended by a narcissistic ego-ideal who undermines the tyrant in order to restore power to the legitimate ruler (Philippides, Livius, Aurelius). In the sequence which follows, as Romulus tries to escape the barbarian invasion, he drops the crown to the floor. When his pursuer arrives on the scene, instead of seizing the crown (in other words, usurping rightful power), he instead crushes it underfoot. If the crown—as traditionally metonymic symbol of rightful authority and just law—is destroyed, then the legitimacy of the status quo can only be restored by an assimilation of its various constituent parts: Romulus (dynastic ruler), Aurelius (democratic leader), Batiatus (armed force), Ambrosinus (wisdom and statecraft), Mira (Otherness), and so on. Given that *individually* each of these character types is flawed, the film seems to suggest that they can only function *collectively* to undermine the tyrant's hold on the throne. In the case of *The Last Legion*, then, the sum of the parts is far greater than the whole.

A similar reflection of the fragmented hero can be found in the 2010 television series *Spartacus: Blood and Sand*, in which the hero works from the very outset to renounce the mantle of Kubrick's intertextual legacy. In some cases, this renunciation takes place quite literally, such as when the Thracian hero rejects his Latinized name by repeating, more and forcefully, "My name is *not* Spartacus"; elsewhere, his total disregard for the political ideal of freedom is underscored by his nonchalance and refusal to form bonds with his fellow warriors, a direct reversal of Douglas' ideological drive for freedom (*Spartacus: Blood and Sand*). Nevertheless, even by the close of the first episode of the series, it becomes patently clear that Spartacus is by no means an amiable, inspirational hero, and the producers of the show make few attempts to disguise his outright misanthropy; he is no leader, he is apolitical, and — aside from his unchecked aggression when provoked — he is not much of a warrior either. One of the critical moments for the series occurs at the end of episode two, in which Spartacus realizes that there is only one way to guarantee his survival: by banding together with the other gladiators of the school, even pledging allegiance to the owner, Batiatus (again), in order to guarantee his freedom. In this respect, the secondary characters of the school embody the various values required to overthrow the corrupt rulers of Rome: Crixus (Manu Bennett) represents the perfect warrior; the Doctore (played by *300*'s messenger, Peter Mensah), imparts the requisite sense of leadership and authority over the gladiators; and Varro (Jai Courtney) serves an ideological function as a free man voluntarily entering the arena to clear his debts and return to his family, leaving the entire political domain to Batiatus (played by John Hannah, in a role reprised from *The Last Legion*). It is, as Varro consistently reminds the audience, only by uniting under the same banner that their individual agendas may adequately be served.

A final example to be adduced here in support of the fragmented hero theory comes in the form of the 2010 remake of *Clash of the Titans*, which allows for a direct comparison with the earlier version. Given that very little of the original plot has been revised, the team's relationship with the hero intimates that a sea change has taken place over the course of the three decades which separate the two films. In the 1981 version, the narrative focus is on Perseus and his quest to win the hand of Andromeda (of which main plot point the secondary quests form a part); though he initially sets out with a handful of soldiers who might be identified as a fragmented heroic grouping, as the film draws on it becomes clear where our sympathies are designed to lie. As each quest is completed, one by one the group is thinned down by circumstances (climbing the mountain, entering Medusa's lair, fighting the giant scorpions, etc.) which force the hero to carry on without any support. In the final showdown, Perseus is unambiguously constructed as a solitary hero, who alone possesses the courage and skill to complete the quest, and to whose muscular arms alone Andromeda's safety is indebted. The ad-hoc group of soldiers in the 2010 remake, however, reflects a distinctly different grouping, one which recognizes the value of diversity, embraces the Other, and from whom Perseus draws the courage to stand against the dark forces of the gods that are pitted against him. While it is again Perseus alone who stands to face the Kraken in the final showdown, the earlier quests of the film draw influence from such a range of other New Epics (*Lord of the Rings*, *Gladiator*, and most of all *Kingdom of Heaven*) that the film can be seen as a kind of mythological road movie, whose power comes from the support of the team, a team which was all but invisible in the 1981 original. To allow one example to speak for many, it is noteworthy that it is only the later version which tries to accommodate any of the monsters—the Djinn warriors who play an integral part in the heroes' journey. The space of only thirty years, then, has been enough to testify to a sea change in audience expectations and generic conventions of the epic hero.

Conclusions

Is this fragmentation, then, symptomatic of a wider pattern in recent invocations of the Epic hero? Certainly it is insufficient to speculate on the basis of a handful of examples drawn from the genre, and especially when these examples have been consciously chosen as the most obvious demonstrations of this fragmentary style. Much more difficult questions are raised, for example, by the adaptation of *The Lord of the Rings*, whose filmic influences can to some degree be traced both vertically in time to the sword and sorcery genre (itself a spin-off from the sword and sandal) and horizontally in context to generic conventions of the road movie/buddy movie, literary adaptations, and the evolution of New Zealand's national cinema. However, the motley group who form the focus of Peter Jackson's film does allow for a similar range of character archetypes (the sagacious elder, the powerful "heavy," the lightning fast weapons expert, etc.), which could easily be seen as a strong influence on recent recreations of Classical Antiquity. On a similar level, it must be conceded that the notion of a group rather than the solitary hero is by no means new to the genre, traceable back as far as the beginnings of the sword and sandal film in the silent era, where in a film like *Cabiria* the *forzuto* Ursus is backed up by a group which collectively aims to depose the unjust and tyrannical rule.

Yet, even taking into account such objections, there is clear evidence that there has been a fundamental change in the ways in which we imagine and characterize the epic hero in the last decade. Films like *Gladiator*, *The Last Legion*, and *Clash of the Titans*, three of the more successful films of the New Epic cycle, demonstrate to great effect that the role of the epic hero has been subject to a fundamental change in the wake of post-classical cinema, the changing tastes of audiences, and developments in masculinity studies in the perception of the ideal-ego. These later offerings try to establish an ideal hero not by a potentially limiting return to male ideals (which are not only outmoded, but also complex and at times contradictory), but instead by demonstrating a much greater and far more democratic fragmentation of heroic virtues. What remains to be seen, however, is the effect that such fragmentary heroes will have on the accuracy (or authenticity) of these historical films, for although it may be necessary to court the much more democratic modern audiences (to whom feudal hierarchies are distinctly unpalatable), there can be no doubt that these groups fundamentally alter the social structures of the past. By devolving the muscular, politico-ideological and gender roles to a group of followers, for instance, these subordinates are being elevated to a broadly equal footing with the hero, which erodes the hierarchy of governance that properly belongs to the Late Roman era, and most certainly would be out of place in a general's relationship with/to his emperor. *Beowulf* alone, for example, would present an interesting opportunity to explore the recreation of these hierarchical relationships over the course of time, and even a surface comparison between *Beowulf* (2007) and *Beowulf and Grendel* (2005) would reveal a strikingly different relationship between the group and the hero; neither, it scarcely needs to be said, bears any real relationship with the strictly vertical feudalism of the original poem.

Even so, these instances of the fragmented hero are sufficient to show, at the very least, that the New Epic hero has returned to the fray to find a very different battle playing out compared to the ones left behind in the 1960s. Where once in *The Robe* the "enemy within" would suffice to allow a patriotic, morally upright leader to vanquish all to the eternal gratitude of his compatriots, the degree of difference among ideological beliefs in the twenty-first century places insurmountable barriers against our heroes—barriers which no amount of Herculean muscle could tear down. In the introductory chapter to his book *Heroes*, Paul Johnson offers an appealing definition of the hero, drawn from Homer, as "a name given to men of superhuman strength, courage or ability" (xii). Where once this might have held true for the Homeric hero, one of the solutions employed by recent epics is to interpret the plural "men" of Johnson's quotation as a very real plurality. These "men" reflect a fragmentation of the heroic role into a loose grouping of individuals who each embody one or more of the qualities demanded of our hero, rather than adopting strict categories of heroic values. By incorporating *all* of these values, the New Epic has offered us a new type of hero motif, one who is no longer superhuman but is, Leviathan-like, merely the sum of the best in each of us. To return to our adage of a society getting the heroes it deserves, perhaps this kind of loose-knit grouping, whose whole is greater than the sum of its parts, might well turn out to be precisely the kind of hero the twenty-first century will need.

Notes

1. By the term New Epic, I mean to indicate the renaissance of films released between 2000 and the present which deal to a greater or lesser extent with classical, ancient, or

mythological topics, and whose emergence is traditionally accredited to Scott's *Gladiator*. One of the most persuasive arguments for this comes in Jeffrey Richards' *Hollywood's Ancient Worlds* (London: Continuum, 2008), in which he argues, "The astonishing worldwide success of Ridley Scott's Roman epic *Gladiator* in 2000 single-handedly revived a cinematic genre that had been moribund for 35 years" (1).

2. For an excellent overview of the problems of the use of this term, see Pomeroy 29–59.

3. This is certainly the argument proposed by David Chapman in his interesting study of the peplum posters and lobby cards of the era, which allow a great deal of speculation on the audiences sought for the films.

4. It is interesting, and somewhat ironic, to note that in *300* (2006, a loose remake of *The 300 Spartans*), King Leonidas should find himself reinvented as a kind of neo-*forzuto* figure, whose exposed body serves as an index of virility, power, and male spectacle. The major difference, however, between *300*'s muscleman and his predecessor in the peplum is that the potency and virility serves as a kind of synecdoche which implies that the whole state of Sparta is cut from the same cloth; in this case, then, the exposed male body serves a politico-ideological function in and of itself.

5. For more on the encoding of agendas in late 1950s and early 1960s Hollywood epics, see Kevin J. Harty, "Agenda Layered Upon Agenda: Anthony Mann's 1961 Film *El Cid*," *Hollywood and the Holy Land: Essays on Film Depictions of the Crusades and Christian-Muslim Clashes* (Jefferson, NC: McFarland, 2010), 161–68; Andrew Elliott, "Chapter One: History, Historiography and Film," *Remaking the Middle Ages: The Methods of Cinema and History in Portraying the Medieval World* (Jefferson, NC: McFarland, 2010); and Alan Lupack, "An Enemy in Our Midst: *The Black Knight* and *The American Dream*," *Cinema Arthuriana: Twenty Essays* (Jefferson, NC: McFarland, 2002), 64–70.

6. Here I am referring to the "history" offered by the film. The historical Romulus did last a little longer than a day, though his reign was indeed over in a matter of mere months.

WORKS CITED

Agora. Dir. Alejandro Amenábar. Mod Producciones, Himenóptero, 2009.
Arroyo, Jose. *Action/Spectacle Cinema: A Sight and Sound Reader*. London: British Film Institute, 2000.
Aziza, Claude. *Le péplum, un mauvais genre*. Paris: Klincksieck, 2009.
La Battaglia di Maratona / Giant of Marathon. Dir. Jacques Tourneur. Galatea Film, 1959.
Beowulf. Dir. Robert Zemeckis. Paramount Pictures, 2007.
Beowulf and Grendel. Dir. Sturla Gunnarsson. Movision, Darklight Films, 2005.
Cabiria. Dir. Giovanni Patrone. Kino Video, 1914.
Cawelti, John. *The Six-Gun Mystique*. Bowling Green, OH: Bowling Green University Popular Press, 1970.
Centurion. Dir. Neil Marshall. 20th Century–Fox, 2010.
Chapman, David. *Retro Stud: Muscle Movie Posters from Around the World*. Portland, OR: Collectors Press, 2002.
Clash of the Titans. Dir. Desmond Davis. MGM, 1981.
Clash of the Titans. Dir. Louis Leterrier. Warner Bros., 2010.
Demetrius and the Gladiators. Dir. Delmer Daves. Twentieth Century-Fox Film Corporation, 1954.
Dyer, Richard. *White*. London: Routledge, 1997.

Ercole l'invincibile / Son of Hercules in the Land of Darkness. Dir. Alvaro Mancori. Metheus Film, 1964.
Ercole, Sansone, Maciste e Ursus gli invincibili / Samson and the Mighty Challenge. Dir. Giorgio Capitano. Films Regent, PE Films, 1964.
The Fall of the Roman Empire. Dir. Anthony Mann. Universal Pictures, 1964.
Le Fatiche di Ercole / Hercules. Dir. Pietro Francisci. Galatea Film, 1958.
Gladiator. Dir. Ridley Scott. Universal Pictures, 2000.
Hark, Ina Rae. "Animals or Romans: Looking at Masculinity in Spartacus." *Screening the Male: Exploring Masculinities in Hollywood Cinema.* Eds. Steven Cohan and Ina Rae Hark. London: Routledge, 1993. 151–172.
Johnson, Paul. *Heroes: From Alexander the Great and Julius Caesar to Churchill and de Gaulle.* New York: HarperCollins, 2007.
Kingdom of Heaven. Dir. Ridley Scott. 20th Century–Fox, 2005.
Lagny, Michèle. "Popular Taste: The Peplum." *Popular European Cinema.* Eds. Richard Dyer and Ginette Vincendeau. London: Routledge, 1992. 163–80.
The Last Legion. Dir. Doug Lefler. Dino Di Laurentiis Company, Ingenious Film Partners, 2007.
Lee, Christina. "Lock and Load(up): The Action Body in The Matrix." *Continuum: Journal of Media and Cultural Studies* 19.4 (2005): 559–569.
Maciste e la regina di Samar / Hercules Against Moon Men. Dir. Giacomo Gentilomo. CFFP, Governor Films, Nike Cinematografica, 1964.
Maciste l'eroe piu' grande del mondo / Goliath and the Sins of Babylon. Dir. Michele Lupo. Eagle, 1963.
Neale, Steve. "Masculinity as Spectacle: Reflections on Men and Mainstream Cinema." *Screening the Male: Exploring Masculinities in Hollywood Cinema.* Eds. Steven Cohan and Ina Rae Hark. London: Routledge, 1993. 9–20.
Nowell-Smith, Geoffrey, James Hay, and Gianni Volpi, eds. *The Companion to Italian Cinema.* London: BFI, 1996.
Pomeroy, Arthur John. *Then It Was Destroyed by the Volcano: The Ancient World in Film and on Television.* London: Duckworth, 2008.
The Robe. Dir. Henry Koster. Twentieth Century-Fox Film Corporation, 1953.
Spartacus. Dir. Stanley Kubrick. Universal Pictures, 1960.
Spartacus: Blood and Sand. Dirs. Michael Warn, Rick Hurst, Jesse Jacobson. Starz Productions, 2010.
Tasker, Yvonne. *Action and Adventure Cinema.* London: Routledge, 2004.
_____. *Spectacular Bodies: Gender, Genre and the Action Cinema.* London: Routledge, 2000.
300. Dir. Zack Snyder. Warner Bros., 2006.
The 300 Spartans. Dir. Rudolph Maté. Twentieth Century-Fox Film Corporation, 1962.
Young, Timothy. "The Mondo-Esoterica Guide to the Peplum." *The Mondo-Esoterica Guide to The Peplum.* 1 Feb 2011. Web.
Žižek, Slavoj. *Violence: Six Sideways Reflections.* London: Profile, 2009.

Reverent and Irreverent Violence
In Defense of Spartacus, Conan, and Leonidas

JOHN ELIA

According to philosopher and playwright Paul Woodruff, reverence is a "forgotten" virtue, praised by ancient peoples across many cultures but lost to the modern world (3). He is surely right: loss of reverence is reflected in the absence of ritual and tradition in contemporary social life; in the incessant drive to innovate, recreate, start fresh; in the degradation of communities and environments; and in thin, ahistorical moral outlooks, which place more emphasis on abstract right and wrong than on particular practices, customs, relationships, and traditions.

Reverence, as Woodruff sees it, is a recognition of one's place in the world, and a capacity to think, feel, and act skillfully in response to that place (4). Heroic narratives were, in classical Greece, important vehicles for sharing an understanding of reverence, and since heroes, because of hyper-ability or semi-divine status, were both sheltered *and* tested by the gods, they needed reverence *and* yet were unusually tempted to forego it. There is no better place to display one's excellence and to lose it than in the *agon*, or contest, especially the contest of war.

Though Conan the Barbarian is surely no Achilles or Odysseus, sword and sandal films are not just fun distractions. They are worth taking seriously. One can find in them intimations of the lost reverence that Woodruff has in mind, so beautifully depicted in ancient heroic narratives such as those of Homer. Like their Greek ancestors, sword and sandal films focus on a hero's journey, making violent contest central to the audience's experience, and putting on display the hero's excellences, whether muscular body or swordsmanship or integrity. While the campier films in the genre surely misunderstand the complexity of violence, more sophisticated entries can be understood to challenge simple conceptions of violence while treating heroic violence as an exercise in testing and confirming the importance of reverence.

Many of the films in the sword and sandal genre are framed by irreverent exploitation and force, which a hero (or heroes) must then work to avenge. Though these films are chock full of fantasy violence and, increasingly, bloodshed, engagement with characters such as Spartacus, Conan, or King Leonidas can deepen one's understanding of violence and its costs, especially violence untempered by heroic reverence. The sword and sandal genre often follows a narrative of return and making whole again, borrowed from Greek epic poetry; however, the best films in the genre show, like their Greek epic counterparts, that the success of violent return is often, if not always, a *myth*. Ultimately, films such as *Conan the Barbarian* (1982) or *300* (2006) can in no way supplant Homer's treatment of war in the *Iliad* or of journey in the *Odyssey*; yet they are about something of the same business.

The Nature of Reverence

Reverence is "to take care never to play the part of god or beast" (Woodruff 220). More specifically, says Woodruff, it is the refined capacity to have the feelings of awe, respect, and shame when these are the right feelings to have (8). Shame is a powerful negative emotion attending to violations of excellence or dignity. Respect is more positive, often a response to the excellence or dignity of others. Awe has largely positive connotations in contemporary society, but also some, perhaps lost, negative ones—to be awed is to stand checked or corrected, put in one's place; awe is responsive to high ideals, godly excellence, natural beauty, immensity, or perfection, and as such can be as terrifying as it is inspiring.

Woodruff's claim is not that modern peoples no longer have the capacity to feel shame, respect, and awe, for that is not the case, and if it were, a call to renew reverence would be misplaced. Rather, it is that this particular constellation of feelings, attitudes, and actions once had a name and a resonance within accepted systems of values (Woodruff talks specifically of ancient Greece and China, though other instances are surely available), and that, in losing track of it, one loses an understanding of the central role that reverence plays in a well-ordered life, family, and community.

Reverence and violence have a complex relationship. Reverence may sometimes require violence and personal risk because to do otherwise would be to fail in some way to honor important values. Yet reverence must always temper violence, since aggressive conflict invites one to lose sight of one's values. Woodruff, in addition to being a playwright and philosopher, is a Vietnam veteran. His book shares some anecdotes about his experiences, but also points to the central ambiguity surrounding violence and reverence. Warring has great costs, both morally and psychologically; probably, he claims, enough to make one eschew war altogether. Yet, says Woodruff,

> I believe that wars can be fought by reverent people. This may be the most controversial suggestion I make here, but it has foundations as deep as Homer's *Iliad*. If it were not so, then we could not pick out, as Homer does, failures of reverence in the opposing armies. A reverent soldier does not go on a rampage, desecrating enemy bodies or killing enemy soldiers who have become harmless. A reverent soldier takes no joy in killing, and he never forgets that the human beings on the other side are just that — human [32].

In spite of all of the pain and suffering violence causes, it happens; the best one can do is to prepare not to forget one's humanity and the humanity of others, and to preserve the values one ought always continue to be awed by, even at the height of conflict and competition.

As Woodruff suggests, epic poems such as the *Iliad* and *Odyssey* are of special assistance here, because while they often dramatize heroic violence, they also emphasize its tragic elements. Recall Achilles's complaint to Agamemnon in Book 1 of Homer's *Illiad*:

> How are you going to get any Greek warrior
> To follow you into battle again? You know,
> I don't have any quarrel with the Trojans,
> They didn't do anything to me to make me
> Come over here and fight, didn't run off my cattle or horses
> Or ruin my farmland back home in Phthia, not with all
> The shadowy mountains and moaning seas between.
> It's for you, dogface, for your precious pleasure —
> And Menelaus' honor — that we came here,
> A fact you don't have the decency to mention!
> And now you're threatening to take away the prize
> That I sweated for and the Greeks gave me [*Iliad* 1.160–171].

Achilles is preparing to help sack Troy, and he is not getting the spoils his valiant efforts deserve. Indeed, he wonders why he is even fighting for Agamemnon. And now Agamemnon has threatened to take away the beautiful Briseis, Achilles's war prize. Achilles had dared to tell Agamemnon to give his own prize, Chryseis, back to her father, in order to mollify Apollo's rage (Chryse, her father, had asked Apollo for help after Agamemnon rebuffed his attempt to ransom her back from the Greeks). Achilles's anger will keep him out of the fight with the Trojans only for so long, however, since he will come to hold himself responsible for the death of his good friend Patroclus, to whom he loaned his prized armor. Indeed, many heroes, on both sides, will die tragically in these battles. The Lycian Sarpedon, for instance, is speared in the leg while fighting for the Trojans; he then takes on the role of supplicant to the Trojan warrior, Hector:

> Son of Priam, don't let me lie here
> As prey for the Greeks. Help me.
> If I must die, let me die in your city,
> Since I will never return to my own land
> To make glad my wife and infant son [*Iliad* 5.738–742].

Achilles himself will violate expectations of care for the dead after he kills Hector and defiles Hector's body. To Hector, Achilles says, "Die and be done with it. As for my fate, / I'll accept it whenever Zeus sends it" (*Iliad* 22.405–406). Achilles's own demise has been foretold: he recognizes that his violation of reverence for the dead and for rituals of mourning are going to cost him; his drive for battlefield glory has gotten the best of him, as Homer helps the audience to understand so clearly.

These tales complicate and test naive attitudes about violence. They recognize that war is an always difficult and sometimes absurd fact of the hero's life, as they depict his conquest and his tragic loss, his excellence and its necessary undoing. As the philosopher Alasdair MacIntyre puts it:

> The Homeric epics are narratives which recount a series of contests. In the *Iliad* the character of these contests is gradually transformed until it is acknowledged in the confrontation between Achilles and Priam that to win is also to lose and that in the face of death winning and losing no longer divide [137].[1]

Reverence is complicated for the hero, since he must have it in order to negotiate his human responsibilities, and yet his special heroic capacities require him to push up against its limits: caught between humanity and divinity, the hero must strive to display his godlike qualities while tragically being disciplined by a mortality he cannot shed.

Reverence and Violence in the Sword and Sandal Film

As a genre, the contemporary sword and sandal epic has its origin in the Italian peplum films of the 1950s and 60s (Bondanella 159–162). Italian cinema's interest in the hero epic prefigures the peplum film, however. The early Italian silent film, *Cabiria* (1914), introduced audiences to the heroic strongman Maciste (an alternative name for Hercules), whose character and characteristics would be reproduced hundreds of times in the ensuing decades, from Hercules and Jason in the Italian pepla to some figures better known to American moviegoing audiences, including Spartacus (*Spartacus* 1960), Conan (*Conan the Barbarian*), and King Leonidas (*300*).

The peplum films had a largely working-class Italian audience, less concerned with great acting and dialogue than with heroes and action (and a movie theater in which they could smoke). Like the spaghetti westerns that would replace them in the 1960s, the pepla had more to do with moral simplicity and the triumph of the hero over the villain than they did with moral sophistication (Bondanella 161–162). Obviously, one should not identify reverence with moral simplicity: proper reverence will require practical wisdom and a refined sense of judgment under complex circumstances. The peplum films can hardly be said to test violence or manifest reverence in the way of Homer's epic poetry. Other films in the sword and sandal genre are not so easy to dismiss, however. Even if the larger framework of good and evil in the sword and sandal genre is simplistic, it does not follow that reverence has gone missing in these films, or that violence is not simultaneously dramatized and called into question. In fact, reverence is a regular theme of sword and sandal films, whether in opposing wrongdoing, unmasking empty ritual or ritual leaders, or in disciplining battlefield violence.

An important aspect of heroic reverence is the wholeheartedness, or sense of mission, that guides the hero in his defense of important values. This is a testament to the power of the cluster of emotions connected to reverence: shame, respect, and awe. Spartacus never wavers in his commitment to free Roman slaves: not in the face of the decimation of his slave army, and not when Marcus Crassus announces, near the film's tragic end, that Spartacus should be immediately crucified. Conan is of similar temper: like the metal his father had once used to craft swords, Conan is unyielding in his commitment to avenge the assault on his childhood village, an event that resulted in Conan's parents' murders and Conan's subsequent enslavement. Spartan King Leonidas of the film *300* is challenged by encroaching Persian forces, cultural aliens whose mores are not Spartan and whose desires for empire seem insatiable. Though they are outnumbered and their defeat is more likely than their success, Leonidas and his Spartan men fight the good fight to preserve their Spartan heritage. Spartacus, Conan, and Leonidas represent a deep loyalty, a purity of reverential commitment, stirred by respect for parents and family, traditions, and moral and political values. Their violence attempts a reverent response to the irreverence and wrongdoing of their opponents.

Spartacus, Conan, and Leonidas are not simple figures. They are approximations of Homeric heroes, especially in terms of the costs they must suffer in their journeys. Like so many of the *Iliad's* heroes, Spartacus and Leonidas end up dead, unable to raise their newborn children. Conan falls in love with one of his quest mates, Valeria, only to lose her in a climactic battle (*Conan the Destroyer* [1984], an altogether "schlockier" film than *Conan the Barbarian*, begins at the site of her funeral pyre). Sword and sandal films can thus recognize that heroic reverence will require suffering, and indeed that a hero's fate is always, as it were, a double-edged sword.[2]

Sword and sandal films also tend to praise proper reverence rather than mere ritual or gesture. One of the staples of the sword and sandal film is the unveiling of false reverence, often in the form of priestly or religious reverence. Spartacus is critical of Roman popular religion and its complicity with slavery, unbridled sexuality, and greed. Conan reviles the power of the cultic priest, Thulsa Doom, who murdered his mother. In *300*, the Ephors, priests in charge of the local oracle, are paid by the Persians to pervert the oracle's pronouncement. Though reverence is often associated with ritual behaviors and forms, empty or play ritual is irreverent and costly. Empty ritual behavior disrespects the values and traditions being ritually preserved while promoting the power of the interpreters and practitioners of the ritual or ceremony (which is especially problematic in a priestly cult, where priests hold a monopoly on these religious services and their attendant powers). Received religious customs are not always reverent.[3]

Finally, sword and sandal films tend to recognize that rituals are often troubling on their own terms, regardless of the attitudes or motivations that practitioners bring to them. The sword and sandal genre regularly uses virgin sacrifice to epitomize the intrinsically irreverent ritual or custom. This trend goes all the way back to *Cabiria*, though it is evident in both of the *Conan* films and others, such as *Clash of the Titans* (1981 and 2010). Similar reactions to intrinsically irreverent customs show up in other films in the sword and sandal genre, such as *Spartacus*'s treatment of slavery, gladiatorial battles, and crucifixion.

Common to films in the genre is a distaste for exploitation and abuse of the vulnerable; yet, in this distaste, interestingly, modern incarnations of heroic epics begin to complicate their own representations of violence in relationship to reverence. In their treatment of specific violent customs or rituals as *intrinsic* markers of villainy, these films apparently succumb to anachronism, since both ritual sacrifice and slavery, for example, were part of Greek religion and culture. That said, historical accuracy is not the aim of these films, not even the more sophisticated ones. Nor is it the most obvious aim of Greek poetry and story-telling. A dramatic or memorable tale is a much more communicative device. Indeed, the best evidence suggests that ancient "singers of tales" would have adorned or redacted their epics as suited to the occasion and the audience (Lord 3–12). Moreover, since the resources for peplum narratives come from a whole mythic background culture, they do still maintain a kind of integrity or texture, in spite of anachronism, and they continue to reflect a concern for reverence, albeit one that their Greek ancestors might not have recognized. Most importantly, sword and sandal films' portrayals of violent contests still resonate with their audiences in forceful, yet ambiguous ways: champions who are suffering, heroes who will die, and the inescapability of external, uncontrollable forces—these are reminders of a person's place in the world, however fictionalized they turn out to be.

Reverence and Violence ... Really?

Perhaps the greatest of the ambiguities for modern audiences accustomed to religious emphases on love and forgiveness, or political conceptions of human rights and dignity, is the deep, apparent conflict between violence and reverence. The Greeks did not share this reaction to violence, and perhaps that is the rhetorical force of Homer's interrogation of it. From a modern stance, however, can reverence possibly be fit to violence?

In general, modern violence possesses the same fundamental ambiguities that Homer recognized nearly three millennia ago. Moreover, reverent commitment to important values is still thought to be central to the ethics of contests and war, even though there is currently more disagreement about whether violence is *ever* justified than any Greek society is likely to have experienced. Though contemporary violence is often different in means (for instance, modern technologies of warfare) and context (terrorism, for example, or the visual depictions of violence common to film, video games, and television) from the violence of the Greeks, ancient lessons about reverent and irreverent heroes are still appropriate to it.

Consider another of Homer's epic heroes, the cunning Odysseus. When Odysseus returns to Ithaca, he unleashes his violent skill on Penelope's greedy suitors. He is backed by the goddess Athena, who has worked on his behalf throughout his tortuous return home: guiding him, inspiring him, sometimes directly intervening in his affairs, such as by clouding others' visions of him as she does on Ithaca. Odysseus's violence is bloody, and yet, in response to the suitors' violations of his estate's hospitality, justified, and even reverent; such is the importance of hospitality to Greek mores. Odysseus's violence is reverent not simply because it is justified, but because it is skillful or excellent as well. Odysseus is an expert with his bow. The suitors have the first chance to use the weapon, and it could mean Odysseus's defeat. They fall short. Only Odysseus has the virtue required to pull the bow. He is not a weak-minded layman trying out his new weapon, but a seasoned veteran who knows why, when, and how to fight.

As readers of Margaret Atwood's *The Penelopiad* (a sardonic retelling of the events of Odysseus's return to Ithaca) know, however, while Odysseus may have been justified in killing the suitors, it does not follow that his treatment of Penelope's maidens is justified or reverent. Odysseus has the maidens hanged, putatively, for some kind of complicity in the suitors' exploits, though these charges seem trumped up. Odysseus's reverent use of violence (both in justification and in means or skill) does not extend to the murder of non-threatening innocents after the fight has been won. Typically, it is the heat of glorified battle that leads to heroic irreverence, as in the cases of Hector and Achilles. Here, it seems to be a much cooler kind of act, and arguably the worse for it, absent as it seems to be of proper reverence and a sense of appropriate shame and respect.

Beautifully controlled violence is central to the sword and sandal film as well, whether in the simple power of the strongman's embrace, or the more terrific violence of the sword, dagger, club, or bow. The heroes of sword and sandal films are jeopardized in some fashion by human irreverence and specially positioned to do something about it. The skillfulness of the violence used by the heroes of these films is sometimes natural: Hercules (of the peplum films *Hercules* [1958], *Hercules the Avenger* [1965], and many others) and Perseus (of *Clash of the Titans*) possess a divine heritage that makes them champions even without considerable practice. In other cases, violent skill is learned, often as a result of an adversary's initial act of irreverence: for instance, Spartacus and Conan are raised as slaves, only to become fighters in blood sports that prepare them for their reverent tasks. Across these films, however, one finds heroes, trained or natural, set to take on irreverence with violent, controlled force and proper ends.

Spartacus, for instance, has a hard-earned understanding of his humanity. His years of enslavement in a quarry, being whipped and beaten, have made sure of that. He has been hardened, so when he is sold off to gladiatorial training, his body and mind are already well-prepared for its discipline. In his training, he quickly distinguishes himself, earning the respect of his fellow gladiators and the scorn of his trainers. After he escapes, Spartacus travels the countryside using his prowess to free slaves and grow an army. He takes prisoners and prizes rather than killing mercilessly. He uses his skills reverently, controlling his violence to the end. Though Spartacus's army is almost wholly slaughtered, and Crassus, who has become a military dictator on pretense of needing dictatorial powers to quell the slave rebellion, is searching for Spartacus in order to publicly humiliate him, Spartacus's soldiers remain loyal to the cause and to their leader. They are systematically crucified along the way to Rome until only Spartacus and Crassus's former slave, Antoninus, are left. Crassus forces them to fight and, in a final act of reverent control of his violent skills, Spartacus kills Antoninus in order to save him from crucifixion. He has borne many costs for leading a slave uprising, though the most uplifting and tragic is yet to come. As Spartacus hangs dying from his cross, his wife, Varinia, and his newborn son are being whisked away from Rome. They see him, and he sees them, though there is nothing that can be done to save him.

One could tell similar stories about Conan's control of his sword or Leonidas's skill in the Spartan phalanx. Of note, however, is that, in the hands of contemporary film writers and directors, great heroes are less apt to suffer because they lose control of themselves than they are because of their reverent commitment to a good cause. Thus, sword and sandal films seem to praise the violence of the warrior in a way that overemphasizes his or her agency, as if even the most skillful warriors never behave badly, which is contrary to what one finds in Homer. Though the best sword and sandal films also show that their heroes impose tragic costs on themselves and others, they may fail to capture the most important lesson a warrior should learn, especially one who can wage war from afar: it is not merely a matter of fate that violence brings about suffering — the hero's own skilled attitudes, desires, and actions are also, and perhaps more centrally, responsible.

Regarding the context of contemporary violence, it is true, and happily so, that most people enjoying sword and sandal films will not be acquainted with the kind of violence and suffering described by Homer. Indeed, the conscription of men for the Vietnam War was American society's last widespread encounter with an unchosen, largely impersonal demand for citizens to contribute to war-making (which is not to say that veterans of the wars in Iraq and Afghanistan have not, like Achilles, wondered why they were fighting). Arguably, in this context, glorification of heroic violence in the sword and sandal films (or in the video games that often now accompany them) so decontextualizes heroic violence and desensitizes us to it as to become irreverent, cheap emotional props for militarism and ethnocentrism.

Furthermore, the sword and sandal films are not uniformly respectful of reverent limits on violence, and this does present a complication, analogous to the complications in Odysseus's treatment of Penelope's maidens. Some recent entries in the genre would seem to succumb to the genre's own association between villainy, empty ritual, and uncontrolled violence. The film *300* began what may become a trend of digitizing violence, enabling a level of spectacle unrealizable in earlier film or television, even if it is hinted at in a couple of scenes of spurting blood and piled bodies in Kubrik's *Spartacus*. The series *Spartacus: Blood and Sand* (2010–present) devotes substantial airtime to digitized blood splatter, decapitation, and battlefield carnage. The anti-realism of these new, gory visuals is, one might maintain, deeply irreverent, for it does not capture anything like the sense of awe, respect, and shame that one can track in Homer's heroes, even when they are slaughtering other warriors on the battlefield; nor does it invite its heroes to suffer because the slaughter inevitably gets out of hand. Similarly, video games that take players on heroic journeys do not clearly invest in them a sense of the tragedy of violence, of its deep, abiding costs, or of the hero's skillfulness in battle somehow tempting him to violate the limits of reverent violence (indeed, at their worst, new entries in the film genre may fail to recognize that there *are* reverent limits on violence, substituting spectacle for meaningful content, just as some video games apparently reward violations of these limits).

Of course, sword and sandal films are in an obvious way intended to decontexualize violence. This is part of their fantasy element. Some of them may decontextualize and glorify violence without recognizing its costs. Yet one can acknowledge all of this while also seeing that the best of these films praise violence when it is justified and controlled by a deep sense of reverence, and that they help to develop an understanding of the hero's mortality and necessary weakness. In these best cases, violence is put into the service of the hero's wholehearted attempt to preserve or promulgate important values, and the hero's efforts are complicated, even if they are not complicated in exactly the manner of Hector, Achilles, and Odysseus.

Masculinity and the Endlessness of Violence

Two additional concerns about reverence and violence in sword and sandal films are worth considering here as well: one is quite new, the other is rather old. The first concern has to do with the connection between violence and masculinity: the sword and sandal genre seems to be guilty of parading around white male violent heroes whose actions more or less reproduce familiar, patriarchal constructions of masculinity for their audiences. Hercules, Spartacus, and Conan are white, muscular, and beautiful. Or consider *300*, where masculinity is put into the service of dominating both women and other "Others" (in this case, the Persians, whose leader is semi-human and androgynous in appearance, and whose mores are arguably perceived to be wrong primarily because they are not Spartan). If masculinity fears androgyny, then reverence appears to be only a masked call to preserve masculine claims to power and control. Indeed, at its strongest, this critique might suggest that reverence itself is nothing more than patriarchy, especially if it justifies masculine violence.

There is no denying that Greek myth and epic poetry champion masculine, heroic values. Yet by vilifying false reverence and empty custom, sword and sandal films arguably erode patriarchal power structures even as they perpetuate them. By endorsing justified, controlled violence, these films sanction violence but also restrain it. As MacIntyre pointed out, the Homeric poems disclose that the hero and the villain are each equally destined to die. Some sword and sandal films obviously have little cognizance of this, even if they recognize that good narratives require some dramatic complications. More complex films in the sword and sandal genre accept the basic ambiguity of the hero's fate, and they respond to it with a reverence that does not blindly adhere to a moral or religious or social code but reminds us of the abiding values of family, friendship, community, sympathy, and humility.

In *Reverence*, Woodruff recounts the story told by Herodotus of King Croesus of Lydia, who thought himself the happiest and most fortunate of all beings. The sage, Solon, upbraided him, "Call no man happy until his life is over" (82). Croesus ignored Solon's counsel, took up arms against Persia, and soon found himself defeated, preparing to be burnt to death. As the fire around him began grow, Croesus spoke aloud, regretfully of course, recounting Solon's advice. The Persian king heard him, was reminded of his own humanity, and ordered the fire extinguished. The story is important because of its reminder that reverence is a basic capacity to feel awe, respect, and shame. Here, as Woodruff points out, the Persian king is not gracious out of some local Persian custom, but because of a fundamental human kinship with Croesus. In the sword and sandal films' violent responses to irreverence, they, too, look not to promulgate a masculine violation of women and other Others (even when they do), nor to perpetuate masculine systems of religious, political, or social organization (even when they do), but to identify and perhaps even to celebrate the great leveling power of being a human, whether hero or villain, slave or king.[4]

A final concern is that the sword and sandal films depict violence as a necessary means of making whole what has been damaged or as the sole means of restoring moral balance and identity. *Conan the Barbarian* offers an easy example, since his aim is to avenge the deaths of his mother and father, not to mention his own enslavement. Conan's quest will not cease until the moral order is restored through violence. Spartacus and the Spartans of *300* bear this out as well. In each case, heroic violence will bring additional violence back upon them as a consequence. Spartacus and Leonidas will never get a chance to "make glad" their wives and children. Muscular Conan seeks to have his love, Valeria, returned to him from the dead in *Conan the Destroyer*, but this return is never fulfilled. Yet much the same was true of the Homeric heroes. Odysseus was not able to rest at Ithaca even after he had slaughtered the suitors, for he was commanded by the blind seer, Tiresias, to leave Ithaca again to make appropriate sacrifices. The quest ends only in the hero's death. He is restless in his pursuits, and never allowed to grow old in peace.

This, finally, is what reverence ought to expect. Going back to Woodruff and MacIntyre, one can see that in the Greek models of these stories, there is no going home again, for even controlled, justified violence will only temporarily set things right, and often it does not do that. As MacIntyre puts it, "For what Homer puts in question, as his characters do not, is what it is to win and what it is to lose.... What the poet ... sees ... is that winning too may be a form of losing" (128). One is rewarded with glimpses of this truth in the sword and sandal film genre as well, reminded by characters such as Spartacus, Conan, and Leonidas of the hero's glory and also his suffering, and of the importance of reverence to a person's sense of place in the world. These films are by no means substitutes for the great works of Greek epic poetry and tragedy; but, like their Greek predecessors, they can both deepen and complicate one's understanding of heroes and of violence, and, as such, they are worth taking seriously.

Notes

1. Similarly, Seth Schein writes about the *Iliad*: "Through parallels, contrasts, and juxtapositions of characters and actions, a dramatic structure is created that forces us to consider critically the traditional heroic world depicted in the poem and the contradictions inherent in this kind of heroism. The overwhelming fact of life for the heroes of the *Iliad* is their mortality, which stands in contrast to the immortality of the gods" (1).

2. Less sophisticated peplum films tend to focus on the upside of fate, or, in other words, victory; more sophisticated films in the genre recognize that fate can mean victory and, at the same time, loss. *Spartacus* most consistently manifests the qualities of complexity; *Conan the Barbarian* and *300* are, though in different ways, weaker on complexity and open to other worries regarding their depictions of violence and reverence.

3. There may be an implicit critique of institutionalized religion in these films, though more broadly they identify the threats of empty ritualized behavior, especially among religious, moral, or political leaders.

4. Of course, it is rare that these films open up their hero roles to women, and when they do, as in *Red Sonja* (1985), for example, we find further evidence of masculine violence and control, though arguably not evidence unique to the sword and sandal film genre. Sonja, often clad in a metal bikini, is clearly intended to satisfy the male gaze (because of the history and power of the male gaze, Sonja must be treated differently than Conan and his codpiece, even though in each case the hero is objectified and reduced).

Works Cited

Atwood, Margaret. *The Penelopiad*. New York: Canongate, 2006.
Bondanella, Peter. *A History of Italian Cinema*. New York: Continuum, 2009.
Conan the Barbarian. Dir. John Milius. Perf. Arnold Schwarzengger, Sandhal Bergman, James Earl Jones. Universal, 1982.
Homer. *Iliad*. Trans. Stanley Lombardo. Indianapolis: Hackett, 1997.
Lord, Albert. *The Singer of Tales*. 2d ed. Cambridge: Harvard University Press, 2000.
MacIntyre, Alasdair. *After Virtue*. 2d ed. Notre Dame, IN: University of Notre Dame Press, 1984.
Schein, Seth. *The Mortal Hero: An Introduction to Homer's Iliad*. Berkeley: University of California Press, 1984.
Spartacus. Dir. Stanley Kubrick. Universal Pictures, 1960.
Spartacus: Blood and Sand. Dirs. Michael Warn, Rick Hurst, Jesse Jacobson. Starz Productions, 2010.
300. Dir. Zach Snyder. Warner Bros. Pictures, 2006.
Woodruff, Paul. *Reverence: Renewing a Forgotten Virtue*. New York: Oxford University Press, 2001.

"Civilization ... ancient and wicked"
Historicizing the Ideological Field of 1980s Sword and Sorcery Films

Kevin M. Flanagan

In their pioneering book *Camera Politica: The Politics and Ideology of Contemporary Hollywood Film*, Michael Ryan and Douglas Kellner chart the modulations in the dominant ideological values of mainstream cinema from the rise of the "New Hollywood" generation of young auteurs through the Reagan-era and the ascendancy of the blockbuster-event movie. Although the word is often used to connote a monolithic and unashamedly profit-driven corporate version of motion picture production, what is generally called "Hollywood" is not wholly absorbed in a single-minded, politically united, and merely reflective mode of film practice (2). On the contrary, Ryan and Kellner write, "In our view, ideology needs to be seen as an attempt to placate social tensions and to respond to social forces in such a way that they cease to be dangerous to the social system of inequality" (14). The political readings that come from popular cinema serve a necessarily correlative function to the daily experiences of spectators, and are tempered by larger indicators like class, race, and sex, funneled through personal taste and experience. Despite their concession that in a large and heterogeneous film culture there will always be movies to serve different political interests, and beyond their recognition of the importance of individual response to the eventual ideological work of a given narrative, Ryan and Kellner maintain that the general set of interests served by American films from the late 1960s until the mid–1980s is marked by a thunderous shift from left-liberal "independent" films concerned with the possibility of collective social action to a conservative-libertarian set that privilege heroic individualism in the face of decaying governmental institutions and social formations. The collective action portended by Haskell Wexler's *Medium Cool* (1969)—with its documentary-like confrontation of the coalescing forces of social inequality — might be seen as typical of several countercultural and political trends of the late 1960s. Yet, by the early 1980s, this collective impulse had symbolically given way to the disenchanted heroics of John Rambo, who in *First Blood* (1982) takes up arms against the society that rejected him, not in the service of a social agenda as such, but rather against the pervasive malaise of an increasingly meek culture disenchanted by the tainted legacy of the Vietnam War (Ryan and Kellner 35).

Ryan and Kellner try to balance their readings of film-texts by taking into account not only individual creative forces, such as the tendencies of writers and directors across a large body of work, but also institutional signposts such as genre. However, their historical methodology mainly identifies genres as they emerged in contemporaneously relevant circumstances: thus, their analysis of such major films of the early-to-mid 1970s as *Airport* (1970), *The Godfather* (1972), *The Exorcist* (1973), and *Jaws* (1975) is not along purely reductive and traditional genre lines (which would likely situate these films as important examples of disaster, gangster, horror, and "when animals attack" thrillers, respectively), but rather first-and-foremost as "crisis" films which variously responded to the legitimacy crisis, in highly metaphorical ways, between the people and the institutionalized power of federal government (Ryan and Kellner 51; Muir 17–20).

Not surprisingly, one of the films which comes to be central to their larger observation about the rightward turn in cinematic production is *Conan the Barbarian* (1982), an origin-story for Robert E. Howard's most famous pulp creation, filtered through the transparent ideological positions of director and co-writer John Milius. Characteristically unable to mince words, Ryan and Kellner describe the film as "a conservative fantasy projection," visualizing a milieu in which "no one can be trusted and where one must fight to survive" (225).[1] The film is significant for the authors because it encapsulates many of the trends which they see as typifying the mainstream cinema of the 1980s. Though they recognize the film's roots in screen fantasy, Ryan and Kellner analyze *Conan the Barbarian* in a chapter called "The Return of the Hero: Entrepreneur, Patriarch, Warrior" (Conan is all three, but so, as they quickly point out, was Ronald Reagan) and focus not on the film's genre pedigree so much as on the film's savagery, its airing of sexual grievance by way of castration anxiety and overbearing phallic imagery, and its lame Oedipal quest structure (225–226; Scott 45). On the whole, *Conan the Barbarian* is seen to most closely align with a larger trend toward "primary-process" thinking in hero-centric movies:

> This vision of society is clearly very primitivistic; it attempts to reduce social life to primary process thinking, that is, to the assertion of the power of natural instinct over rational arrangements. In many of the new hero films, metaphors of nature and primitivism abound, and the great enemy is often an image of extreme rationality, science, intellect, or technology. Nature is the primary metaphor in the hero films because the ideal of the free individualist which the hero seems to promote

is itself based on the assumption that individualism is more "natural" than something like rational state planning, which is too distant from nature [Ryan and Kellner 222].

Ryan and Kellner read *Conan* as a pioneering, trend-setting motion picture of the time, one to be aligned with Stallone's Rocky and Rambo films, the notorious Chuck Norris movies made with Cannon Films—especially *Invasion U.S.A.* (1985), in which Norris's Matt Hunter, roused from his idyllic home in the Everglades by invading guerrillas, singlehandedly stops a communist invasion of the United States—and even the original *Star Wars* trilogy, especially as it pertains to Luke Skywalker's trajectory of personal discovery.

While this analytical approach certainly does given recent movies a sense of contemporary urgency, Ryan and Kellner's relative dismissal of the traditional parameters of genre classification does not help place movies like *Conan the Barbarian* in a long view, one sensitive to similar productions over the course of film history (some of which long predate the late 1960s, the start of the period under consideration in Ryan and Kellner's study). Understanding *Conan the Barbarian* as indicative of a new brand of heroism is one thing, but generally ignoring older modes of heroic characterization displaces the novelty of the newer tendency. What I propose, then, is to outline the structural, iconographic, and ideological characteristics of genres and genre productions that directly prefigure Conan's once-groundbreaking blend of sword and sandal and sorcery, a formula which dominated the "heroic fantasy" films of the early-to-mid 1980s (Worley 198–212). While I still side with Ryan and Kellner in viewing Conan's screen heroics as espousing a distinctively conservative ideology, I propose to test this pedigree against the longer heritage of strong-man films (the Italian Maciste films of the silent era), early (American) superhero serials, and Italian pepla (the genre and production cycle that most directly anticipates *Conan the Barbarian*). One could even go so far as to claim that *Conan the Barbarian*— and its wave of sword and sorcery epics such as *The Sword and the Sorcerer* (1982, Albert Pyun), *The Beastmaster* (1982, Don Coscarelli), *Deathstalker* (1983, James Sbardellati), *Hundra* (1983, Matt Cimber), *Red Sonja* (1985, Richard Fleischer), and *Conan the Destroyer* (1987, Richard Fleischer)—are period-sensitive revitalizations of the seemingly moribund sword and sandal moment.

More to the point, the earlier sword and sandal movies, especially the Italian pepla of the 1950s and 1960s, can be characterized as something more nuanced than merely or reductively "conservative." In their figuration of the preservation and/or restoration of order, their general narrative subservience to the marriage plot, and their various attention to the positive aspects of civilization, these films can be understood as working through a largely liberalist political posture. That is, beyond their generic tendency toward exceptional heroism and battles of good against evil, these films implicitly endorse a set of values that translates to a "good" version of citizenship for the postwar liberalist state.

Tellingly, the 1980s sword and sorcery films embody many of the neoliberalist contradictions that emerged over the course of the 1970s but solidified during the Reagan years: the privileging of unregulated, mercenary agents in search of personal profit (remember that the Conan of the two 1980s films is a sword-for-hire); the structural overvaluation of the individual and the small heroic band over any form of widely collective enterprise; and an insistence on showing how deregulation and a reduction of socially dictated laws aides powerful, motivated individuals (a rough explanation of why these sword and sorcery films largely operate out of frontier towns, where relative lawlessness suggests the possibility of personal advancement) (Bourdieu).[2] Put bluntly, these sword and sorcery movies (for the sake of clarity, my label for the 1980s generic make-over of the sword and sandal films of the 1950s and 1960s) offer conflicted layers of social and ideological representation: on the one hand, they are explicitly about dead political systems (monarchy, empire, the nation-state *polis*, the nomadic barbarian kingdom), yet their plots cannot help but trace the contemporaneously important ideological values of postwar Western cinema.

The heroic adventure movies under consideration retain trace elements of venerable modes of storytelling, from oral-epic formations such as Homer's *Odyssey* (eighth century B.C.), or even slightly more contemporary swashbucklers like Alexandre Dumas's *The Three Musketeers* (1844). Providing a full account of the transmutation of these sorts of narratives, across national and generic boundaries, is far outside of the scope of this essay. Instead, what was to become the mature sword and sorcery film of the 1980s can be narratively and iconographically situated within a few prescient moments in the social history of cinema.

My emphasis on visual representations deals, in part, with the very aggregate nature of such labels as "sword and sandal" and "sword and sorcery": these labels do not ascribe an abstract psychological term (horror), or suggest an experience delivered through a specific mode of performance (the musical), but instead provide a group identity through the material accoutrements—the props, costumes, and types of supernatural possibilities which achieve magical visualization on screen (Neale 16). For example, a lineage which dates back to the kind of "pre-historic" mode of heroic strong-man films inclusive of the Italian Maciste cycle from the 1910s and 1920s, resuming with the 1930s and 1940s American super-heroic serials, and settling at the "boom" decade (late 1950s through mid-to-late 1960s) of the Italian pepla provides a general representational framework for the sword and sorcery epics. What emerges is not a strict story of a genre evolving, or finally assuming a stable form after a long process of combination and re-combination, but rather a case where the realities of production cycle success at the box office meet a set of abstract ideological assumptions that temper a set of dominant messages.

The early Italian film industry excelled at crafting large-scale historical spectacles. Titles such as the *Last Days of Pompeii* (1908, Luigi Maggi), *The Fall of Troy* (1910, Giovanni Pastrone), and *Quo Vadis?* (1913, Enrico Giozzoni) featured massive sets, lush costumes, and established a successful cinematic showcase for acts of physical heroism (Worley 169). Given Italy's relatively recent unification in 1871 (after a series of wars and revolutions over the course of the nineteenth century), these epics of an idealized Roman past served as points of idealistic nationalist projection: the greatness of the contemporary Italian state could be exported as a screened idealization of a storied past (Roberts 722–724, 727). Of course, epic historical visualizations of the early silent feature era were not the sole provenance of Italy. D.W. Griffith's celebrated *Intolerance* (1916), although an American production, proposes an equally ambitious and spectacular frame for the ancient world. Yet Italy excelled at a version of heroic spectacle that, in its earliest iteration, reaches a zenith with Giovanni Pastrone's *Cabiria* (1914) (Usai 125, 127).

Cabiria is an historical drama set during the Punic Wars. Scripted by nationalist poet Gabrielle D'Annunzio, it principally concerns the kidnapping of a young girl at the hands of Carthaginian pirates. *Cabiria* operates on a strictly defined logic of good versus evil, with the Carthaginian interlopers very obviously caricatured as insidious, an odious threat to the Roman people. According to Paolo Cherchi Usai, "The success of *Cabiria* was due to the character of the slave Maciste [Bartolomeo Pagano], whose athletic prowess made him a favourite with audiences" (129). The character of Maciste is constructed as a loyal, morally righteous strong-man with a soft-spot for beauty and a knack for restoring order. His popularity yielded many sequels, including *Maciste* (1915, Vincenzo C. Dénizot), *The Testament of Maciste* (1920, Carlo Campogalliani) and *Maciste in Hell* (1925, Guido Brignone), making them "the first in a tradition of 'strong-man' films, an athletic variant on the adventure film, whose protagonists are endowed with extraordinary physical strength and untarnished simplicity of emotion" (Usai 129). Moreover, *Cabiria* provided a veritable blueprint for the Italian pepla that were to thrive in later decades. According to Patrick Lucanio, "It remains for *Cabiria*, more than any other Italian spectacle, to serve as the mold from which the renaissance of Italian spectacles in the 1960s — which included a revival of the Maciste character — was formed" (8).

Despite *Cabiria*'s centrality to the sword and sandal lineage in question, *Maciste in Hell* provides a far stranger, more magically-plotted progenitor for the sword and sorcery films of the 1980s. Lucanio relates that this feature even played in New York in 1931, signaling an early American interest in Italian strong-man films (212). Maciste, introduced in a contemporary setting as simply a strong and kindhearted man, is targeted by demons and brought to Hell. Figures of Roman mythology (Pluto) and the Christian tradition (Nimrod) enliven what is otherwise an excuse to have Maciste fight his way through hordes of demons and devils. The ideological assumptions of the film are populist and overt: Maciste moralistically uses his working class brawn against evil, which at times is coded as aristocratic, over-indulgent, and exploitative. For example, man-demons in tuxedos, behaving as upper-crust layabouts, tempt Maciste and question his propriety. Despite the sumptuous visuals and truly inspiring costume and set designs, *Maciste in Hell* already signals the "primary-process" thinking that Ryan and Kellner pin on *Conan the Barbarian*. Brawn and moral certitude best trickery and mental skill. Usai calls *Maciste in Hell* "the apotheosis of kitsch," a bold claim perfectly encapsulated by the film's supernatural ending (129). Seemingly trapped for all eternity in the netherworld, Maciste is brought back to life and his world thanks to the prayer of a child, earnestly delivered on Christmas Eve.

American adventure serials (both earth-bound and fantastic) provide another template for the episodic, thrilling exploits of Italian pepla and the 1980s sword and sorcery cycle. These popular stories—significant examples include *The Lost City* (1935), *Flash Gordon* (1936), and *Undersea Kingdom* (1936)—follow many of the ideological assumptions of the later genres. In addition to an unmistakable binarization of "right" and "wrong," these serialized stories espouse explicitly colonialist positions (the featured adventurers, scientists, and professors are somewhere between fortune-seekers and agents of Empire engaged in the discovery and plunder of new lands); use Orientalist short-hand to code evil empires and threatening locals as Eastern and non-white; and tend to reduce complex political transactions and questions of moral appeal to perfunctory physical conflicts with predictable endings. Many of the overt schematizations are familiar from the above discussion of the early Italian spectacle, but in this context were likely sourced from the literary inheritance of such authors as Edgar Rice Burroughs (the Tarzan tales) and H. Rider Haggard (*King Solomon's Mines* [1885]).

William C. Cline describes the function of heroes in this era of the American serial as a set of typifications that seem to be directly imported into the Italian peplum film of the 1950s and 1960s:

> The Hero (with whom the audience was to identify) had to be immediately recognizable as a stalwart of Truth and Right. There could be no questionable aspects to the character. Knowing in the first chapter that they had a long way to go together, the audience expected a hero to be trustworthy and dependable. They had to be able to believe that he was smart enough and daring enough to undertake what they knew was going to be a rough job. His bravery and courage had to be—from the opening scene on—a matter of accepted fact [5].

The primary villains in these serials have a similarly proscriptive function. Cline relates that the figure of the villain "was the 'threat'—to the hero, to the heroine, to national security, to society at large," and that "brute strength was part of his total armory, but the real danger lay in his ability to conjure up plots that would unquestionably draw the hero and his forces into dangerous situations" (5). Like many melodramatic forms of stage and screen, the villain is often characterized through an hysterically Orientalist point of view. In the lineage that I am tracing from serial, to peplum, to American sword and sorcery epic — excluding differences in available technology, access to magic, and superficial appearance — there is an evident similarity between the monomaniacal villainy of Ming the Merciless (from *Flash Gordon*), Queen Fazira (from *Samson in King Solomon's Mines* [1964, Piero Regnoli]), and Thulsa Doom (from *Conan the Barbarian*).

As with the Italian spectacles already discussed, the points of ideological identification in American serials are delineated for an audience even before the film begins. In addition to sporting frequently recurring character types, these serials inhabit a narrowly defined set of plots, situations, and settings. Cline relates that, as entertainments more widely cast as action and adventure cliffhangers, these serials tended to be organized as Westerns, mysteries, jungle stories, historical costume adaptations (*The Three Musketeer*s, for example) and science-fiction/fantasy tales (28). Despite certain cosmetic differences, serials can be understood as a territorializable genre in their obvious fulfillment of one of Rick Altman's hypothetical claims that details how genres come to be. He writes, "In order to be recognized as a genre, films must have both a common topic ... and a common structure, a common way of configuring that topic" (23). Moreover, the American serial — as with the somewhat posthumously understood historical Italian spectacle/epic —conforms to another of Altman's hypothetical precepts, namely that "before they are fully constituted through the junction of persistent material and consistent use of that material, nascent genres traverse a period when their only unity derives from shared surface characteristics deployed within other generic contexts perceived as dominant" (36). We can ascribe recurrent ideological and narrative assumptions to the serial even as its images vary.

The primary, and seemingly obvious, point of unity in the Italian peplum cycle of the 1950s and 1960s is iconographic. Swords, sandals, and approximations of the peplum tunic are the common accoutrements featured in these films, from Pietro Francisci's popular *Hercules* (1958) to *Knives of the Avenger* (1965, Mario Bava). As such, a preliminary understanding of these movies as a similar set of texts might be sourced in the above observations by Steve Neale, or in Colin McArthur's observations about recurring visual icons in the American gangster film in his book *Underworld USA* (1972). A mutual emphasis on less generalizably recurrent elements— mythological and historical source material (as mainly relates to the Mediterranean world); narratives that focus on heroism and moral righteousness; value ascribed to physical strength and sacrifice for one's people —cuts closer to the heart of the films. In fact, the sword becomes the dominant figuration: while Lucanio urges viewers to think of peplum more in terms of their obsession with a sense of moral certitude and their almost comic sincerity or insistence on goodness, physical skirmishes and a pervasive reliance on the logic of "might makes right" are still hallmarks of the genre (5–6). Thus, a preliminary and schematic reading of sword and sandal films finds in them an inherit conservatism, consistent with earlier Italian spectacles and American cliffhangers.[3]

Lucanio usefully sketches the prototypical "mythologem," the melodramatic form that essentially characterizes all pepla, whether they be what he has termed "Mytho-history" (appealing primarily to an appearance of, or lip-service to, actual historical events) or "Mytho-fantasy" (situating their genre credentials firmly outside any historical sphere in favor of fantastic invention) (34; 38):

> An evil force comes to power through treachery and oppresses an innocent group that remains powerless against the oppressor until one man — although a few films use a woman — leads the group in righteous rebellion against the oppressive power. A final head-to-head confrontation wherein the hero slays the villain assures victory and freedom for the oppressed people, and the narrative then ends with marriage [29].

There are a few implicit conditions of setting, *mise-en-scène*, and narrative that help further tie these claims to ideological assumptions. In order for the evil antagonist to loom as a threat, there has to be some condition of order (a kind of civic or social harmony) present at the beginning of the tale. Further, as the general reliance on the marriage plot attests, the defeat of the oppressor or interloper and the restitution of virtuous leaders serves not only to reassert the idealized status quo from earlier in the tale, but also put to rest any sense of a legitimacy crisis. For example, *Hercules Unchained* (1959) contains contests between brothers Eteocles and Polynices over their claims to the throne of Thebes. In this instance, neither would properly restore tranquility to the body politic. The brothers die in their conflict with one another and the priest Creon assumes control by popular means. The new leader suggests a nascent paradise regained.

As either vaguely historical (usually set in pre-modern, proto-European milieus) or blatantly fantastic stories, these sword and sandal films outwardly feature older formations of social order. Monarchical kingdoms, empires, and thoroughly militarized nation-states are common. How, then, might we theorize the political worlds presented in these films as being directly applicable to the contemporary moments of their initial release or exhibition? One way is through the sort of projection that Ryan and Kellner do, but with a slightly modified set of terms.[4] Therefore, rather than view pepla as straight-forwardly conservative, perhaps the somewhat counter-intuitive "liberalist" label will help further explicate the sorts of assumptive political work that these films tacitly support.

Susan Braedley and Meg Luxton note that the classic definition of liberalism, as derived from eighteenth and nineteenth century European thinkers like Hume and Locke, values an individual's freedom from oppression, servitude, and coercive (tyrannical) political power above all else (7). This freedom can be upheld through the capitalist marketplace — although this belief is nowadays tied more closely to the more recent phenomenon of neoliberalism — but it is often upheld through the vigorous efforts of a centralized governmental sovereignty: the nation-state, *polis*, the leadership tacitly endured by the people. After an initial recovery from the damaging legacy of World War II in the 1950s, Western economies used Keynesian economic principles privileging full employment and welfare polities: this was a time of "embedded liberalism," under which "a social and moral economy (sometimes supported by a strong sense of national identity) was fostered through the activities of an interventionist state" (Harvey 11). F. A. Hayek speaks of "self-generating" or "spontaneous order" in social affairs, of "an order which made it possible to utilize the knowledge and skill of all members of society" (43). This is a way of thinking that supports an abstract sense of a common good, but one which refuses to bow to directed coercion. In many pepla, one gets the sense that the forces of good have an implicit faith in the value of a strong nation-state or kingdom.

Of course, there are strongly hierarchical relationships embedded in pepla: the heroic strong-man becomes more valuable to the maintenance of order than the lowly foot-soldier, while the heir to the throne can still be imagined to live a life of central importance. The point is that the values that are central to sword and sandal films—civic virtue, good and desirable forces positioned as inevitably triumphant over bad, and a sense of renewal after periods of disequilibrium — are values that also inform good citizenship in postwar Western economies. A notoriously simple-minded set of movies like these Italian sword and sandal pictures can come to be read as obsessively insisting on the continued importance of behaviors that are essential to statist and patriotic democracies, even though they embed them in ancient and mythical worlds populated by cartoonish heroism.

The thread of similarity between sword and sandal and "sword and sorcery" movies is clear, at least on a visual level. Sword and sorcery movies, like their progenitors, generally enact epic adventure stories through sword-bearing, sandal-wearing, and tunic-donning heroes. Visual cues signal constructions of good (white tunics, physical beauty, athletic grace, strength) and evil (dark colors, physical deformity, Oriental, decadence). There remains a strong delineation between, on the one hand, the exceptional hero and his/her small cohort and, on the other, the disposable herd of common soldiers and townspeople on the narrative's periphery. Heightened moral certitude, restoration narratives, and clearly demarcated (though, in the case of films like *Conan the Barbarian* and Paul Verhooven's visceral *Flesh and Blood* [1985], slightly less schematic) conceptions of good and evil remain essential. In this way, they already inherit an inherently conservative ideological tradition. Additionally, as with Italian spectacles, American cliffhangers, and Italian pepla, sword and sorcery texts can be considered an already-hybridized genre. They are more widely ordered as "fantasy" films. Like pepla, they can be given a qualified generic position, such as "heroic fantasy" (Worley 162).[5] Such distinctions are also necessary given the somewhat tenuous set of films that could be culled under the rubric of "fantasy," a loaded label that David Butler comes to use as representing "an impulse rather than a single coherent genre" (43). A provisional checklist of fantasy titles from the period suggests the heterogeneity of the genre by the early 1980s. As points on a spectrum, Warren Beatty and Buck Henry's *Heaven Can Wait* (1978), Ralph Bakshi's *Lord of the Rings* (1978), Terry Gilliam's *Time Bandits* (1981), and Frank Oz and Jim Henson's *The Dark Crystal* (1982) could scarcely be ideologically and iconographically farther apart. Overall, sword and sorcery films can be seen as indicative of a widespread American revitalization of screen fantasy more generally, but the strand of Italian sword and sandal films in particular.

If sword and sandal films were noteworthy for having cobbled together narratives through a fantastic combination of ancient myth, popular history, and pure imaginative speculation, then sword and sorcery films likewise owe a debt to an established body of literature. Robert E. Howard and later followers L. Sprague de Camp and Lin Carter provide a varied literary template from which films like *Conan the Barbarian* and *Red Sonja* molded mixed-source screen narratives. Howard's interest in composite world-building is illustrated by his mythological history "The Hyborian Age," which assembles elements of vanished civilizations, verified ancient history, and pure fabrication into a time and place suitable for his brand of heroic adventure (Howard). In this instance, authorial originality comes from a selective reading of history, streamlined through a set of political and ethical assumptions that accentuate certain elements of an invented past at the expense of others. The world that could accommodate Conan needed to be filled with danger, had to be only tenuously civilized, and, in order to inspire superhuman heroism, had to belie a permanently Hobbesian state of conflict and distrust. Although films like *Red Sonja*, *Fire & Ice* (1983, Ralph Bakshi), and *The Sword and the Sorcerer* are borne of similar circumstances, Howard's overtly political template for the mode of fantasy that comes to be understood as sword and sorcery is best illustrated through the film of *Conan the Barbarian*.

Critics have reacted virulently to Howard's politics (which are partially determined through his historical selectivity) as represented on page and, through the lens of John Milius, on the screen. For Hans Joachim Alpers, this sort of reductive heroic fantasy looks alarmingly like fascism. He lists overlapping structural parallels:

> The ideologies thereby propagated [in heroic fantasy] are: magic-mystic understanding of the world, i.e. mystification of relationships that could be grasped by the intellect; right of the stronger as the principle of societal organization; glorification of violence, particularly killing; oppression of women; emphasis on the racial superiority of the Nordic (Aryan) type; fatalism toward hierarchic structures and their consequences, such as wars; the fuehrer principle; the greatest butcher of them all shall determine our fate; imperialistic policy; and anti-intellectualism [31].

Writing on the film version of *Conan the Barbarian* for *Film Comment*, Carlos Clarens muses, "You would think that if Conan had not already existed in print and drawing, Milius would have invented him," after which he proceeds to list the director's debts to the myth of Siegfried, Nietzschian will-to-power, and Wagner (27).[6] These sympathies come as no surprise for Milius, who as Richard Combs relates, mentioned how his vision of Conan would have been popularly and enthusiastically received in 1930s Germany (167).

According to Ryan and Kellner's methodology, certain latent political formations surface (or are submerged) by the dominant ideological tenor of the day. Along with Andrew Britton and Robin Wood, Ryan and Kellner read the social circumstances and dominant ideological attitude of the United States under Reagan as enabling an otherwise fringe attitude like Milius's to prosper (Ryan and Kellner 217–219). In the wake of economic stagnation and botched military operations under Jimmy Carter, the ascendancy of Ronald Reagan to the presidency gestured to an iconic shift in representations of American dominance: individualist and militaristic free-market ideology came to rule the day. Andrew Britton's characterization of this "New Right" attitude speaks to the genuinely utopian dimension of Reaganite thought, some valences of which find a home in the brutally ahistorical fantasy of *Conan the Barbarian*:

> The utopianism of the new radical right has two dimensions. On the one hand, it looks back from a position of geriatric post-imperial decrepitude (Great Britain) or of recently humiliated and increasingly embattled hegemony (the United States) to a vanished golden age in which the nation was great and the patriarchal family flourished in happy ignorance of the scourges of abortion and a soaring divorce rate, gay rights and the woman's movement. On the other hand, it anticipates a gorgeous reflowering of capitalism in which the good things will be born again under the aegis of the microchip once a flabby body politic has been slimmed down and its cancerous growths excised [9].

In "80s Hollywood: Dominant Tendencies," Robin Wood aligns the wider film culture, of which *Conan the Barbarian* is a part, with a set of extremely reactionary positions that seek to re-institute a Freudian "law of the father" complicit with patriarchal capitalism (2). Generally speaking, the sorts of critical claims made against the broad spectrum of popular movies produced during Reagan's presidency apply to *Conan*. Yet turning to its characterizations, the organization of its diegesis, and the punitive economic assumptions that the film makes in the name of high adventure helps complicate this general understanding of Conan, Milius, and sword and sorcery as "conservative" by instead drawing attention to the particular ways in which the text voices an emerging and ambivalent neoliberal world.

The narrative of *Conan the Barbarian* hinges on a somewhat inarticulate seeking of revenge. In the long view, the movie charts Conan's origin and early adventures, leading up to his alliance with Subotai and Valeria, and their battles with Thulsa Doom's Snake Cult. While Conan is largely motivated by revenge, both for the deaths of his parents and for the eventual loss of Valeria, he is also driven by personal glory, the promise of wealth, and power. It is no coincidence that, when asked "What is best in life?," Conan's seemingly conditioned response is "to crush your enemies, see them driven before you, and to hear the lamentations of their women" (*Conan*). As much as the film seems to be about honor and redemption for a transgression against the family, it also paints a picture of a world of mercenary opportunism and the reluctant embrace of civilizing infrastructure.

After the Nietzschean epigram "That which does not kill us makes us stronger," the film opens with scenes of a young Conan being initiated into the values of his small village. He learns of the powers of the Earth god Krom, watches the forging of weapons, and witnesses the life-world of the warrior. The culture to which he is heir is evidently hierarchical and patriarchal. Soon, vicious marauders led by Thulsa Doom massacre the village, killing all of Conan's family and positioning him for a life of slavery. His time spent monotonously pushing a gigantic wheel (whose purpose is never entirely made clear) presumably provides Conan with the otherwise incredulous physique of actor Arnold Schwarzenegger. The hero, through Milius's choice of "lingering low-angle close-ups [that] focus on the handsome face, the bared chest, the long hair flowing in the wind," is positioned as a monstrously strong, yet malleable and adaptable, conqueror figure (Bell-Metereau 49). After the period of brute servitude, Conan comes to compete as a gladiator, whereupon the genesis of his skills are explained.

If earlier strong-man films forgo any nuance of characterization beyond their already-arrived-at status as morally pure warriors, then *Conan the Barbarian* overcompensates in the other direction. As a prized fighter, Conan is introduced to the possibilities of civilization: he is taught to read and appreciate literary production, is given women as prizes, forms personal bonds through training, and becomes acquainted with magic, a mysterious practice most closely associated with Eastern figures. Despite Conan's friendship with mentor-figure The Wizard (played by Mako), he remains somewhat positioned against magic as a result of his having been socialized into the elemental faith in Krom. Over the course of his adventure, Conan questions Krom's relevance (as an ancient wilderness god) to his journeyman and reluctantly cosmopolitan lifestyle. Despite his relative upholding of basic lessons derived from this god—most centrally, the importance of combat—Conan moves away from his childhood faith in favor of the promise of personal satisfaction: wealth, women, fame, and incessant questing.

Furthermore, Conan's long period of physical and mental training justifies his eventual role as a largely self-sufficient agent of fortune. He variously uses stealth (as with his team's infiltration of the Tower of the Snake Cult), brawn, and calculated trickery (his masquerade as a cultist before the final confrontation with Thulsa Doom). He seizes opportunities for wealth—the rumors of riches in the Tower, and his decision to risk life and limb in order to get them, illustrate his capacity for greed — and seems ill at ease with settling too long in a single spot, preferring instead to adventure in search of far-flung treasures. On this somewhat abstract level, he is an ideal neoliberal subject: pliant and posed for success in any number of contingent circumstances; individualistically motivated; relentlessly competitive; dissatisfied with centralized authority (including the "good" King Osric, whom he reluctantly aides in rescuing Princess Yasmina); and predisposed to his personal (that is, privatized) allegiances, which remain unconnected to sovereign political entities.

Generally speaking, neoliberalism distinguishes itself as "an agenda of economic and social transformation under the sign of the free market" during a "mad heroic phase" that was coincident with the rule of Ronald Reagan in the United States and Margaret Thatcher in Great Britain (Connell 22). It has been read as a massive program of income, power, and social agency along the lines of market efficacy: the rich get richer while the poor become poorer. Through this "financialization of everything," economic elites solidify their hegemonic position (Harvey 33). While this has played a part in maintaining some aspects of traditional (white, Protestant, male, educated) wealth, it has also rewarded visionary entrepreneurs who have made quick fortunes through technological and service-based innovations, including Bill Gates or Mexican telecommunications magnate Carlos Slim (Harvey 34). As such, individual and corporate organizational models are favored more than those that are collectivist and state-sponsored. Pierre Bourdieu laments two of the larger tendencies of life under neoliberalism:

> First is the destruction of all the collective institutions capable of counteracting the effects of the infernal machine, primarily those of the state, repository of all of the universal values associated with the idea of the *public realm*. Second is the imposition everywhere, in the upper spheres of the economy and the state as at the heart of corporations, of that sort of moral Darwinism that, with the cult of the winner, schooled in higher mathematics and bungee jumping, institutes the struggle of all against all and *cynicism* as the norm of all action and behaviour [Bourdieu].

Conan might be read as a primary-process projection of this mindset. Driven by personal goals and exceptional ability, he negotiates institutional barriers— religious formations, monarchs like King Osric, imposed forms of social decorum — through his strength, ability, and cunning. Aided by a select group of hierarchically subordinate friends, he overcomes challenge after challenge. Instead of seeking collective support, he is motivated by opportunities for fame and wealth.

One of the most characteristic positions of neoliberalist logic is to turn away from state formations— both the strictly bordered nation-state and super-forms like communism — in favor of deregulated markets and the bucking of individual and corporate restraint (Harvey 10). Here, Conan's attitude toward "civilization" becomes more than just incidental and personally idiosyncratic.

Conan's first encounter with a city — perhaps the most visibly and materially obvious emblem of centralized governmental power — is accompanied by Subotai's warning: "Civilization ... ancient and wicked" (*Conan*). Conan has never before encountered such a built-up, bureaucratized, and regulated place. A sequence shows Conan and Subotai's initial engagement with the sensations of the city. While seemingly enchanted by the opportunity and cultural exchange possible by the metropolis, Conan is disgusted by the stink, overcrowding, pre-prepared foods: in short, the betrayal of his survivalist and independently agrarian roots. Moreover, the people of Conan's tribe have already been idealized by the movie as noble, independent, traditional, and dependable. Suddenly, Conan is thrown into the midst of cranks, conspiracy theorists, cultists, prostitutes, and decadent libertines. The fantasy projection of the central, liberalist state — here, a chaotic, dangerous, and seductive city — comes to ensnare Conan in a sequence of events that complicates his personal mission. This is not the under-siege, but idealized and recuperable, Thebes of *Hercules Unchained*. The invented allegorical image of the liberalist state in *Conan the Barbarian* seems almost beyond repair.

Conan does gain power, fame, and money, thanks to his skill and the devotion of his friends. He never fully swears himself to any cause, but rather seeks opportunities that lead to personal wealth (his gladiatorial and thieving exploits) and calculated vengeance. The movie ends with a wonderfully ambivalent image. Conan is seated on an impressive throne, in lavishly ornamental armor, bearing a solemn, contemplative, and somewhat disappointed look. By this point, his quest for revenge has long-since ended. Supposedly staged at a late moment in his adventures, after Conan has amassed enough wealth and favor to start his own kingdom, this image exposes the tension underlying the application of contemporary neoliberalist logic to a fantastic tale of a far-off land. Having conquered the world through a lived application of ideal neoliberal subjecthood, Conan seems bored and despondent. He has institutionalized his own state control and rules with apparent wisdom. Curiously, he is not shown to be surrounded by adoring citizens, or in the middle of his capital city's civic life. Instead, he is perched on his abstract, purgatorial throne. By neoliberal logic, he has gained the world, and done so on his own terms. Yet, this image suggests that he is left without equals, colleagues, or rivals. In short, his methods have left him without connective humanity.

Conan the Barbarian is an exceptional and widely-lauded 1980s sword and sorcery film, and can be viewed as the point of emulation for the rest of the production cycle. Other films from this era feature revenge plots (*Red Sonja*), mercenary protagonists (*The Warrior and the Sorceress* [1984, John C. Broderick]), and characterize civilization with suspicion (*Hundra*), though none do so with as much alacrity or élan as Milius's contested epic. While I have traced a mixed-source genre lineage for the sword and sorcery film — one that can engender ideologically conservative readings at each stage — and have provided this to illustrate an alternative means of characterizing some of the provocative claims made about these sorts of films given by Ryan and Kellner, I have also suggested that the sword and sandal genre can be alternatively theorized through the allegorical emplacement of liberalism and neoliberalism.

While this analysis deliberately stops with the coincident moment of Reagan's presidency and *Conan's* triumphal box-office, a continued re-focusing on the political regimes that parallel the periodic revitalizations of the sword and sandal genre could help elucidate the contemporary situation. A number of high profile films—not least among them *300* (2006, Zack Snyder), *Pathfinder* (2007, Marcus Nispel), *Prince of Persia: The Sands of Time* (2010, Mike Newell), and a high concept remake of *Clash of the Titans* (2010, Louis Leterrier)—have been released to enthusiastic audiences during this ever-more entrenched period of neoliberal logic. In these films, an accelerated recycling of familiar genre cinema—one increasingly dependent on direct remakes and adaptations of video game properties—meets (at some level) the widely-reverberating aftershocks of worldwide financial crises, the recent memories of Western wars in the Islamic world, and global anxieties about the promise of peace in our time. At the very least, a continued monitoring of the ideological mindset of popular genre cinema serves as an early warning siren for larger scale social anxieties of the contemporary moment.

Notes

1. Ryan and Kellner see fantasy as being a particularly loaded delivery-system for political assumptions. They write, "Detachment from the constraints of realism allows fantasy to be more metaphoric in quality and consequently more potentially ideological. Fantasy replaces an accurate assessment of the world with images that substitute desired ideas or feared projections for such an assessment" (244).

2. In "The Essence of Neoliberalism," Pierre Bourdieu characterizes a mature form of political neoliberalism as "a programme of the methodological destruction of collectives" (Bourdieu). Moreover, "neoliberalism tends on the whole to favour severing the economy from social realities and thereby constructing, in reality, an economic system conforming to its description in pure theory, that is a sort of logical machine that presents itself as a chain of constraints regulating economic agents" (Bourdieu).

3. These are the dominant messages highly visible in a schematic reading of the genre. Counter-positions have been articulated. Alec Worley has pointed out the potential for these films to germinate gay fandoms (172–173). Moreover, Italian pepla, especially when viewed in horrendously dubbed prints, are fitting illustrations of what Jeffrey Sconce, in "'Trashing' the Academy: Taste, Excess, and an Emerging Politics of Cinematic Style," calls "paracinema," a kind of legitimated "bad movie" that challenges the seriousness of institutionalized academic film study while at the same time providing some room for subversive interpretation.

4. I should note that Ryan and Kellner do, in fact, use the terms liberalism and neoliberalism, but generally in already politically constituted ways. Thus, left-liberalist comes to characterize films of collective social action, whose numbers dwindle and stagnate by the mid–1970s, while (right)-neoliberalist films unabashedly support market ideology. I am attempting to complicate this based on how the terms have been applied in intervening years.

5. Curiously, "heroic fantasy" is a term that Alec Worley most closely aligns with the creations of Robert E. Howard, including Conan.

6. Assigning straightforward ideological intentionality to *Conan the Barbarian* is complicated somewhat by the fact that the script was a collaboration between John Milius and Oliver Stone. In subsequent work, Stone has proven anything but politically dogmatic and inflexible.

Works Cited

Alpers, Hans Joachim. "Loincloth, Double Ax, and Magic: 'Heroic Fantasy' and Related Genres." Trans. Robert Plank. *Science Fiction Studies* 5.1 (1978): 19–32.
Altman, Rick. *Film/Genre*. London: BFI, 1999. Print.
Bell-Meterau, Rebecca. "Sylvester Stallone and Arnold Schwarzenegger: Androgynous Macho Men." *Acting for America: Movie Stars of the 1980s*. Ed. Robert Eberwein. New Brunswick, NJ: Rutgers University Press, 2010. 36–56. Print.
Bourdieu, Pierre. "The Essence of Neoliberalism." *Le monde diplomatique*. Trans. Jeremy J. Shapiro. Dec 1998. Web. 06 Sept 2010. <http://mondediplo.com/>.
Braedley, Susan, and Meg Luxton. "Competing Philosophies: Neoliberalism and the Challenge of Everyday Life." *Neoliberalism and Everyday Life*. Eds. Susan Braedley and Meg Luxton. Montreal: McGill-Queen's University Press, 2010. 3–21. Print.
Britton, Andrew. "Blissing Out: The Politics of Reaganite Entertainment." *Movie* 31/32 (Winter 1986): 1–42. Print.
Butler, David. *Fantasy Cinema: Impossible Worlds on Screen*. London: Wallflower Press, 2009. Print. Short Cuts.
Cabiria. Dir. Giovanni Pastrone. Perf. Umberto Mozzato, Bartolomeo Pagano, Lidia Quaranta. Itala Film, 1914. Film.
Clarens, Carlos. "Barbarians Now." *Film Comment* 18.3 (May/June 1982): 26–28. Print.
Cline, William C. *In the Nick of Time: Motion Picture Sound Serials*. Jefferson, NC: McFarland, 1984. Print.
Combs, Richard. "*Conan the Barbarian*." *Monthly Film Bulletin* XLIX, 572 (1982): 167–168. FIAF. Web. 25 Sep 2010.
Conan the Barbarian. Dir. John Milius. Perf. Arnold Schwarzengger, Sandhal Bergman, James Earl Jones. Universal, 1982. Film.
Connell, Raewyn. "Understanding Neoliberalism." *Neoliberalism and Everyday Life*.Eds. Susan Braedley and Meg Luxton. Montreal: McGill-Queen's University Press, 2010. 22–36. Print.
Harvey, David. *A Brief History of Neoliberalism*. New York: Oxford University Press, 2005. Print.
Hayek, F.W. "The Principles of a Liberal Social Order." *Liberalism: Critical Concepts in Political Theory*. Vol. 1. Ed. G.W. Smith. London: Routledge, 2002 [1967]. 41–56. Print.
Hercules Unchained [*Ercole e la regina di Lidia*]. Dir. Pietro Francisci. Perf. Steve Reeves, Sylvia Lopez, Gabriele Antonini. Galatea Film, 1959. Film.
Howard, Robert E. "The Hyborian Age." *The Conan Chronicles: Volume 1: People of the Black Castle*. Ed. Stephen Jones. London: Millenium/Orion, 2000 [1936]. 1–24. Print.
Lucanio, Patrick. *With Fire and Sword: Italian Spectacles on American Screens, 1958–1968*. Metuchen, NJ: Scarecrow Press, 1994. Print.
Maciste in Hell [*Maciste all'inferno*]. Dir. Guido Brignone. Perf. Bartolomeo Pagano, Franz Sala, Umberto Guarracino. Cinès-Pittaluga, 1926. Film.
McArthur, Colin. *Underworld USA*. London: Secker and Warburg, 1972. Print.
Muir, John Kenneth. *Horror Films of the 1970s*. Jefferson, NC: McFarland, 2002. Print.
Neale, Steven. *Genre and Hollywood*. New York: Routledge, 2000. Print. Sightlines.

Roberts, J.M. *The Penguin History of the World*. New York: Penguin, 1995. Print.
Ryan, Michael, and Douglas Kellner. *Camera Politica: The Politics and Ideology of Contemporary Hollywood Film*. Bloomington: Indiana Universtiy Press, 1990. Print.
Sconce, Jeffrey. "'Trashing' the Academy: Taste, Excess, and an Emerging Politics of Cinematic Style." *The Cult Film Reader*. Eds. Ernest Mathijs and Xavier Mendik. New York: McGraw Hill, 2008. 100–118. Print.
Scott, James. "The Right Stuff at the Wrong Time: The Space of Nostalgia in the Conservative Ascendancy." *Film & History* 40.1 (Spring 2010): 45–57. *Project Muse*. Web. 20 July 2010.
Usai, Paolo Cherchi. "Italy: Spectacle and Melodrama." *The Oxford History of World Cinema*. Ed. Geoffrey Nowell-Smith. New York: Oxford Universtiy Press, 1997. 123–130. Print.
Wood, Robin. "80s Hollywood: Dominant Tendencies." *CineAction!* 1 (Spring 1985): 2–5. Print.
Worley, Alec. *Empires of the Imagination: A Critical Survey of Fantasy Cinema from Georges Méliès to Lord of the Rings*. Jefferson, NC: McFarland, 2005. Print.

Homer's Lies, Brad Pitt's Thighs

Revisiting the Pre-Oedipal Mother and the German Wartime Father in Wolfgang Petersen's Troy

ROBERT C. PIRRO

> As Troy was being shot it was rumored ... that my calves were too thin and had to be digitally altered for the film. How idiotic can one actually be to believe that it would be technically possible to alter a body part frame for frame for an entire film. Anyway, we wore knee high boots.
> — Brad Pitt (51)

> At the beginning of the Fifties, as the German economic miracle began, our life was rather sad and gray. My parents seemed to me to be bitter. As a result of the Hitler catastrophe, Germany lay more or less in rubble and ashes, in every respect.... To look forward, build a new life, and forget all the horrors — that was the dominant feeling. Then the Americans arrived with their love of life.... At the cinema, there were the Westerns, with those endless landscapes, there was Rock 'n' Roll and Elvis Presley. That brought a feeling of enormous release and freedom, the feeling of a wonderful alternative to all that we saw around us. The most seductive, however, were the great heroes of the cinema.
> — Wolfgang Peterson (Ich liebe die grossen Geschichten 50–1)

In an incisive analysis of the sword-and-sandal epic *Spartacus* (1960), Ina Rae Hark argues that the Kirk Douglas vehicle both partakes in, and critically thematizes, the scopic nature of cinema. Drawing upon feminist film critic Laura Mulvey's pathbreaking essay "Visual Pleasure and Narrative Cinema," Hark points out, "A male may very well find himself situated in positions analogous to those of the fetish or object of punishing voyeurism Mulvey describes as women's in cinema's classic scopic regime" (151). Women in film tend to end up in that position, according to Mulvey, because men seek to alleviate the castration anxiety provoked by the otherwise pleasurable scopophilic act of making women the object of their gaze. One cinematic response to that anxiety, which for Mulvey is exemplified in *film noir* classics and the cinematography of Alfred Hitchcock, is to inflict pain on women for provoking male anxiety by constructing film narratives in which female characters are watched, pursued, and punished. The other response is to "disavow castration by the substitution of a fetish object or turning the represented figure into a fetish" (311). For Mulvey, this response is characteristic of Josef von Sternberg's directorial style, in which, "the beauty of the woman as object and the screen space coalesce; she is no longer the bearer of guilt but a perfect product, whose body, stylized and fragmented by close-ups, is the content of the film and the direct recipient of the spectator's look" (311).

Of the many film genres "contain[ing] episodes in which a male protagonist's enemies make a spectacle of him," Hark singles out peplum films (151). Set in cultures open both to "homoerotic practices" and to the elaborate public humiliation and torture of criminals and conquered enemies, peplum films were known for very skimpy styles of dress, especially for male leads (Hark 151). In taking a slave revolt of gladiators against ancient Rome as its subject, *Spartacus* follows the peplum convention of making an issue of the scopic treatment of the hero. Unlike female characters, whose treatment as objects of the male gaze is coded as natural and unproblematic, "males played by movie stars become spectacularized or commodified, these narratives assert, only because the rightful exercise of masculine power has been perverted by unmanly tyrants" (Hark 152). Although the makers of *Spartacus* gesture at transcending this convention, by, for one example, having the hero take a principled stand against his followers' staging of a gladiatorial combat between captured Roman soldiers or, for another example, allowing the female lead (played by Jean Simmons) to voice her opposition to being made a spectacle for the pleasure of others, Hark finds the film's promise to "define a human subjectivity independent of another's subjection" to be unfulfilled (153).[1] At film's end, Spartacus is forced to kill his best friend in an impromptu gladiatorial combat organized for the viewing pleasure of his aristocratic Roman nemesis, Crassus, and is then crucified along the Appian way with the rest of his followers.

In bringing Mulvey's psychoanalytic treatment of cinematic scopophilia to bear on *Spartacus*, Hark offers a way to understand the significance of a distinctive aspect of peplum films, the scopic treatment of the classical or mythic heroes as played by their male leads. Her analysis only goes so far, however. In the first place, the use of Mulvey's framework, in which the castration anxiety of male filmmakers and audience members is the crucial factor driving the scopic treatment of female (and male) characters, neglects a powerful, alternative psychoanalytical approach to understanding the bases of cinematic pleasure: Gaylyn Studlar's "Masochism and the Perverse Pleasures of the Cinema." Drawing upon the work of Gilles Deleuze and shifting the psychoanalytic focus from oedipal issues of castration anxiety centered upon the father-son relationship in the genital stage to pre-oedipal issues of maternal care of, and control over, infants in the oral stage, Studlar suggests as a second source of cinematic pleasure a "masochistic fantasy ... in which the subject (male or female) assumes the position of the child who desires to be controlled *within* the dynamics of the fantasy" (607). The importance for later adult development of experiences in the pre-oedipal stage of infant care originates in the infant's absolute dependence on, and primary identification with, a caretaker who in most cases is a woman. In this early stage of development, the sense of boundaries between self and environment is, by turns, inchoate and rudimentary and the "infant's experience is a cycle of fusion, separation and refusion with its mother" (Chodorow 73). In addition to bliss and contentment, this situation is also bound to generate frustration, ambivalence, and anxiety (Chodorow 70). For Studlar, this preoedipal environment of contradictory stimuli forms the basis for a masochistic response:

> Both love object and controlling agent for the helpless child, the mother is viewed as an ambivalent figure during the oral period. Whether due to the child's experience of real trauma ... or to the narcissistic infant's own insatiability of demand, the pleasure associated with the oral mother is joined in masochism with the need for pain [606].

Taking issue with Mulvey's oedipal reading of von Sternberg, Studlar argues that a psychoanalytic approach emphasizing the effects of the preoedipal configuration of helpless infant and all-powerful mother offers more insight into the psychological resonances of the films of von Sternberg featuring Marlene Dietrich, "with their submissive male masochist, the oral mother embodied in the ambivalent, alluring presence of [their female lead] and their ambiguous sexuality" (607). In a similar way, some features of *Spartacus* singled out for special consideration by Hark, including the narcissistic Crassus's evocation of Rome as an overwhelming figure of female power and attraction — "There, boy, is Rome, the might, the majesty, the terror of Rome. No man can withstand Rome.... You must serve her, you must abase yourself before her, you must grovel at her feet, you must love her" — take on a different and clearer aspect when viewed through the prism of Studlar's masochistic framework (qtd. in Hark 166). That framework can also explain the psychological appeal of the "material tragedy" embodied in the film's final scene of the crucified Spartacus as originating in pleasurable identification with the afflicted hero (Hark 169).

Focusing on transplanted West German auteur-turned-Hollywood A-list director Wolfgang Petersen's 2004 sword and sandals epic, *Troy*, this chapter will contend that the exhibitionist treatment of peplum heroes and the male leads who play them is best appreciated from a psychoanalytical perspective that remains attentive to the legacies both of preoedipal issues of maternal presence and power and of oedipal issues of paternal rivalry. In its presentation of Achilles, a male hero whose desire for everlasting fame through exhibition of the self in mortal combat is frustrated by the machinations of a paternal rival, *Troy* invites a psychoanalytical approach attuned more to the masochistic basis of cinematic pleasure. Such an approach finds that while Achilles begins the film in a situation of oedipal rivalry, he ends by opting for a symbolic return to preoedipal fusion with the maternal.

By way of demonstrating the utility of taking a more comprehensive psychoanalytical approach, the analysis of *Troy* to follow will also illustrate the importance of political context for understanding the distinctive mix of oedipally-driven sadistic and preoedipally-driven masochistic meanings to be found in a given peplum film. Born in Nazi Germany during World War II, Petersen came to his vocation as a film director and to the sword and sandal genre with a sensibility importantly formed by his experiences of West German life in the early postwar years, a time when issues of masculine crisis and issues of political crisis were conflated in nationally distinctive ways. In such a physically and morally wrecked country, relating to remote fathers who had been away from home for extended periods and who, after their return, were closemouthed about their wartime experiences, was difficult, and this made further investment in the maternal connection with its substratum of preoedipal issues all the more tempting. In taking on *Troy*, his only peplum film to date, Petersen revisited a key text of his German school days (Homer's *Iliad*) and afforded himself the opportunity cinematically to revisit pre-oedipal issues of maternal care and oedipal issues of paternal rivalry reminiscent of his postwar childhood and youth.

The Duel

Troy begins with a duel. On a dusty plain, two armies approach and come to a stop. From each army, a chariot bearing a king rolls slowly forward. The leaders dismount and meet. With a proprietary look, King Agamemnon admires the army of Thessaly and, in response to the Thessalian king's refusal to place his army at the disposal of Agamemnon's empire-building ambitions without a battle, Agamemnon makes an offer: let each king send out his champion to fight and thereby settle the larger political dispute. The Thessalian king can hardly believe his good luck. Over his shoulder, he calls out the name of his champion and from behind the first ranks a real brute of a man, standing a head above the rest, heedlessly pushes his comrades aside to await confidently the Greek champion. Yet, the advantage is with Agamemnon (as he knew full well when he made his offer), because the champion of the Greek army is Achilles, the greatest warrior of his time. Achilles does not come forward at Agamemnon's call, however. He is, as an irritated Agamemnon soon discovers, back in camp.

The film cuts to the camp and a boy messenger who enters Achilles' tent to find him (played by a buffed up Brad Pitt) undressed and sleeping in a tangle of naked women. Roused from his slumber, Achilles suits up and mounts his horse before the awed gaze of the boy, who nevertheless has the temerity to offer an assessment of the challenge awaiting Achilles: "That Thessalian you are fighting. He is the biggest man I have ever seen. I wouldn't want to fight him." From atop his mount, Achilles, in an earnest tone, tells the boy, "That's why no one will remember your name" (*Troy*). Back at the plain, Achilles arrives on horseback to the cheers of the soldiers of the Greek army, as they part and make way. Reaching the front rank, he makes a quick and unworried estimate of his challenger, dismounts, and strides purposefully forward past Agamemnon. Incensed at having been kept waiting, the Greek king sneeringly broaches the possibility of having Achilles whipped for his impudence. His own pride now injured, Achilles turns around and begins to stalk off the field, inviting Agamemnon to fight the duel himself. Nestor, the king's advisor, pulls Achilles up short with a plea before the ranks of the army to spare the soldiers a battle that would cost many of them their lives.

Reluctantly, and with a contemptuous aside to Agamemnon — "Imagine a king who fights his own battles" — Achilles reverses direction to bring the duel to its foregone conclusion (*Troy*). The pace of events quickens. A medium close-up shot frames, against the backdrop of the Greek ranks, the torso and head of Achilles as he determinedly draws a sword and rushes forward. A close-up head shot of the Thessalian champion's scarred face follows as he turns around to the army of Thessaly and impatiently elicits a cheer of support from his comrades. Turning back to his adversary, he gamely and accurately throws one spear, then another, but Achilles with his powerfully compact body and swiftness of step stops one with his shield and avoids the other with a graceful torquing of his torso. Just as the Thessalian champion frees his own sword, Achilles is upon him with a quickness that is enhanced by the slow motion pacing of the shot. In a final leap, Achilles launches himself upward on a trajectory that has him rising above and to the flank of the giant and then plunging his sword downward into the Thessalian's vitals. The giant body collapses to its knees and then flops lifelessly forward. The Greeks cheer offscreen and then onscreen, in the background of a shot of Nestor and a grim-looking Agamemnon in near close-up. A close-up of Achilles follows and then a shot of the front ranks of the army of Thessaly, abashed and silent, as Achilles (his back to the camera) contemptuously struts before them, calling out a further challenge: "Is there no one else?!" (*Troy*). A suitably impressed Thessalian king appears at his side to ask his name — "Achilles, son of Peleus" is the reply — and to direct him to bring Thessaly's royal scepter to Agamemnon, his king. Achilles ignores the proffered scepter and turns on his heels, dismissively saying, "He's not my king" (*Troy*).

The film's opening is a virtuoso shot sequence, perhaps the best shot sequence of the film and worth describing in detail for two reasons. First, it illustrates Petersen's skill at working within the conventions of the peplum or sword and sandal genre. In particular, the Thessaly sequence features such conventions as the prominent display of well-muscled male bodies, the staging of a contest of strength and skill, the mass choreography of lavishly-costumed extras, and the spectacle of a noble hero putting himself at risk for the good of the people. It also invites the kind of scopic analysis Hark applies to *Spartacus*. With the exception of the naked female companions in Achilles' tent, male bodies are the ones that are fetishized (Achilles) or phallicly punished (the Thessalian champion).

Secondly, the sequence is worth describing because the duel agreed upon by Agamemnon and the king of Thessaly and fought by Achilles and the Thessalian champion establishes a relational dynamic between king, champion, and army/people that infuses the rest of the film narrative with distinctive psychological and political meanings. (Of no small relevance, in this regard, is the fact that the opening Thessaly sequence is a pure invention of Petersen and his screenwriter; there is no basis for it in the text of *The Iliad* or, for that matter, in any of the ancient references to Achilles.)[2] In this dynamic, an older, ugly, power-hungry politician comes into conflict with a younger, beautiful, glory-seeking hero whose deeds rouse the admiration of the army and threaten the politician's sense of control. Here, an instructive contrast can be drawn with the key dynamic of *Spartacus* as analyzed by Hark. In that film, single (gladiatorial) combat is a punishment scopically visited upon the male hero for the sadistic viewing pleasure of the villainous Romans (within the film narrative) and the moral disapprobation of members of the film-going audience. In *Troy*, by contrast, single combat is not a sadistically-imposed punishment. It is, rather, a duty enjoined by the hero's nemesis (who nevertheless gets no viewing pleasure from it) and accepted (masochistically) by the male hero for the purpose of gaining the admiration of his fellow warriors and their posterity (within the film narrative). As this chapter will argue, this difference correlates with the latter film's presentation of its hero not primarily as a victim (or perpetrator) of scopic sadism but as a masochist, for whom "only death can hold the final mystical solution to the expiation of the father and symbiotic reunion with the idealized maternal rule" (Studlar 609).

The Muscle-Bound Male Body and Death

Troy's release formed part of a third wave of sword and sandal cinema, which arguably first took impulse with the rousing popular and critical reception of Ridley Scott's *Gladiator* (2000), starring Russell Crowe as Maximus, the virtuous Roman general who is unwillingly drawn into a bloody imperial power struggle. Scott's film revisited the plot of Anthony Mann's 1964 Hollywood epic, *The Fall of the Roman Empire*, whose poor performance at the box office helped to bring to an end the genre's second wave. The peplum phenomenon initially appeared in the Italian cinema of the silent age, on the heels of the 1908 release of Luigi Maggi's *The Last Days of Pompeii*, and its popularity lasted into the early Twenties.

Considered one of the masters of first wave sword and sandal epics, Giovanni Pastrone became world famous after the release of *Cabiria* (1914), which not only stunned film audiences in Europe and America with the director's virtuoso staging and camera work but also gave birth to several sequels based on one of the film's characters, Maciste, a slave "played by a non-professional actor named Bartolomeo Pagano, whose muscular exploits turned him overnight from a Genoa dockworker into a star" (Bondanella 6). *Cabiria*'s Maciste became the prototype of the muscle-bound heroes of classical myth and antiquity that would figure so prominently in the Fifties and Sixties revival of peplum films, whose plots "centered on the need for muscle-power to resolve almost any problem (including, in one film, the thermonuclear bomb)" (Frayling 73). In an analysis of Second Wave peplum, Michèle Lagny notes that "one of the dominant themes of the genre is that of virile strength" (171). *Troy*'s adherence to this convention is apparent in the muscularly enhanced body of Brad Pitt, who reportedly worked out six days a week for months as part of his preparation for the role of Achilles. Much of the internet chatter around the film concerned Pitt's physique, including details of his workout routine and questions about whether his apparently impressive thighs were digitally enhanced or the product of stunt doubles. In an interview, Petersen gave "a ten minute soliloquy on Pitt's physique," noting his amazement at "the proportion of Brad Pitt's pectoral muscles" (Tyrangiel 66).

Just as Second Wave peplum "directors patently linger on their actors' physique, often highlighting it by drawing a parallel with statues," so *Troy* repeatedly offers close-ups of Brad Pitt's face, arms, and torso, in shots that give him the solidity and presence of a classical bust (Lagny 171). This is particularly true in the sequence leading up to his ship's landing on the Trojan beach, when, dressed in a toga-like cloak and gesticulating grandiloquently, Achilles calls forth his Myrmidons' fighting spirit by reminding them of the greatest reward mortal combat promises: immortality through the remembrance of great deeds. (Petersen: "I ... love [the scene] when Achilles lands on the beach at Troy and calls to his soldiers, 'Go get your immortality.' You get this sense that this is maybe a dark kind of crazy guy, right? But he has enormous dreams" [Tyrangiel 72].) An intimation of that reward is forthcoming at the conclusion of the succeeding battle sequence as Achilles, perched on a ridge in a statue-like pose, receives the acclaim of Greek warriors massing on the beach. By way of reinforcing that link between hero and classical art work, the beach landing sequence includes shots of Achilles standing by a piece of statuary, in this case the golden statue of Apollo at the entrance of a Trojan temple. (Significantly, he decapitates the statue to show his disregard for popular belief in the gods after his lieutenant wonders aloud about the prospects of divine retribution in response to the Myrmidons' plundering of the temple.)

In visualizing Achilles in the form of classical statuary, *Troy* not only emphasizes his "virile strength" in the tradition of peplum, but the film also gestures to his impending doom. As Angela Dalle Vacche, referring to the operatic qualities of the early peplum tradition in Italian film, has written, "By modeling itself on a motionless sculpture, the body in opera points to a single component of cinema — the still frame of photography — and to the feeling of death that hangs over the arrested image" (6). Applied to the sword and sandal genre, Studlar's analysis reveals a deeper layer of meaning in generic convention of likening the well-muscled bodies of male leads to statues and suggests that the mark of death that is on *Troy*'s classically-posed Achilles has very much to do with the masochistic pleasures of cinema.

In simultaneously evoking immortality and death, *Troy*'s image of Achilles-as-classical-sculpture raises the question whether the hero's desire for everlasting fame prolongs, in altered form, those childishly unlimited desires for maternal love and acknowledgement, which carry over powerful, inchoate pre-oedipal experiences of the not-altogether-distinguishable infantile ecstasies and torments of fusion with, and separation from, the mother. In this regard, it is interesting that the last person in Phthia Achilles consults before deciding whether to participate in Agamemnon's expedition to Troy is his mother, Thetis. The encounter, which has no precedent in *The Iliad*, takes place in a setting whose features evoke maternal plenitude and fusion. Thetis stands knee deep in a tidal pool, an intermediate zone between earth and sea, blurring the features of both. Rising conspicuously behind her in the rock face is a jagged vertical crack. Gathering sea shells, she tells Achilles that she is going to make him a bracelet, like the ones she made for him when he was a boy. He raises the question of whether he should go to Troy and she answers by starkly posing the alternatives: remain in Phthia, marry, have children, die peacefully in old age, and be forgotten or go to Troy, fight heroically, die young, and be remembered. (In *The Iliad*, the doom of Achilles is considered more or less a settled matter by Achilles' mother: "Since indeed your lifetime is to be short, of no length" [Lattimore 70].)

Psychoanalytically-speaking, the alternatives posed by Thetis can be framed as, on the one hand, a post-oedipal option, in which the son gives up his rivalry with the father and takes a mother substitute as wife, and, on the other, a pre-oedipal option, in which the son opts for infantile re-fusion with the maternal. (How regression to a state akin to pre-oedipal relations can marry immortality and death is perhaps best seen on consideration of the pre-oedipal mother in one her negative guises: the "archaic mother." Her "monstrous desire" is to "reincorporate and destroy all life" (Creed 139).) Much more than *The Iliad*, *Troy* frames Achilles within an oedipal rivalry. Examination of the political context of Petersen's early life reveals why this might be so and who the father of this oedipal rivalry might be.

The Early Postwar German Context

If Achilles is implicated in an oedipal rivalry with a father figure, it is not with his biological father, Peleus, who makes no appearance in film (or poem) and to whom scant reference is made. As it turns out, the paternal rival in question is Agamemnon, who, of all the characters of *The Iliad*, undergoes the greatest metamorphosis in the adaptation of his role to *Troy*. To be sure, there is much overlap with the Homeric source material. As in the epic poem, *Troy*'s Agamemnon is anxious about his authority as leader of the Greek army and extremely hostile toward Achilles for his refusal to show him proper deference. In both film and epic poem, Achilles nearly comes to fatal blows with Agamemnon over the latter's decision to claim Achilles' war captive, Briseis, as his own. As in the epic poem, *Troy*'s Achilles sits out the fight between Greeks and Trojans until Patroclus is killed by Hector, then engages and kills Hector, refuses the body the proper rites, and only relents in response to the supplications of King Priam.

Among the film's most obvious departures from *The Iliad* is its portrayal of Agamemnon. In the first place, *Troy*'s Agamemnon is old enough to be Achilles' father, a generational divide that is missing from *The Iliad*. (The only reference in that poem to the age difference between Achilles and Agamemnon is Agamemnon's off-handed statement, "And let him yield place to me, inasmuch as I am the kinglier and inasmuch as I can call myself born the elder" [Lattimore 202].) Secondly, *Troy*'s Agamemnon is cast as a modern power politician — "a really modern type ... a politician who wants to establish a world empire and destroy everything that stands in his way," Petersen said in an interview with Martin Wolf (158). At every turn in the film, he seems a coldly calculating leader, willing to break agreements to extend his empire (as when he agrees to his brother Menelaus fighting a duel with Paris while fully intending to violate the terms of the duel), huddling with his chief advisor, Nestor, in his map room savoring the prospects of conquering Troy ("I always thought my brother's wife [Helen] was a foolish woman but she's proved to be very useful") or recognizing what Patroclus' death at the hands of Hector means for Greek prospects in the war ("That boy just saved the war for us") (*Troy*). The epic poem's thin-skinned and impulsive paramount war chief, insecure about his command over the Greek kings but solicitous of his army's well-being, only distantly resembles the Agamemnon in the map room sequence, who sweeps his horse hair crop across the map, saying, "If Troy falls, I control the Aegean!" or who fulminates, "Before me, Greece was nothing! I brought all the Greek kings together. I created a nation out of fire-worshippers and snake eaters! I build the future, Nestor, me!" (*Troy*). Petersen would later note in an interview with Tobias Kniebe that the biggest deviation of the film from *The Iliad* involved Agamemnon: "Our worse crime against the original poem was in how we killed him off" (4).

Contemporary political circumstances may have had a role in Petersen's reshaping of Agamemnon. In public interviews, such as the one he gave to Wolf, he implicitly draws a parallel between Agamemnon's imperial ambitions and the Bush administration's foreign policy: "Actually, although Homer composed it almost 3,000 years ago, *The Iliad* says a lot about our world. Agamemnon, for example ... is, for me, a really modern type. I don't want to name any names but politicians still exist today who want to establish world empires and destroy anything that stands in their way" (158). Brad Pitt, who, one imagines, had ample opportunity on the set to discover Petersen's political take on the film he was shooting, responded in May 2004 to Tobias Kniebe's suggestion that *Troy* might offer lessons to the contemporary world by saying, "I'm sure of it. Just look at our current war of aggression. That war shows that we as a society have made no progress over the last thousand years" (51). The Bush administration's foreign policy is also the backdrop against which film historian Christine Haase reads *Troy* as an antiwar film. The film "reflects Petersen's ideological convictions which seem ... acutely aligned with postwar German attitudes ... in sharp contrast to the belligerent rhetoric and actions of the Bush administration around the time of *Troy*'s production" (91).

The Bush and Iraqi invasion references point to a larger political context plausibly explaining the genre's reemergence in the first decade of the new millennium: the post–Cold War rise of the United States as unchallenged world superpower with military bases across the world and military spending far, far in excess of any potential rival.[3] It was no great imaginative leap to analogize the status of the United States to the Roman Empire. Thus, for example, a May 2002 *New York Times* Ideas and Trends column entitled "All Roads Lead to D.C." reported a growing consensus among historians and foreign policy experts that the United States was an empire and should act like one on the world stage (Eakin). Revealingly, the image that accompanied the article was a still photo from the reputed breakthrough film of peplum's Third Wave, *Gladiator*, showing Emperor Commodus (played by Joaquin Phoenix) receiving the acclamation of the Roman masses.

While the newfound popularity of imperial analogies, especially among the sort of foreign policy elites who might have had the ear of Bush Administration officials, is a plausible context for understanding the timing of the most recent peplum revival, it is not the most important context for understanding the form and meaning of the discourses on masculinity and politics presented in *Troy*. The more relevant context is suggested by the World War II references in the map room sequence. The use of the map as prop and the boilerplate dialogue evokes classic World War II film epics like *Battle of the Bulge* (1965) or

The Battle of Britain (1969). And filmgoers might easily read the sequence's strutting empire builder Agamemnon as a Hitler dressed up in archaic robes. This latter parallel is further suggested by Nestor's declaration that "Hector commands the finest army *in the East*" as he tries to temper Agamemnon's eastward-looking imperial ambitions (*Troy*, emphasis mine).

One of the major effects of Hitler's war of aggression was the physical destruction and moral collapse of Germany, a degradation that decisively shaped the conditions of Petersen's childhood and school years. Born in 1941, Petersen was a member of a postwar generation, many of whose members wondered about the nature of their fathers' complicity with the criminal policies of the Nazi regime and found it difficult, if not impossible, to ask, or get answers to, painful questions. This was no less an issue for Petersen. When asked what he had heard from his parents about the Hitler years and the war, he said: "My father was uncommunicative. My mother, by contrast, was frank, which I appreciated" (1997 165). Further complicating relations with his father was his father's pattern of infidelity, which, Petersen attests, cast a shadow over family life (Ich liebe die grossen Geschichten 47). It also probably intensified his mother's adoration of her only son: "Yes, it's true, I always got whatever I wanted from her. She threw her educational principles to the winds in order to make me happy" (Petersen 62). In school, which he attended until 1960, "there was no serious coming to terms with the Third Reich" (1997 166).

In response to the gap in generational memory and the burdens it placed on familial relationships, some members of the generation born before or during the war chose to explore their families' wartime past imaginatively. "What emerged was a genre of *Väterliteratur* in the early 1980s in West Germany, in which sons and daughters probed their fathers' involvement in the Third Reich" (Kosta 220). If any work of Petersen's can be assimilated to this genre it is his 1981 adaptation of *Das Boot*, Lothar-Günther Bucheim's fictionalized account of his wartime service in the German U-Boat fleet. The film, which Petersen wrote and directed, recounts how a U-Boat captain (played by Jürgen Prochnow) shepherds his mostly young and untested crew through a dangerous 1941 North Atlantic tour that is punctuated by several depth charge attacks. The last of these attacks, in the Strait of Gibraltar, nearly sinks the sub, but under the calm and determined leadership of their captain, the crew members keep their nerves, pull together, and get their ship operating again. At film's end, the now seasoned crew and their stoic captain steam into port to a somewhat ragtag hero's welcome, only to be decimated by an Allied air raid.

A huge box office hit in Germany and abroad (six Oscar nominations and the record U.S. gross for a German-language feature film), *Das Boot* met with harsh criticism from some prominent film reviewers in Germany (Haase 75–6; Petersen 1997, 173–4). Among the most serious charges to be lodged against the film was that its portrayal of a mostly apolitical crew led by a captain openly disdainful of Germany's Nazi leadership served to obfuscate the criminal nature of Nazi Germany's war aims and conduct as well as the co-responsibility of German soldiers in supporting the war. In the words of one film scholar, Petersen's desire "to represent the horror of war but not the horror of Nazi ideology" formed part of a "process of exonerating the soldiers, and, by extension, the public themselves" in both Germany and the United States (where inconvenient questions about responsibility for American military involvement and conduct in Vietnam were already being elided in such war films as *The Deer Hunter* [1978], *Apocalypse Now* [1979], and *First Blood* [1982]) (Prager 244, 255).[4]

While Brad Prager does not reference *Väterliteratur* in his critique of *Das Boot*, he does interpret the U-Boat captain as a "father-protagonist" with whom viewers are invited "to identify" and for whom they are invited to "mourn" (247). In the scene showing the U-Boat's departure for the North Atlantic, the captain says of his new crew, "They're just kids, nurslings who belong at their mothers' breasts" (*Das Boot*). This "radically gendered discourse," Prager writes, "is no surprise, as the film is in many respects about turning the boy soldiers into responsible men, primarily in the image of the captain, who appears as the submarine's father figure" (249).

For his part, Petersen, who remembered his father's silence about the war and his mother's confession to being "enraptured" by Hitler and being taken in by the "glamour" of the propaganda and entertainment films of the early years of Nazism, believed that he had written and directed an anti-war film, whose gritty realism exposed the negative consequences of the fascist glorification of war through appeals to young men's sense of honor and toughness (1997 165–166). In the context of this article's topic, *Das Boot* is important as a point of comparison with *Troy*, Petersen's only other war film and a vehicle for his indirect, if perhaps also inadvertent, return to concerns about family relationships and the strains placed on those relationships by German history. On this view, *Troy* constitutes, broadly speaking, a kind of time-delayed peplum variant of *Väterliteratur*. That Petersen chose Greek myth rather than Roman history as material for his one foray into the peplum genre further suggests the significance of his personal biography and his native country's history.

During the 1950s' and 1960s' peplum revival, "the Italians preferred Greek mythology, or comic-strip mythologies of their own making," while Hollywood producers were drawn to a more historically-based (or, in the case of biblical epics, text-based) peplum films focused on the politics of empire (Frayling 73). In both of its national variants, peplum film was known for its ambition both to entertain and (however clumsily) to teach lessons of moral or political value (Lagny 170; Brunetta 332–3). Among the themes taken up in Hollywood's Rome-centric films of the time were the hubristic tendencies of "totalitarian" leaders, the clash of *raison d'état* with the divine will, and the vindication of egalitarian values (Lagny 174). As a Hollywood production, and in comparison with *Gladiator*, *Troy* is an outlier for its focus on Greek myth, although, in accordance with American tastes, Petersen's treatment of the epic material is realistic. In an 2004 German newspaper interview with Kniebe, Petersen suggests that his background as a "humanistically educated *European*" made him an attractive choice to take over direction of the Warner Brothers project (3, emphasis mine). What Petersen elides in this account are the national dimensions of his affinity with Homer. It is hard to overstate the longstanding importance of Homer and Greek poetry to German elite education and literate culture. Since the mid-eighteenth century publication of Johann-Joachim Winckelmann's pathbreaking book, *Geschichte der Kunst des Alterthums* (*The History of Art Among the Ancients*), in which ancient Greek art is held up as a model of cultural expression, German literati and philosophers have made artistic and intellectual engagement with ancient Greek poetry a priority. Homeric epic and Greek tragedy came to be seen by thinkers as diverse as Goethe, Hölderlin, Hegel, and Nietzsche as antidotes to the fragmentation, division, and alienation of modern life. Engagement with the figures of Greek poetry and myth became a means for imagining new and purportedly more worthy ways of orienting German cultural and social life, especially during and after times of major political upheaval. This philhellenic impulse would come to shape the modern German educational system, particularly the emphasis placed on Greek language training and the Greek classics in Gymnasium, the German equivalent to college prep schools in the United States.

In the same 2004 interview, Petersen enthusiastically relates how his Gymnasium education introduced him to Achilles and Hector. Achilles is "very much oriented to himself. He makes his own rules, refuses to follow the orders of anyone, and stands outside the community. He is the rebel. And he pursues immortal fame through deeds that will outlast time." Conversely, Hector is the "exact opposite, a noble soul, who considers the common good more important than his own desires. He would be happy loving his wife, his father, his son, his country. And he fights only because all that is endangered." For Petersen, as he revealed to Kniebe, these differences were already perceptible "in my student days at the humanistic Gymnasium in Hamburg as we read *The Iliad* in the original" (2). When pressed to name his personal favorite as a student, Petersen equivocates at first, saying that both heroes are admirable, and that when making *Troy* he deliberately chose to forego the typical Hollywood approach of telling the audience who is good and who is bad. Yet, Petersen does eventually express a preference for Achilles: "To really appreciate and understand Hector, one needs to be more mature. Achilles is a great rebel. When one is fifteen and pimply and feels ill at ease in life, then he is the attractive figure" (3).

Even while admitting to a past preference for Achilles, Petersen hedges that preference by attributing it to teenage awkwardness and immaturity. One may well wonder what effect his being a *German* teenager, living in a country devastated by war, occupation, and partition, and lacking a close relationship to a remote father who remained silent on the subject of the war, had on his preference for Achilles over Hector. After all, by his own account, the latter hero stood for love of father and of country, among other things. The Hollywood films on which Petersen built his career—*In the Line of Fire*, starring Clint Eastwood as a grizzled Secret Service agent trying to make amends for his self-perceived failure in Dallas in 1963, and *Air Force One*, starring Harrison Ford as a president who single-handedly foils a terrorist hijacking and saves his family in the process—did not lack for patriotic themes or positive father figures, but they were set in the United States where, as Petersen said in a German newspaper interview at the time of *Air Force One*'s German release, one could feel good about being patriotic: "After the war, we Germans were not allowed to display patriotic feelings.... It was nice for me ... to get my share of good patriotic feelings (through *Air Force One*), feelings that I have never had before" (Krämer 79). If making American-themed films in Hollywood allowed Petersen to display feelings, and tell stories unburdened by German history and his postwar upbringing, his return to Homer and to the theme of war could well have reactivated emotional affinities and burdens from his past. So, for example, Achilles returns (from Petersen's reading of him in his Gymnasium days) as the outsider hero or rebel. Revealingly, what he now rebels against is patriotism, specifically the sort of patriotism that enlists men in the cause of someone else's campaign of empire building or entangles them in the machinations of power politics. During Agamemnon's map room tirade, the Greek king declaims, "Achilles is the past! A man who fights for no flag, a man loyal to no country!" (*Troy*). In another scene, Achilles, brooding in his tent after his withdrawal from the fight at Troy, laments that "soldiers fight for kings they've never even met" and tells Patroclus, "Don't waste your life following some fool's orders" (*Troy*).

Achilles' critique of the sacrifices that kings (and countries) demand from ordinary soldiers parallels the attitude of the U-Boat captain in Petersen's 1981 war film. That the anti-patriotic message of *Troy* recalls Petersen's postwar West German upbringing is confirmed by the family drama in which that political message is nested, the rivalry between a rebellious son (Achilles) and an overbearing father figure (Agamemnon).

On one level, that rivalry is centered on differing valuations of politics. The foremost politician on the Greek side, Agamemnon, "has no honor," Achilles tells Odysseus, when the latter comes to Phthia to enlist him in Agamemnon's campaign against Troy (*Troy*). What Achilles means by this has already been demonstrated in the Thessaly sequence; Agamemnon does not fight his own battles—he uses other men to do his fighting for him. What makes Agamemnon's leadership especially dishonorable is that it not only enlists men in wars in which they have no real stake, it also demands of those men that they give the credit and acclaim of their own martial deeds to Agamemnon. In essence, Agamemnon's politics brings dishonor to all. This corrosive dynamic is made plain in a scene set in Agamemnon's tent on the Trojan beach after Achilles and his Myrmidon warriors successfully spearhead the Greek landing in the face of fierce Trojan resistance. After washing off the blood and gore of battle, Achilles is called to the tent (a luxurious contrivance built over Agamemnon's beached ship) where he is treated to the spectacle of the various Greek kings—including the king of Thessaly, Agamemnon's erstwhile battle opponent now turned imperial flunky—effusively praising Agamemnon for "his" great victory and laying lavish gifts at his feet. After another fawning tribute, this one from Nestor, Agamemnon notices Achilles' disapproving presence and dismisses the other kings so that he and Achilles can "have it out" in private. The significance of the ensuing scene for the film's overall view of politics is anticipated by a departing Odysseus, who tells Achilles, "War is young men dying and old men talking. You know this. Ignore the politics" (*Troy*) The back and forth between Agamemnon and Achilles that follows bears only a distant relation to the scene that dominates the first book of *The Iliad*, in which Agamemnon takes Briseis, Achilles' battle prize, and Achilles is stopped from attempting to kill Agamemnon through the intervention of Athena. *Troy*'s Agamemnon does take Briseis and Achilles does contemplate an attack on Agamemnon, but the centerpiece of the scene is a hostile exchange unique to the film and expressive of the basic conflicts that structure the film's narrative:

> ACHILLES: Apparently you won some great victory.
> AGAMEMNON: Perhaps you didn't notice. The Trojan beach belonged to Priam in the morning. It belongs to Agamemnon in the afternoon.
> ACHILLES: You can have the beach. I didn't come here for sand.
> AGAMEMNON: No you came here because you want your name to last through the ages. (Pause.) A great victory was won today. But that victory is not yours. *Kings* did not kneel to Achilles. *Kings* did not pay homage to Achilles.
> ACHILLES: Perhaps the kings were too far behind to see. The soldiers won the battle.
> AGAMEMNON: History remembers kings, not soldiers! [*Troy*].

This passage makes clear the terms of the conflict between the two. Achilles pursues immortal fame, a reward he believes rightly accrues to those individuals who accomplish great deeds on the battlefield. Agamemnon stakes a claim for the preeminent value of politics based on the capacity of those highly skilled in its uses (i.e., himself) to achieve all ends of any significance: territory, immortal fame, even sexual access.

In making Briseis the last in a series of prizes claimed by Agamemnon, the scene feminizes the other prizes—territory and everlasting fame—and frames the conflict between Agamemnon and Achilles as one fought on the grounds of masculinity. It isn't the first time territory is feminized in the film. As the Trojan troops assemble to repel the beach landing, Hector calls to them: "Troy is mother to us all. Fight for her" (*Troy*). To the extent that the conflict between Agamemnon and Achilles can be envisioned as a masculine struggle over a feminized prize, it invites analysis in terms of the classic oedipal struggle between a father (or father figure) and son. This would mean that Briseis is a mother figure for Achilles. When Achilles decides, after recovering Briseis, to leave the war and take Briseis home as his consort, she does enact the role of mother figure or substitute, which, according to Freud, is the role every wife plays to some extent. However, the death of Patroclus forecloses this post-oedipal resolution for Achilles. What remains for Achilles is the other option outlined by his mother back in the tidal pool of Phthia before his departure for Troy: early death and immortal fame. Or, to put this option in psychoanalytical terms, Achilles chooses pre-oedipal fusion with the maternal which manifests itself in his masochistic yearning for fame through self destruction.

Significantly enough, Achilles' masochism finds clearest expression when he is in the company of Briseis. After rescuing her from an attempt by Agamemnon's henchmen to torture and rape her, Achilles brings her back to his tent where she angrily rejects his attempts to minister to her wounds. Challenging her religious beliefs, he points out a contradiction in her pious aversion to the warrior ethos. He then offers an alternative "theology" based on the provocative notion that the gods masochistically envy humans for the fragility of their lives: "The gods envy us because we're mortal. Because any moment might be our last. Everything is lovelier because we are doomed" (*Troy*). Looking at her battered and bloodied face, he attempts to sway her to this masochistic perspective when he says, "You will never be lovelier than you are now" (*Troy*).

The camera cuts to a shot of the Greek beach encampment at night, under a bright moon and with the ocean surf sounding in the background. Intended as part of a montage sequence to signify the passage of time, the shot carries symbolic weight in and of itself with its prominent references to traditional symbols of maternal infinitude and plenitude: the eternally cycling phases of the moon and the expansiveness of the ocean (Creed 135). The next shot frames Achilles' sleeping face in close-up as a hand slowly presses a knife against his throat. "Do it!" Achilles says, inviting his own death. "Nothing is easier." Surprised, the knife wielder Briseis asks, "Aren't you afraid?" Achilles responds, "Everyone dies. Today or fifty years from now. What does it matter?" (*Troy*) He grips her shoulders and urges her again to slit his throat. Then, with her knife still at her throat, he maneuvers her downward and pulls her gown from her legs. Only after he kisses her does Briseis relax her grip on the knife. The mix of sadistic and masochistic gestures not only endows the sex scene with a certain frisson, but it also gestures to the desire for pre-oedipal regression that, according to some scholars, forms one of the bases for adult sexual pleasure: "People come out of the earliest mother-infant relationship with the memory of a unique intimacy which they want to recreate" (Chodorow 194).

Achilles' masochistic pursuit of a condition akin to pre-oedipal fusion with the maternal finds its final expression in his death scene, at which, significantly, Briseis is again present. After Briseis kills Agamemnon (thereby attesting, one might argue, to her symbolic enactment of the role of archaic mother whose preoedipal presence completely overshadows the father) and is rescued from the retaliation of Agamemnon's guards by Achilles, the two embrace. Paris appears and sends an arrow through Achilles' heel. A close-up shot of Achilles' face in agony is followed by slower motion shots, cutting back and forth between Paris and Achilles, the former sending arrows on their way, the latter responding with expressive grunts of pains as each arrow finds its mark. After taking a third arrow in his torso, Achilles seems less pained, more accepting. As a panicked Briseis reaches him, he calmly says, "It's alright. It's alright." He grasps a lock of her hair, smells it, and looks content: "You gave me peace" (*Troy*). Sending her away, he topples over, just as Greek soldiers enter the temple. In a crane shot pulling up and away, the audience sees Achilles sprawled on a long, narrow rectangular swath of grass as soldiers approach from all directions to stand before the body and gaze upon the fallen hero. The rectangular patch in which he lies, recalling as it does the vertical crack in the rock face of his mother's tidal pool, symbolically returns Achilles to the life-giving and death-dealing body of the archaic mother. The struggle between Achilles and Agamemnon over the sympathy of the army, over sexual access to Briseis, and over the more lasting place in human memory is finished, at last. Achilles has finally gotten what he (masochistically) wanted from the start: immortal fame at the cost of his life. Or, to put it another way, he has been "incorporated" into the immortal memory of the people, as his mother promised.

Conclusion

> *I noticed that my mother would have walked through fire for her children. She really would have. By contrast, my father was more caught up in his own world.... My father considered my ambition to be a film director to be nonsense, a delusion. He wasn't acquainted with the world of cinema. My mother took my ambitions seriously because she knew me and paid careful attention to me.*
> — *Wolfgang Petersen (Ich liebe die grossen Geschichten 45 – 46)*

Wolfgang Petersen has long presented German film scholars and critics with something of a puzzle. His work in 1970s West German television and cinema fell squarely within the conventions of New German Cinema — topical films that engaged pressing issues of social relevance such as the "brutality of public life" or "the alienation of urban youth" (Hake 174). After the box office success of *Das Boot* (1981) and *The Never Ending Story* (1984), he moved to Hollywood and became an A-list director making high budget, slickly produced, commercially-oriented genre films that bore no apparent relation to his prior work. Had Petersen, in the American tradition, completely remade himself? Haase argues that Petersen did not shed his native film training and culture and that even his most popular and commercial Hollywood films retain a progressive and critical political edge. She characterizes his Hollywood style as exemplifying an "aesthetic of hybridity," part of whose basis is the continuing influence of a German past that he never explicitly references (95). As with his other Hollywood productions, *Troy* exemplifies this aesthetic. Unlike his other Hollywood films, however, *Troy* offers relatively more direct access to his German past; in particular, to the educational culture and dynamics of family relations in a country that had been ruined by its embrace of Nazism.

Buoyed by the attention and encouragement he received from an adoring mother, whose own susceptibility to the attractions of cinema he apparently inherited, Petersen came early to appreciate the power of film, especially Hollywood film, to fascinate and enchant audiences. It was, after all, Hollywood cinema that allowed him to escape for hours at a time from the physically drab and morally compromised world his father's generation had inadvertently helped to fashion. Taking his mother's and cinema's side did not mean escaping the burdens of his father and national history, however. Highly skilled in the techniques of cinematic enchantment and covetous of box office success, Petersen has nevertheless found ways to integrate moral and political critique into the entertaining stories he tells. In choosing to work on a peplum film, Petersen found a genre congenial to marrying entertainment values with didactic purposes. In taking on a peplum film based on *The Iliad*, Petersen found the perfect vehicle for infusing that cinematic marriage with the memories and passions of his own upbringing.

To be sure, Petersen's path to *Troy* is an unusual one when considered beside the paths other directors have taken to working in the peplum genre. His path, with its distinctively German aspect, nevertheless remains a convenient point of departure for understanding not only how issues of masochistic pleasure find potent expression in the generic conventions of the peplum but also how national histories differently condition the receptivity of directors and audiences to the masochistic appeal of peplum films.[5]

Notes

1. For more on these scenes, see Hark 159 and 156.
2. Petersen refers to his relationship with the film's screenwriter David Benioff as a "partnership" in a discussion concerning changes made to the Homeric source material (Kniebe interview 4). As "one of just a handful of Hollywood directors who have earned the right to final cut," Petersen would have had unlimited leeway in shaping the film plot (Haase 64). Further evidence that the Thessaly sequence was mainly his invention is the fact that scenarios in which two characters engage in a duel are common in his films (Haase 85; Kniebe interview 1). All translations from the German are mine unless otherwise noted.
3. The social-political context of First Wave peplum was, according to Irmbert

Schenk, the conditions of Italian society in the throes of early twentieth century economic and political change. In a country deeply divided along class, regional, and cultural lines, and overextended militarily by a political elite with neocolonial ambitions, sword and sandal films, with their mythic images of strength and power, provided Italian moviegoers with an emotionally satisfying alternative to social and political reality (Schenk 183–4). For a people whose sense of identity was so fractured and whose self image was marked by a national inferiority complex, peplum films' showcasing of muscle-bound heroes could foster consolatory fantasies of individual and collective power and efficacy (Schenk 185–6). Scholars of Second Wave peplum tend to relate the popularity of peplum heroes to Italians' transition in mid-twentieth century from agricultural to industrial work, from rural to city life, from subsistence economies to a consumer society: "The peplum affirmed the worth of male physical strength in a rapidly industrializing society ..." (Nowell-Smith 94). In *La Battaglia di Maratona* (1960), a film that Lagny considers in many ways characteristic of the genre, the hero Philippides "tends to prefer the country but is not hostile to the city" (167). Made on the cheap and in assembly-line fashion at Rome's Cinecittà Studios, Second Wave peplum films often affirmed the values of rural life at the same time that they were themselves the products of processes of standardized mass production and globalized mass consumption (Brunetta 332). Pierre Leprohon also notes Second Wave peplum's reliance on cutting-edge technologies such as color film and panoramic lenses (173–4).

4. For more on apologetic films on Vietnam, see Prager 239.

5. In this regard, one might speculate about the significant role that male audience goers of the generation of Italians born during wartime had in giving impulse to the Second Wave peplum revival of the late 1950s. Like their contemporary Petersen, they also experienced national episodes of wartime defeat and postwar scarcity in which issues of masculine crisis coincided with issues of political crisis.

WORKS CITED

Bondanella, Peter. *Italian Cinema from Neorealism to the Present*. New York: Continuum, 1990.
Brunetta, Gian Piero. *Cent'anni di cinema italiano, 2*. Bari: Laterza, 1991.
Chodorow, Nancy. *The Reproduction of Mothering*. Berkeley: University of California Press, 1999.
Creed, Barbara. "Alien and the Monstrous-Feminine." *Alien Zone: Cultural Theory and Contemporary Science Fiction*. Ed. Annette Kuhn. London: Verso, 1990. 128–142.
Dalle Vacche, Angela. *The Body in the Mirror: Shapes of History in Italian Cinema*. Princeton, NJ: Princeton University Press, 1992.
Eakin, Emily. "All Roads Lead to D.C." *New York Times*. 31 Mar 2002. Web.
Frayling, Christopher. *Spaghetti Westerns: Cowboys and Europeans from Karl May to Sergio Leone*. London: Routledge & Kegan Paul, 1981.
Haase, Christine. *When Heimat Meets Hollywood: German Filmmakers and America*. Rochester: Camden House, 2007.
Hake, Sabine. *German National Cinema*. London: Routledge, 2008.
Hark, Ina Rae. "Animals or Romans? Looking at Masculinity in *Spartacus*." *Screening the Male: Exploring Masculinities in Hollywood Cinema*. Eds. Steven Cohan and Ina Rae Hark. London: Routledge, 1993. 151–172.
Kosta, Barbara. "*Väterliteratur*, Masculinity, and History: The Melancholic Texts of the 1980s." In *Conceptions of Postwar German Masculinity*. Ed. Roy Gerome. Albany: SUNY Press, 2001. 219–242.
Krämer, Peter. "The Spectre of History in the Age of Globalisation: Notes on German Hit Movies and Hit Makers at Home and in the US." *Shifting Landscapes: Film and*

Media in European Context. Eds. Miyase Christensen and Nezih Erdogan. Newcastle: Cambridge Scholars, 2008. 69–85.

Lagny, Michèle. "Popular Taste: The Peplum." Trans. Peter Graham *Popular European Cinema*. Eds. Richard Dyer and Ginette Vincendeau. London: Routledge, 1992. 163–180.

Lattimore, Richmond. *The Iliad of Homer*. Chicago: University of Chicago Press, 1951.

Leprohon, Pierre. *The Italian Cinema*. Trans. Roger Greaves and Oliver Stallybrass. New York: Praeger, 1972.

Mulvey, Laura. "Visual Pleasure and Narrative Cinema." *Movies and Methods, Volume II*. Ed. Bill Nichols. Berkeley: University of California Press, 1985. 303–315.

Nowell-Smith, Geoffrey. "Peplum." *The Companion to Italian Film*. Eds. Nowell-Smith, James Hay, and Gianni Volpi. London: Cassell, 1996. 94–95.

Petersen, Wolfgang. "Einmal voll zuschlagen." Interview with Martin Wolf. *Der Spiegel* (October 5, 2004). 158–159.

_____. "Homer ist, wenn man trotzdem lacht." Interview with Tobias Kniebe. sueddeutsche.de (October 5, 2004).

_____. *Ich liebe die grossen Geschichten*. Ulrich Griewe. Cologne: Kiepenheuer & Witsch, 1997.

Pitt, Brad. "Ich bin ein alter Knacker." Interview with Roland Huschke. *tip* (May 6–19, 2004): 50–52.

Prager, Brad. "Beleaguered Under the Sea: Wolfgang Petersen's *Das Boot* (1981) as a German Hollywood Film." *Light Motives: German Film in Perspective*. Eds. Randall Halle and Margaret McCarthy. Detroit: Wayne State University, 2003.

Schenk, Irmbert. "Von Cabiria zu Mussolini: Zur Geburt des monumentalen Historienfilms in Italien." *Die Spur durch den Spiegel*. Eds. Malte Hagener, Johann N. Schmidt, and Michael Wedel. Berlin: Bertz und Fischer, 2004. 179–192.

Studlar, Gaylyn. "Masochism and the Perverse Pleasures of the Cinema." *Movies and Methods, Volume II*. Ed. Bill Nichols. Berkeley: University of California Press, 1985. 602–621.

Tyrangiel, Josh. "Troy Story." *Time* 163:19 (October 5, 2004): 66–72.

An Enduring Logic
Homer, Helen of Troy, *and Narrative Mobility*

LARRY T. SHILLOCK

> *Interpretation is not an isolated act, but takes place within a Homeric battlefield, on which a host of interpretive options are either openly or implicitly in conflict.*
> — *Fredric Jameson*

It is a curious fact that narrative has long been the province of men. In the *Iliad* and *Odyssey*—the precursors of today's sword and sandal films—it is men who go on journeys and, as strangers, wash up on familiar shores. It is the men of classical literature who travel to war, sail for commerce or piracy, encounter unknown peoples, pilgrimage to sacred sites, and narrate their adventures. And thus it is men whose mobility, as paradigmatically represented in myth, initiates and complicates plot. As the narratologist Jurij M. Lotman observes, "Characters can be divided into those who are mobile, who enjoy freedom with regard to plot-space, who can change their place in the structure of the artistic world and cross the frontier ... and those who are immobile, who represent, in fact, a function of this space" (167). Mobility is at base gendered, since characters and readers are "constrained and defined within two positions of a sexual difference thus conceived: male-hero-human, on the side of the subject; and female-obstacle-boundary-space, on the other" (de Lauretis 121). Famously, Helen of Sparta contests such foundational constraints when, as wife to Menelaus, she leaves her married homeland and travels to Troy with Paris. In the process, she enacts a spatial imagination at odds with those who control women's bodies and thereby provokes, to borrow a phrase from Fredric Jameson, "strategies of containment" relating to honor and gender (53–54). Her mobility—personal and erotic—does more, of course, than set in motion the Trojan War, since Helen's actions provide the occasion for the *Iliad* and *Odyssey* as well as for the many plots which treat Homer as a narrative exemplar. It follows that Helen's uncharacteristic migration speaks to the potential of different plots that lie latent in Homer's epics and therefore in narrative more generally. At issue here is not the primary role of myth in plotting, a role that classicists and narratologists alike emphasize, so much as how Helen's example returns through the master trope of mobility to provoke recent sword and sandal films on Troy and thereby contest the character types and plot functions available to women in them.

Evoking a Tradition

It has become a scholarly commonplace to note that the *Iliad* and *Odyssey* begin the literary canon and yet are near endpoints of an existing oral genre. Homer's works, Seth L. Schein explains, are "product[s] of a Greek poetic tradition that may have been as much as a thousand years old by the time the epics were composed, [emerging] probably in the final quarter of the eighth century B.C., and that had roots in a still older Indo-European poetic tradition" (3). Scholars first inferred the presence of this pre–Homeric tradition by noting the recurrent elements — the words, epithets, phrases, types of description, rituals, subjects, themes, mythological references, and so on — that serve as formulae which singers and, later, rhapsodes perform (see, e.g., Parry; Lord). Following Mikhail Bakhtin, we might say that Indo-European life in common was made possible by the utterances of its everyday speech genres. These, in turn, got absorbed into the secondary speech genre of oral poetry that the Greeks formalized through performance and discipleship. In this model, individual utterances, speech genres (be they simple or complex), and the literary and extra-literary strata of national languages weave and are rewoven through song (Bakhtin 65–66). The resulting catalog is available to speakers, whether sanctioned or not, which ensures that speech can be put to emergent purposes and plots.

The *Iliad*'s back story begins when Paris, the prince of Troy and son of Priam, travels to Sparta where, in a grave breach of hospitality, he seduces Helen, the wife of Menelaus. Together, Paris and *orea Eleni* depart for Troy to live as husband and wife. Menelaus and his elder brother, King Agamemnon, raise an army in response and sail, with perhaps one thousand ships, to Troy, where they intend to claim Helen, if not also the walled city's wealth. Rebuffed, they begin a war. The *Odyssey*'s back story commences a decade later as the victorious Greek federation leaves Troy ablaze and seeks its home-coming, now enriched by plunder, its men now aroused and distracted by slave-wives.

Homer's interdependent works represent the two faces of ancient epic. One face — that of the gods — is distant and proximate. From their sanctuary on Olympus, the gods observe humans. So too do they shape-shift and move among the mortals. In both cases, the gods use men as pawns in their quarrels and for entertainment. Tactically, the gods disrupt the Trojan War, adding to its body count. They complicate as well the *nostoi*-story of Odysseus and his men, testing their endurance with hardship and loss. Throughout, the gods play favorites, betraying and disturbing at will. Odysseus, for his part, is fated by them to spend almost as long getting home as he spent warring at Troy. Goddesses contend for his affections, becoming obstacles to his mobility before either releasing or being overcome by him. Calypso, for instance, plots to have him for her husband and only reluctantly allows him to leave her island; Circe enthralls his men only to become enthralled in turn. Athena, so deadly in the *Iliad*, travels repeatedly to aid Odysseus so that his journey home—its own masterplot—can occur and the suitors get killed. Understandably, the ancient Greeks respond to the gods' interventions with fear that takes the form of worship. Their rituals propitiate the gods and goddesses, earning their care and perhaps even forestalling fate.

The second face of ancient epic belongs to warriors, those men who endure a trial (*peira*) in battle and strive, alongside their compatriots, for imperishable glory (*kleos aphthiton*). Living and fighting heroically bring honor, provided that both occur under maximum duress and are met courageously. The greatest renown occurs when a warrior is affirmed by enemies and friends alike and granted immortality by a singer, typically as part of dying on the battlefield. Odysseus is semi-divine, a hero, and therefore atypical. Ever resourceful, he contributes the idea of the Trojan horse, leaves the enclosure-gift to sack the city, and survives the fighting, unlike others that Homer dotes on. Later, in the *Odyssey*, he is surprised to hear the story of Troy sung by Demodocus, the famous singer, a meta-commentary which suggests how quickly history is refashioned as myth. Marking the penultimate point in his travels, the song causes him to relive his suffering. King Alcinous observes Odysseus' anguish and asks why he mourns when "hear[ing] of the fate of the Greeks and Trojans. / This was the gods' doing. They spun that fate / So that in later times it would turn into song" (8.624–26). Here Homer's *Odyssey* is unequivocal: oral song, a kind of weaving, results from and compensates for the suffering induced by the gods.

Like Odysseus, Helen of Argos is one of the few characters to span the *Iliad* and the *Odyssey*. She too is semi-divine, having been born of the violent union of Zeus and Leda, a figure aptly named as Nemesis. Helen is the daughter of King Tyndareus and sister to Castor, Pollux, and Clytemnestra. As a young woman, she marries Menelaus and gives birth to Hermione. Thus she deserts her husband, daughter, and married homeland by leaving Sparta with Paris for Troy. Conflicting accounts explain her motivation but concur that Helen chooses a younger not an older man, mobility over stasis, travel rather than domesticity. Importantly, Helen journeys across the Mediterranean, a domain traversed by classical gods and men, not women, a time-space where ill winds bring tragedy. As Tim Cresswell observes, mobility "operate[s] within fields of power and meaning" (10). Helen's leaving is thus a double affront — to her husband and to her social station. "For nearly three thousand years," Bettany Hughes observes, "she has been upheld as an exquisite agent of extermination" (2).

Despite being a catalyst of the war, Helen is offstage as the *Iliad* begins. Nine years have passed, and she is now much-spurned. Homer's invocation begins *in medias res* and, by so doing, signals her importance even as it effaces her history. Like the modern scholars who follow Homer, it focuses on the actions of men, asserting that "Achilles' rage" has "cost the Greeks / Incalculable pain, pitched countless souls / Of heroes into Hades' dark" (1.1–4). Homer's proleptic invocation is more complex than it appears, since it confers responsibility on Achilles and Zeus, shifts temporal registers, and confuses consequence and cause (Genette 36–37). After the fact, readers learn that Chryses, Apollo's priest, has come to Troy to beg Agamemnon to accept ransom for his kidnapped daughter. Despite the bounteous offer, Agamemnon rebukes Chryses, who prays to Apollo for revenge. A nine-day plague of arrows then routs the Greeks.

Homer is interested in more than godlike rage or heroes' fates, for the epic's first book turns on the tension between story and narrative, mobility and immobility. Because Helen's flight dishonors Menelaus, it must be righted with a compensating, and more powerful, display of force. Yet that response fails. Now, much later, the Greeks cower, under attack: "death-fires crowd the beach" (1.60). True to form(ula), Achilles calls an assembly to determine what is to be done. There, following Calchas' prophetic reading, he and Agamemnon taunt each other unforgivably. A flurry of movement then begins around them. Chryses returns to Chryse. Athena, roused to action by Achilles' desire to murder Agamemnon, arrives from Olympus. Satisfied that Achilles will not kill his fellow king, she returns to the hall of the gods. Agamemnon sends heralds to take "fair-cheeked Briseis" from Achilles, who was his war prize in the fight for Thebes (1.336). Briseis leaves for Agamemnon's tent to warm a rival's bed. Twice dishonored, Achilles prays to Thetis, the daughter of the Old Man of the Sea. She arrives and promises to speak to Zeus. Simultaneously, Odysseus sails with Chryses' daughter and one hundred oxen that will be sacrificed to appease Apollo. Thetis arrives on Olympus and persuades Zeus to risk Hera's wrath and "Give the Trojans the upper hand until the Greeks / Grant my son the honor he deserves" (1.540–41). Thus do rage and loss bequeath betrayal.

With fine economy, Homer's exposition represents the characters and conflicts around which the narrative turns, confident that listeners know their bases in myth. To develop, his narrative must then define its plot-spaces: the Greek beachhead, the plain where much of the fighting occurs, and Troy. At stake are two questions. Will the Trojans drive the Greeks into the sea or home? Will the walls of Troy hold? The central issues are thus movement and, as an index of plot, succession. Unpredictably, Homer chooses delay, working against the propulsive force of the invocation. In effect, rage must wait rather than be expressed in violence. Even as Agamemnon's forces anticipate Odysseus' return, Achilles "the great runner [stands] idle by his fleet's fast hulls" (1.517). How the Greeks will breach the frontier plot-space of Troy without he and his fifty ships of men is unclear. Responding to the structural conflict between motion and stasis, the epic shifts to representing battles that gain little ground.

In terms of plot, the Achaean Greeks camp on the beaches and fight on the plain of Troy because Helen left Sparta. She might have loved Paris, been seduced by him, or even responded to a god's erotic incitement without causing war; but by enacting the determinative plot function of absentation, to borrow from Vladimir Propp's taxonomy, she spurs Menelaus, Agamemnon, and the federation to treat her leaving as an abduction and depart in response. Upon arrival, Menelaus asks about Helen (the function of reconnaissance), gains information (delivery), and demands her return (a counter-action). Spurned, he must fight to regain what he lacks or return dishonored, outcomes which are two sides of a dilemma and function as well. What energizes this emergent doubleplot is thus more than a desire to redress lost honor, for the *Iliad* reflexively foregrounds the dynamic of narrative and modulates its progress.

Because mythic sources precede the *Iliad*, Homer can borrow from the oral tradition in ways that focus attention on his warrior-heroes. Yet Homer does more than merely borrow; he compensates for reducing Helen's role in the plot by weaving the stories of battle with references to women experience. His story requires, for instance, the Judgment of Paris, a prior set-piece which contributes to the misjudgment of Helen, Paris, Priam, Agamemnon, Menelaus, and Achilles and sets a causal chain in motion that affects thousands. So too does it require the inspiration made possible by the Muses. The emergent plot turns as well on goddesses who travel to Troy and determine events. More prosaically, Homer foregrounds the conflicts which arise around Chryseis and Briseis, the prisoners whose erotic service rewards Agamemnon and Achilles for heroism. These women are not mere tokens; they, too, impact the action, since mistreating the first leads to widespread death, and appropriating the second generates the rage that so clouds the thinking of Greek leaders. It is therefore difficult to see — amid the comings-and-goings of book one — how "the *Iliad* is the story of Achilleus," as Richmond Lattimore confidently asserts or, more to the point, how its story, like narrative more generally, names men as subjects and women as both non-man and plot-space (17; de Lauretis 167). Hence readers would do well to question whether classical narrative, from its paradigmatic origins in Homer, is actually the province of men.

Ecphrasis and Narration by Other Means

Helen enters book three when Iris, the herald-goddess, comes in disguise to report that Menelaus and Paris will soon fight to the death over her. At the time, she is working the loom silently, "designing into the blood-red fabric / The trials that the Trojans and Greeks had suffered / For her beauty under Ares' murderous hands" (3.128–30). When Iris adds that the war may soon end, Helen dresses and leaves the room crying in quiet anticipation. Unlike King Priam, who cannot bear to watch his son fight Menelaus, Helen goes to the Scaean gate to see the combat. As she arrives, the Trojan elders speak warily of her almost inhuman desirability: "Whatever she is let her go back with the ships / And spare us and our children a generation of pain" (3.167–68). Homer doesn't say if Helen overhears, focusing instead on her confession to Priam:

> Death should have been a sweeter evil to me
> Than following your son here, leaving my home,
> My marriage, my friends, my precious daughter,
> That lovely time in my life. None of it was to be,
> And lamenting has been my slow death [3.182–86].

Decrying her decision to journey with Paris, Helen uses the first-person pronoun seven times in five lines, a fact which does not dispose readers in her favor. Once atop the western wall, Helen answers Priam's questions—aiding the war effort by identifying the Greek heroes by name and quality—and calls herself a "shameless bitch" (3.190). That she ends book three in Paris' bed speaks to how amenable she is to the power of others' desire and plotting. Clearly, she is a narcissist-pariah whom the gods manipulated and may manipulate again.

The Helen who weaves and the Helen who, under Iris' influence, laments are at base similar, for each are narrators of a sort. The first Helen works the loom silently. Her account there is set against a "blood-red" background or history; together, the images represent Trojan and Greek trials and their attendant suffering. As she weaves, she signals key moments in a multi-temporal, yet unspoken, plot. Weaving in the epic has a reflexive dimension as well since it parallels Homer's signifying practices. In other words, his text narrates Helen's ecphrasis, which is a trope whose root terms mean "out" and "speak" and therefore signals mobility and orality. Her outspoken narration thus has the selective force of a singer transposed to women's material culture. By extension, Helen works in two Homeric temporalities by weaving signs of heroic suffering, which she in part compelled, and by telling Priam her abject state of mind. Despite her separation from and considerable repression by others, then, Helen tells her stories. It follows that readers see weaving as recompense for her failings and language as a field of action. Plot is not just for men or heroes or even singers; as "the organizing dynamic of a specific mode of human understanding," to borrow from Peter Brooks, its utterances and forms—however repressed—can return to serve women as well (7).

It would of course be a mistake to exaggerate Helen's influence on the *Iliad*. She spends the epic in Troy, occupying a feminine plot-space, and waits more than she acts. Achilles, for his part, offers a variation on her example, since, by withdrawing from battle, he and his men initially reside in a less-masculine plot-space too. Together, Helen and Achilles are thus obstacles to peace as well as to narrative resolution for much of the plot. Homer fills the gap created by their absence with other warriors and battles but also with women. As the epic nears its conclusion, the *Iliad* again foregrounds a profound conflict — the negotiations, between Priam and Achilles, over Hector's corpse — that it counterpoints to women's actions. The concluding book shows, for instance, that Hera and Athena remain steadfast in their hatred, refusing to forgive Paris for spurning them and "honor[ing] the one who fed his fatal lust" (24.35). Thetis laments in advance the death of Achilles. Iris interrupts Priam's mourning and compels him to go to Achilles and retrieve his son's body. Hecuba sees that her husband prays properly before traveling to the enemy's camp. Andromache cries for Hector, certain that Troy will fall and "All the solemn wives / And children you guarded will go off soon / In the hollow ships, and I will go with them" (24.782–84). Thus are plot resolutions — death for heroes, sexual slavery for women — announced and shown to be gendered. In the process, Homer's heroic song shifts from the warriors to the embattled civilians, from outside on the plain of Troy to inside its walls. The latter plot-space is populated by older men, women, and children, and yet Homer insists upon its parallel resonance. Even Helen's second, self-absorbed oration has a kind of grace as she recounts Hector's kindness. Rage, unleashed, again vies with pathos for our attention. Thus do the gods spin the fates of humans, like so much carded wool, as Homer weaves mythic elements into a final, shared tableau.

By ending the *Iliad* before the *Odyssey* begins, Homer emphasizes the epics' interdependence, since it falls to his second song to explain details unrepresented by the first. Bridging the two is a reflexive emphasis on spinning. In a remarkable metapoetic turn, Helen's work at the loom anticipates Penelope's focus as silent but significant weaver. For her part, Helen weaves as the *Iliad* more or less begins; Penelope weaves as the *Odyssey* more or less ends. Helen, a foreigner, fears that the Greek soldiers will storm Troy. Penelope, by contrast, is at home, surrounded by familiar objects and servants, but also repressed by circumstances. Having broached the walls of her palace, the suitors seek her hand — indeed, her kingdom — in marriage, should Odysseus not return in time. Like Helen, then, Penelope is at odds with those who share her plot-space; unlike her, she is devoted to memory, not forgetting, and her epic to "alternate story patterns," itself an ecphrastic metaphor (Slatkin 228). She responds as Helen does, with seclusion, work, and sadness, and weaves a different object, a burial shroud, which will honor her father-in-law upon his death. Famously, Penelope weaves by day, keeping the suitors at arm's length, and unweaves by night. Her ecphrasis stalls—and thereby protects—her own marriage plot from revision by men.

Penelope treats the burial shroud as a social responsibility, a necessary response to Laertes' abject condition and widower status. A form of women's work, it is also a means by which women make and sustain culture. Thus it is a mimetic object at once functional, with respect to ritual, and immanent to the text—a sign, that is, of the braided tissue of signification and reading (see, e.g., Barthes 159; Snyder 193–95; Filson-Rubin 151–52). Moreover, as Penelope labors, undoes her weaving, and elaborates what had been woven, she produces an object that differs from Helen's but shares the same aesthetic practice. The imaginative substitution of Penelope for Helen, of burial shroud for storycloth, of ecphrasis for ecphrasis, reinforces our sense that women narrate in ways that may elude men's notice. The two faces of epic representation—that of the gods and heroes—should therefore expand to include a third: women and their signifying practices, since both comment upon and extend Homer's Ur-narratives in space and time.

Mobility and Genre Hybridity

In the last sixty years, two films have helped to expand Helen's authority beyond that accorded her by the *Iliad*. The first was directed by Robert Wise and shot in Italy. Dubbed into English, *Helen of Troy* (1956) is a CinemaScope peplum, complete with departures from Greek myth and not-quite-supernaturally attractive stars. Its women wear bullet bras under peplos; its men have glistening skin. Wise introduces Helen by placing her outside of domesticity. She is on a beach and has found Paris, who apparently escaped drowning at sea by tying himself to the mast of a ship, an invention with a clear debt to Odysseus' fight with Poseidon. From the first, Wise's Helen is unapologetically mobile, which may well be the film's signature innovation. She is free to rescue Paris from his immobility and, soon thereafter, to nurse him to health. Helen has a kind of subjective mobility as well, since she represents herself to Paris as a slave, not as someone who is married to a king, before their contentious love takes form.

Of greater interest for my purposes is *Helen of Troy* (2003), a USA Network miniseries, which has its own revisionist intentions. It begins with a voice-over from Menelaus, whose role inverts the Muses' gender and implies other inversions will follow. From the first, his remarks interpolate viewers by addressing them directly: "You may have heard the story of Helen, a woman whose beauty launched a thousand ships and started the most famous war in history." Once Helen departs, "ten thousand men, the best that the gods and dreams of glory could have fashioned ... [were] led by my brother, Agamemnon, the mightiest of the Greeks, and Achilles, who could strike down ten warriors with one blow." As Helen's witness-victim, he will tell "the real story" (*Helen*).

The film opens with a weave of images that move forward and back in time. In the first image, Helen disrobes and walks among drunken royals before standing — in a sequence worthy of a 1980s seminar on feminist film theory — on a platform, alone. The kings and princes have formed a political federation to ensure that Helen's husband is protected from the betrayals her beauty may inspire. They insist upon seeing Helen naked before she marries Menelaus to see if their decidedly homosocial alliance is needed. The opening sequence then shifts to the mini-series' second episode. Helen has fled to Troy, and now the federation's ships amass to revenge her infidelity — a tragedy in the making, as indicated by the ships moving across the screen from right to left. The assault on Troy's beachhead ensues before the film cuts to Helen inside the city. A quick image of Troy's citizens fleeing the federation's soldiers from the angle of fate follows before we see Helen while an off-stage Priam reflects on whether to protect her and therefore fight the Greeks. Clytemnestra, wife of Agamemnon and Helen's sister, then has two scenes. One represents a marriage proposal; the other alludes to domestic happiness with her daughter, Iphigenia, and beloved sister.

A pattern emerges from these initial images. Director John Kent Harrison and writer Ronni Kern use the voice-over to announce crucial plot points, moving from domesticity to battle and back. Like Homer, they rely on our knowledge of mythology to limit their exposition. In the process, Harrison ties words in the voice-over to the image of those characters and events. Thus, we hear and see Helen, the ships, war, the valiant struggle, the golden walls of Troy, Agamemnon, Achilles, Paris, love, and so on. The approach is like the often-scorned technique of mickeymousing song and dance movements through editing; and yet, it produces a clever weave of word and image, summary and incident, oral and visual signifier. Together, the compound signs also announce individual plot functions, including, in rapid order, reconnaissance, delivery, departure, counter-action, and wedding. Tension is thus created before the storyline proper begins. Viewers soon infer that legend and the *Iliad* are to serve Helen and her story at least as much as history and the godlike rage of heroes.

An insightful reworking of myth opens the film proper. Hecuba is in labor, and a very young Cassandra runs through the palace, in a deft tracking shot, shouting, "Kill him, kill him." Her childish command is prescient, since Alexandros has not been born and thus no one knows his gender. Frightened by the vision, Cassandra declares to King Priam that "If he lives, Troy will burn" (*Helen*). As its back story begins, then, *Helen of Troy* changes legend twice, since Cassandra is too young to have been made a seer by the gods and her vision appropriates a dream in which Hecuba gives birth to a firebrand that spreads flames over the city. The double revisions speak to the role of children in the mini-series. More directly, they elevate Cassandra and, by extension, such younger women as Helen and Clytemnestra over their mothers, a peplum convention. Persuaded, Priam orders his newborn, swaddled in a purple weaving, to be thrown from the highest point on Mount Ida. But Alexandros is left to die, not killed. A shepherd finds and raises him, thereby starting the parallel editing—of Paris and Helen's back story—that follows.

The audience is shown the young shepherd, now in a flash-forward, years later. Tracking an errant goat, he enters a cave and meets Hera, Athena, and Aphrodite. It is the Judgment of Paris repurposed. Each woman offers a bribe for his vote in the impromptu, and ill-advised, contest. Speaking last, Aphrodite holds out a golden apple and promises the world's most beautiful woman to him if he selects her. The apple makes a portal through which he sees Helen and she, from a distance, sees him. Wordlessly, Paris chooses love over glory in battle. Helen, in equal wonder, touches his cinematic image in the puddle below her.

Both images dissolve into a shot of Helen on horseback, which introduces the motif that enables the Trojan defeat. A joyful and accomplished rider, she has left the city's walls and its domestic constraints. Her relationship with the horse is both sensitive and mutual. Indeed, it calls diegetically to her three times as she walks to a bluff-edge alone and looks at a train of men coming to see her family. The camera, conventionally enough, captures King Atreus and princes Agamemnon and Menelaus in an over-the-shoulder, high-angle establishing shot. But, as Helen watches, it changes to her point of view. By allying Helen with the cinematic apparatus, Harrison increases her authority and signals her agency. From the first, then, she is less an object of representation and more its subject. It follows that we see what Helen selects for us to see, and even her reactions, shown in shot/reverse shot, are thoughtful. Pollux, the heir to the throne, arrives to admonish her, saying, "You know you can't go outside of the city walls. Father is furious." Apparently, Helen disobeys as she sees fit— and often. "Come on," Pollux orders. "Let's get you back and dressed.... You can't go to a wedding looking like that" (*Helen*).

At this point, Helen is not *orea Eleni* but an older girl. Tall, gangly, lacking screen make-up, she is energetically curious, not conventionally feminine. Information about royals coming from Mycenae interests her more than her sister's marriage proposal and wedding. Classicists expecting Helen to be stately and ethereal encounter, instead, a spirited and rambunctious adolescent (see, e.g., Roisman 144). Pollux, for his part, would school her in femininity so that she is proper, a goal that shades off into propriety and property. Despite his injunctions, Helen arrives late to the formal greeting with King Atreus, leaving Tyndareus—who has no presence in the *Iliad*—to introduce only his "most beautiful and obedient" daughter. As Agamemnon tells Clytemnestra that he will take her for his wife, Helen interrupts the proposal and captivates the princes. Tyndareus would have her go to her room and be properly (re)dressed, but the princes intervene. Unhappily, he introduces her as "my youngest, still a child—an untamed and disrespectful child" (*Helen*). The contrast between Helen and Homer's narcissist, Helen and Clytemnestra, is pointed.

In *Helen of Troy* we meet a free spirit who borrows actions from the domain of the masculine and repurposes them; thus her mobility, not immobility, is often at issue. Harrison's camera obediently follows as Helen walks, rides, looks, strides the palace's halls, and sails the Aegean. It will fall to Pollux to tell her what she does not know: "Your beauty, your spirit, it makes men weak" (*Helen*). Spiritedly, it will fall to Helen to tell him what only Paris may sense: she has had a vision and is uninterested in princes who visit and proposals and marriages because, defying tradition, she has made her marriage-choice.

That future is delayed when Theseus, the king of Athens, enters the palace and kidnaps her. Kidnapping is narrative sleight-of-hand, at once a complication and form of misdirection. Common in classical warfare, as the examples of Chryseis and Briseis suggest, it removes Helen from her parent's care—putting her into the masculine world—even as it infantilizes her. A foreigner, Helen thus washes up onto new shores, where she comes to love her captor, even offering herself to him before he is ready to love her. The rapid succession of departure and arrival emphasizes Helen's unfeminine mobility; enacting her desire for Theseus extends mobility, as an organizing trope, to eros. In the process, the miniseries spans past and present, weaving Helen's story into a modern genre, the sword and sandal film, as Theseus kills four Trojans during the kidnapping and, in turn, is mortally wounded when Pollux arrives to rescue Helen. She does not seek rescue—itself a re-gendering—and is horrified as Theseus kills Pollux and thus denies her a brother and Tyndareus an heir.

The problem here may be with a different kind of descent. Derived, in part, from Homer's epics by way of Italian cinema, sword and sandal films elevate warriors, with their metonymic swords, over the citizens in sandals who get positioned as audience. Such spectacles focus on war, hand-to-hand combat, the debasement and revenge of former slaves, the toppling of murderous regimes—not a trans-tribal love story or a girl's coming-of-age. Content with Helen as narrative catalyst, Homer mentions her "seventeen times in the *Iliad*—[but] on eight occasions her name is coupled with the word *ktema*, 'treasure' or 'possession'" (Hughs 80). He compensates for such a strategy of containment, first, by representing goddesses and women other than Helen in action, and second, by granting women an even more expansive role in the *Odyssey*. *Helen of Troy*, for its part, reasserts Helen's narrative primacy and thereby inverts aspects of the very genre it occupies.

To be sure, there is any number of historical reasons why such an inversion should give viewers' pause. Few of these, however, pertain to the workings of plot. As Bakhtin shows, speech genres are anonymous forms that may be dialogically altered by anyone who knows the proscribed utterances and can reimagine them. Propp, for his part, insists that the elements, functions, and characters in wondertales and myth are open to substitution and inversion. A stepdaughter, for instance, may be persecuted by a father, mother, visitor, witch, or other magical figure. Her persecution is a constant; the plot's structure stays the same despite differing villains. By extension, a young man or, through inversion, a young woman might go in search of a lover, friend, magical potion, or lost relative. Here the functions of departure and absentation endure and are more or less gendered as the sought-for person or sought-for object changes. Like characters in general, women characters resist their object-status and can do so because plot, too, is structurally — if not practically — anonymous. Plots vary, therefore, as a result of how the available, because mythological, functions are used. Narrative is thus more at odds with sociality than studies of ideology often attest.

A Marriage Deferred

With Pollux dead, *Helen of Troy* expands the role of its heroine, inside and outside of domestic life. As Menelaus, in voice-over, explains, "The great kings of the Aegean were drawn to Sparta like moths to the flame" (*Helen*). He, Odysseus, Achilles, Agamemnon, and others arrive to assess the elderly king's daughter and kingdom. The eligible among them vie for Helen. Tyndareus recognizes their ambitions and stands her before them, even as his son's funeral bier burns. The scene shows Helen, in a gauzy fabric that reveals her breasts, to the gazing men. "By your actions," he rages at her in a tightly framed two-shot, "you have left me without love or hope and Sparta without its future king" (*Helen*). Here, "actions" is a telling metaphor for gender insubordination as well as a synecdoche for plot — since Aristotle's *Poetics* the structural spine of story. The camera then cuts to an over-the-shoulder shot of men's shields and the bier, occupying the mid-ground, and Helen and Tyndareus, in the background. Spatially, war and parental obligations clash. "It should have been you who died," Tyndareus exclaims, pulling her roughly. Walking towards the kings and princes, he rages, "Is there any among you who will take this cursed woman? Is there any among you who wishes their home devastated, his country brought to ruin, his heart broken beyond repair? I leave her to you" (*Helen*). His interdiction is a curse; the men then violate it by casting lots for her. The twin functions of interdiction and its violation signal that they do so at considerable risk.

As princess, Helen is the sought-for person in Propp's taxonomy and is therefore positioned in/as feminine plot-space. Menelaus shows as much by watching her intently, spurning the ritual occasion. Agamemnon, too, is visibly captivated; Achilles, who says he "fears nothing," is silent before her and thus showcases a double denial. As Helen stands within touching distance of Pollux's body, Harrison contrasts her grief with the men's erotic distraction. Breathing in smoke, charcoal, and burning flesh, she mourns, silenced and abandoned. Observant because he has married well, Odysseus cautions that "Tyndareus is right" about the danger she poses, adding, "The path to her bed is strewn with ash and death" (*Helen*). The other men grasp only that they could easily fight over her and vow to join forces, rather than compete for a woman, however beautiful. *Helen of Troy* thus elevates its central character to womanhood by killing the two men, and therefore the two sympathetic authority figures, who know her best. Shortly thereafter, Tyndareus and Atreus die, empowering Menelaus, who wins Helen and Sparta, and Agamemnon, who becomes king of Mycenae.

The brothers are brutes, ambitious and unfeeling. Menelaus is the false hero in Propp's list of characters; his brother, the patient villain. They compel Helen to debase herself, naked, before the kings and princes. Shown during the voice-over that begins the film, the full scene foreshadows what she can expect of marriage. In an unexpected reversal, Helen sees Paris, for the first time in person, as she is displayed. He recognizes rather than objectifies her, in defiance of the political economy of the gaze (see, e.g., Mulvey; Doan). Now the film makes two crucial turns in its (proto)feminist reimagining of the *Iliad*'s back story. It sets them up by showing Helen trying to kill herself, as her mother purportedly did, only to be saved by Paris. He is as endangered as she, since Menelaus and Agamemnon plan to kill him once they learn enough about Troy to make diplomacy unnecessary. The first turn then occurs as Helen saves Paris from assassination, which shows her ability to wield weapons and foil plots even in a culture that powerfully constrains a woman's mobility. The larger point here is that her reversal is undertaken for love, and against authority, as a way to change the structure of the artistic world she will inhabit.

Earlier, we met a young Helen who resists being someone's war prize. To Theseus, she explains, hyperbolically, "You must have me confused with my sister. I'm not the daughter of Tyndareus who does what anyone says" (*Helen*). Now we meet a woman whose actions extend from defying fathers to resisting kings whose power extends over life and death. Her decisiveness is modulated by foresight and thought — in a phrase, by the capacity to plot; her disobedience is put in the service of a will that undercuts sociality. The gods do not compel this Helen to love and rescue Paris. She decides to do so, her mind unclouded by romance or lust and cognizant of love's potential consequences. Together, the two flee on horseback so that Paris and his men may sail for Troy. At the dock, Helen stays behind, justifying her choice until, in a second instance of reciprocal yearning, she turns, runs along the harbor's edge, and leaps— the camera tracking her all the while — into the water. Characteristically, she chooses mobility, spatial and erotic, rather than the social immobility that the Greeks and marriage require. On the masculine domain of a ship, she transgresses the gendered divides of myth and narrative together.

The energy of the plot cannot continue to be hers, since *Helen of Troy*, in its second and final segment, shades off into a sword and sandal hybrid that seeks to expand its audience. We see as much as Agamemnon prepares his men for invasion, a time-honored set piece. Aggrieved, Menelaus now asks for his brother's help in avenging Helen's flight. He receives it with a caveat: Agamemnon will have the war prizes, once Troy falls, and Menelaus receive no tribute. Only then is the Greek federation recalled. Achilles soon comes to the forefront of the plot, although without his Homeric hatred of Agamemnon. He is eager to fight, not sulk over a woman from a feminized plot-space, and thus he epitomizes the warrior caste's pursuit of imperishable glory. His armor is cross-hatched, not encompassing, the better to show off his body; and his head is shaven, extending what Maggie Günsberg calls the "body-as-spectacle" focalizing of peplum (104). *Helen of Troy* emphasizes his masculine forcefulness by eliding his shield, one of the most powerful instances of ecphrasis in history (18.461–652) and, following Rene Girard, a mimetic object (146). It comes to Achilles from Hephaestus at the behest — unsurprisingly — of Thetis. Like Helen and her weaving, the shield honors the determinate tensions joining war and homeland, glory and domesticity, and thus is too feminine for a film hero. In keeping with the peplum's model of masculinity, Achilles is also less fleet of foot than muscle-bound. Readying for war, other men like him spar with Agamemnon, their burnished muscles set off by thick loincloths.

Agamemnon must transport the armies he has mustered to Troy in the face of calm seas. Called to account for them, Calchas explains that Artemis will provide a following wind in exchange for his daughter's life. Agamemnon's lone humanizing tendency, to this point, has been his fatherly devotion, but he appeases the goddess and has Iphigenia — who resembles Helen and is a sign of innate domesticity — brought through a horrible gauntlet of armored warriors. Acting as a father and king, he kills his daughter and thereby what remains of his femininity as well. In response, the film reverts to its structure of parallel editing; only now, it sets the love of Paris and Helen, near Troy, against the preparations for war in Mycenae. Domesticity recedes even further in importance as it conflicts with imperial ambitions. Peace still abides, but as the federation's ships appear on the horizon, the plot turns in Homer's direction. Helen, so central to the mini-series, moves towards its margins but not, as her *Iliad* counterpart did, in silence and shame.

At stake is the gender-divide signaled by the space of Troy itself. Prompted by Calchas' insight, the Greek federation travels far to penetrate its walls. The warriors who will do so embody a primal masculinity, unhampered by women or children. The minimal domesticity they allow in their camps serves only the purposes of war. Troy, by contrast, is a center of trade and wealth. Its well-dressed citizens speak of beauty, compassion, kindness, and mercy which, by comparison to what audiences see at the Greek beachhead, are feminine virtues. Paris pointedly contrasts the Greek treatment of women with that of the Trojans to rouse the assembly. A woman, Cassandra, is Troy's seer and so speaks of returning Helen to her husband, not pursuing war. Indeed, the plot of the final installment leaps forward to year ten of the conflict, aided by her very public vision. The structural equivalent of the mini-series' opening sequence, it is marked by an adroitly cross-hatched set of images. As Cassandra narrates over the flash-forward, her words and the images often align. The sequence becomes a visual analogue of a woven fabric — of masculine femininity — and thereby recalls Helen and Penelope's work at the loom. Addressing the Trojans and film audiences simultaneously, Cassandra predicts that

> for ten years the Greeks will pillage our country and attack our gates. For ten years they will raid the southern shores, enslave our neighbors, fatten themselves on their butchered cattle, and become rich with spoils. And our friends will flee here and flee here [and] flee here until these walls are packed with broken people and our city is filled with sorrow, our streets flooded with tears, until there will not be one of us with food to eat, water to drink, or air to breathe [*Helen*].

Priam interrupts, demanding that Troy speak with "one voice," which is his, but Cassandra will not be silenced (*Helen*). A story of the future-as-fated cannot be Troy's, and so her competing vision is repressed when she, now an obstacle to plot, is jailed, a space which qualifies as the most potent affront to agency short of death. Her freedom is doubly gone because its enabling conditions — narration and mobility — are to be compromised for years.

Helen of Troy cuts to the Greek camp, where Agamemnon decides, paradoxically, that it is time to retreat and attack. If the Greeks, to this point, have fought more with force than tactics, their king now intends to do the reverse. How they might do that goes unsaid as the film crosscuts to Mycenae, where swans are shown from a slightly high angle. They are the sign of Leda and Zeus and therefore of Helen. The camera tilts up and tracks to the left, showing a member of the royal household walking, before emphasizing a woman's right hand and arm. The camera tilts again to reveal Clytemnesta, standing alone; to the unidentified man, she says, "When the outcome of Troy is determined, I wish to know it" (*Helen*). The moving camera, a sign of emphasis, is itself a mark of mobility. Harrison then cuts back to Troy, as if to imply that Clytemnestra's presence is an afterthought.

It is a measure of Harrison and Kern's resolve that Helen's own mobility is not sacrificed to the exigencies of the sword and sandal film. Because the mini-series subsists on the principle of imaginative substitution, it can refine the Homeric tradition so that Helen is an active presence in its traditionally masculine plot. It does so, most easily, by using gaps in Homer's timeline to embellish her character and that of other women. Given how minor a diegetic role Helen plays in the two epics, it is easy to insert a new love scene, for instance, after a day's battle or as part of her back story. Crucially, the mini-series also changes the characters who once acted in myth or Homer's epic while retaining their actions and plot functions. For example, when Menelaus and Paris fight over Helen in the *Iliad*, their battle occurs early in the epic, if late in the war. The idea for doing so is Paris.' In the mini-series, by contrast, the idea is Agamemnon's. From a plot perspective, the person who proposes the function of a difficult task and thereby compels the hero and villain to struggle — another such function — is of little importance. What matters is that a fight occurs and is represented. The outcome of their battle in the *Iliad* looks to be tragic for Paris, as Menelaus drags him back to the Greek lines by his helmet. However, Aphrodite snaps the strap holding the headgear, covers Paris "in mist, and loft[s] him into / The incensed air of his vaulted bedroom," where he will entice Helen into having sex (3.408–09). The broken strap returns, as does the covering mist, in *Helen of Troy*, but Agamemnon's poisoning of Paris — a plot invention — now dominates the sequence. The function of trickery, rather than Paris' receipt of a magical agent, is its focus. Paris escapes the combat because he and Menelaus recognize that his branding — another such function — is significant only because the blade that cut him was poisoned dishonorably. Hector, not Aphrodite, pulls Paris to safety. Thus is Agamemnon exposed as the character-villain, not the peplum hero.

The two episodes also end differently. In the *Iliad*, Helen upbraids Paris, wishing for his death at the hands of "a real hero"; her allegiance is clearly to Menelaus. The filmic Helen supports her beloved, cheering his unanticipated survival (3.457). Matters then worsen for Troy when Hector steps in, with Paris incapacitated, and challenges Agamemnon, in effect substituting himself for his brother. Achilles, seeking glory, then takes up the challenge for Agamemnon, becoming a substitution for a substitution. Helen taunts Achilles from Troy's western wall, telling Hector, "He hungers only for glory; if you do not feed him, he will starve"— strong words coming from the catalyst of a ten-year war (*Helen*). Priam and Hecuba also tell Hector not to fight, but he dies at spear point before the assembled armies. In the *Iliad*, by contrast, Hector and Achilles meet in book twenty-two, and only after Hector runs from his foe three times around the city. Athena comes from Olympus and interrupts his flight, assuming the form of Deiphobus, Hector's favorite brother. S/he persuades Hector to stand his ground, promising to fight with him. Again, Priam and Hecuba plead with Hector to come into the city and avoid Achilles, but he refuses. Suddenly realizing that he is alone, Hector proposes to Achilles that they agree to return the loser's body for a ritual burial rather than treat it as spoils. Achilles rejects the offer, too angry at Hector for killing Patroclus, who was wearing his armor at the time. Dressed as Achilles, Hector suffers a fatal wound to his throat that enables him to narrate pathetically. Beyond the death of Hector, then, Homer directs our attention to the multiple substitutions— Breseis for Chryseis, Patroclus for Achilles, Athena for Deiphobus— informing his story. *Helen of Troy* borrows Homer's logic so that, at the level of plot, it may expand the role of Helen in particular and women more generally. Such women borrow actions from the domain of masculinity and make them their own. These are risky but exhilarating moves in an epic-peplum hybrid.

The most important plot substitution, from Helen's perspective, occurs after Hector dies but before the Trojan horse arrives in *Helen of Troy*. Helen grieves for him by mobilizing decisively. First, she goes to Cassandra, who is still in jail. "I will do anything to save him," she says of Paris, "anything. Tell me what to do" (*Helen*). Emboldened by Cassandra's ambiguous response, she leaves under cover of night for the Greek camp — a foolhardy action — to offer herself to Agamemnon and so end the war. In the process, Helen does what the Greeks cannot: breach the walls of Troy, changing both her plot-space and plot-function. Once outside the walls, she watches as Achilles drags Hector's body with his chariot; he is motivated to do so not out of rage over Briseis and Patroclus, as in the *Iliad*, but as part of a brutal strategy to debase the Trojans and inspire the Greeks. Helen then kneels before Agamemnon and offers him "a trade: the daughter of Zeus for the body of Hector." "You think that's enough?" he asks, unmoved. "You think my daughter's death was for nothing?" (*Helen*). In effect, she offers her sexual and narrative slavery, re-engendering herself as non-man and object in the deal. He responds that her offer and body and uncharacteristic mobility are "nothing." "There is no trade," Agamemnon adds. "Not you, not Troy, not even my own life will balance the scales" after Iphigenia's death (*Helen*).

The *Iliad* offers a parallel scene but with quite different characters. The person who absents himself from Troy and attempts to redress Hector's abduction is Priam. He does so after Iris, mediating for him and his interests on Mount Olympus, arrives to give him the function of a difficult task. He departs for the Greek camp where, initially, his arrival goes unseen and his identity unrecognized. Prostrating himself before Achilles, not Agamemnon, Priam speaks of his advanced age and asks his enemy to recall his own elderly father. The two men, in a recognition scene informed by tragic pathos, then weep together alone. The ransom delivered, Achilles releases Hector's body to Priam, who returns to Troy with it, his lack redressed, his difficult task resolved. The *Iliad* ends on that profound, and temporary, reconciliation.

By transposing the core plot functions of the Priam/Achilles encounter to Helen's meeting with Agamemnon, *Helen of Troy* increases one woman's role in a peplum-hybrid. In the process, however, it risks feminizing a plot-space that is heroic and separate and therefore consummately masculine. The Greek camp is not feminized as such, since Agamemnon refuses Helen's offer, becomes distracted, and thereby enables her escape. Tellingly, their encounter *qua* substitution gives the audience a view of how the logic that undergirds plot works and can enable new substitutions. One soon occurs as Clytemnestra, having learned of the fall of Troy, travels there, like Helen before her. Asserting her own mobility at sea — the domain of sailors, not of a woman alone — she arrives as the war prizes are being sorted. Harrison tracks her progress in Priam's palace by moving from right to left and filming her through cross-hatched window coverings that are analogues to her clothing. Violating the 180-degree rule, he then shows Clytemnestra surprising her husband in his bath with two women who, in their nakedness before authority, recall Homer's Chryseis and Briseis. She pauses to greet a naked Helen and, disturbed, sees her sister's bruises and trauma, both of which occurred during her rape by Agamemnon. Doubly emboldened by the loss of Iphigenia and the signs of Agamemnon's violence, *Helen of Troy*'s obedient second sister assumes the defiance of Helen and casts a woven shawl over her husband. Immobilized by her net-like weaving, a sign of scheming traditionally associated with the word *metis*, he is helpless as she looms over him, pulls a knife from her clothing and, screaming, stabs him repeatedly. Blood disperses through the pool, and Agamemnon floats, facedown, on his stomach. Thus, he is violated both by a woman's violence and usurption of plot.

Clytemnestra has killed the king whom *Helen of Troy* called "the mightiest of the Greeks," a task that no Trojan warrior could accomplish. As re-imagined by Kern and Harrison, her action offers a satisfying — and feminine-induced — climax to a brutal war story. Few parts of narrative are less gendered, of course, than the climax, since it is often where protagonist and antagonist face off, fight in hand-to-hand combat, and one or the other dies. The marriage-function, associated primarily with women and marriage plots, possesses a later temporality, since it typically comprises the denouement. It follows that Kern and Harrison have done something else remarkable by repurposing the oft-told tale of Agamemnon's death in the *Odyssey*. In Homer, it occurs because Clytemnestra, having committed adultery with Aegisthus, sees to her husband's murder. Thus does Agamemnon's *nostoi*-story end with sexual betrayal. Homer uses Clytemnestra's horrid example at strategic points to elevate Penelope and to counterpoint women and warriors. One would think that removing Clytemnestra's negative example would compromise Penelope. And yet, the reverse occurs when readers of Homer see *Helen of Troy* in light of the *Odyssey*. Penelope, shining among women, can now be seen as separate from Clytemnestra, as subjectively distinct rather than as a representative of a shared sex-class. Penelope's ecphrasis-plot subsequently grows in authority, since her resolute thinking stands on its own without another woman's illustrative contrast. She will be judged and judge — a fate that her testing of Odysseus underscores. Such an ancillary effect speaks to the power of women's lives and signifying practices, even in epics devoted to war and homecoming.

An Enduring Logic of Return and Plot Creation

Helen of Troy ends as the legend which enables its story began: with a journey. Bereft, Helen pauses to mourn the death of Paris. Menelaus interrupts her, asking, "What will you do?" His focus on "will" ascribes agency to Helen — a princess without a brother or king, a once sought-for person who is less a sought-for object than a dishonored war prize. His utterance also recognizes her power to decide. She answers, questioningly, "I will follow," thereby echoing him. "I accept," Menelaus says quietly, and they walk single-file into the negative space of the future (*Helen*). Their progress dissolves into the mini-series' closing image. It is of Troy, which was discovered by Heinrich Schliemann in the nineteenth century. In this way, the miniseries ends badly for its central figure but not as badly as it might have, as the virtual erasure of Helen from *Troy* (2004), the Brad Pitt-led sword and sandal film, illustrates. The strategies of containment that arose in response to Helen's transgressions with Paris succeed in *Helen of Troy* and, so great are the resulting losses, they cannot but fail. As the double provocation of Helen in Homer's epics and in epic filmmaking shows, mobility is a master trope for narrative and also a prize that may temporally elude the sexual division of labor.

After her death, Helen was worshiped by Greek women, young and old, and I cannot help but think that her mobility, every bit as much as her beauty, was its basis. Homer's warrior-heroes, Achilles' rage, Odysseus *nostoi*-story, sword and sandal spectaculars—all subtend women's stories and the masculine-feminine actions represented in them incompletely. Different plots, however repressed, linger like the archeological fragments of Troy, awaiting excavation and reuse. Patiently, they signal that other stories endure in the very logic of narrative, in myth as it is passed to us orally, since it is through the dialogical functions of substitution, extension, and inversion that the next stories—perhaps even the next women's stories—are to be sung and heard.

Works Cited

Bakhtin, M. M. "The Problem of Speech Genres." *Speech Genres & Other Late Essays*. Eds. Caryl Emerson and Michael Holquist. Trans. Vern W. McGee. Austin: University of Texas Press, 1986. 60–102. Print.

Barthes, Roland. "From Work to Text." *Image Music Text*. Trans. Stephen Heath. New York: Hill and Wang, 1977. 155–64. Print.

Brooks, Peter. *Reading for the Plot: Design and Intention in Narrative*. New York: Vintage, 1985. Print.

Cresswell, Tim. *On the Move: Mobility in the Modern Western World*. New York: Routledge, 2006. Print.

de Lauretis, Teresa. *Alice Doesn't: Feminism, Semiotics, Cinema*. Bloomington: Indiana Universtiy Press, 1984. Print.

Doane, Mary Ann. *Femmes Fatales: Feminism, Film Theory, Psychoanalysis*. New York: Routledge, 1991. Print.

Felson-Rubin, Nancy. *Regarding Penelope: From Character to Poetics*. Princeton, NJ: Princeton Universtoy Press, 1994. Print.

Genette, Gerard. *Narrative Discourse: An Essay in Method*. Trans. Jane E. Lewin. Ithaca: Cornell University Press, 1980. Print.

Girard, Rene. *Violence and the Sacred*. Trans. Patrick Gregory. Baltimore: Johns Hopkins University Press, 1977. Print.

Helen of Troy. Dir. John Kent Harrison. Perf. Sienna Guillory, Matthew Marsden, and John Rhys-Davies. USA Cable Entertainment, 2003.

Helen of Troy. Dir. Robert Wise. Perf. Rossana Podesta, Jack Sernas, and Sir Cedric Hardwicke. Warner, 1956.

Homer. *Iliad*. Trans. Stanley Lombardo. Indianapolis: Hackett, 1997. Print.

_____. *Odyssey*. Trans. Lombardo. Indianapolis: Hackett, 2000. Print.

Hughes, Bettany. *Helen of Troy: Goddess, Princess, Whore*. New York: Knopf, 2005. Print.

Jameson, Fredric. *The Political Unconscious: Narrative as a Socially Symbolic Act*. Ithaca: Cornell University Press, 1981. Print.
Lattimore, Richmond. "Introduction." *The Iliad of Homer*. Trans. Lattimore. Chicago: University of Chicago Press, 1951. 11–55. Print.
Lord, Albert B. *The Singer of Tales*. 2d ed. Eds. Stephen Mitchell and Gregory Nagy. Cambridge: Harvard University Press, 2000. Print.
Lotman, Jurij M. "The Origin of Plot in the Light of Typology." Trans. Julian Graffy. *Poetics Today* 1.1–2 (1979): 161–84. Print.
Miller, J. Hillis. *Ariadne's Thread: Story Lines*. New Haven: Yale University Press, 1992. Print.
Parry, Milman. *The Making of Homeric Verse: The Collected Essays of Milman Parry*. Ed. Adam Parry. London: Oxford Universtiy Press, 1971. Print.
Propp, Vladmir. *Theory and History of Folklore*. Ed. Anatoly Liberman. Trans. Ariadna Y. Martin and Richard P. Martin. Minneapolis: University of Minnesota Press, 1984. Print.
Roisman, Hanna M. "Helen and the Power of Erotic Love: From Homeric Contemplation to Hollywood Fantasy." *College Literature* 35.4 (2008): 127–150. Web.
Schein, Seth L. "Introduction." *Reading the Odyssey: Selected Interpretive Essays*. Ed. Schein. Princeton, NJ: Princeton University Press, 1996. 3–32. Print.
Slatkin, Laura M. "Composition by Theme and *Metis* of the *Odyssey*." *Reading the Odyssey: Selected Interpretive Essays*. Ed. Seth L. Schein. Princeton: Princeton University Press, 1996. 223–37. Print.
Synder, J. M. "The Web of Song: Weaving Imagery in Homer and the Lyric Poets." *Classical Journal* 76 (1980–81): 193–96. Print.
Troy. Dir. Wolfgang Petersen. Perf. Brad Pitt, Eric Bana, Orlando Bloom, and Diane Kruger. Warner, 2004.

"By Jupiter's Cock!"
Spartacus: Blood and Sand, *Video Games, and Camp Excess*

DAVID SIMMONS

Spartacus: Blood and Sand began airing in January 2010 and quickly gained notoriety for its often explicit visual content. Barry Garron's piece on the season for *The Hollywood Reporter* reflects the views of many critics when he suggests that while the graphic depiction of sex and violence might be an increasingly acceptable means "to shore up a story" on film, television requires greater narrative depth, something Garron believes *Spartacus: Blood and Sand* lacks: "With such thin stories each week, it's small wonder that sex and violence are used to take up the slack" (Garron). Garron and his fellow critics may be missing the cue, however; *Spartacus: Blood and Sand*'s emphatic use of visual excess is intentional, allowing the series to operate as a vehicle for the pleasurable extremes that certain pop cultural texts often offer. Concomitant to this notion is the impression that while criticism concerning contemporary television has undoubtedly embraced a range of shows that combine genre elements with sophisticated and "adult" narratives (science-fiction in *Battlestar Galactica*, comic books in *Heroes*), there still exists an inability to engage with those shows that operate in a predominantly camp mode, those that place an emphasis on a type of excess that often revels in its own lack of seriousness. This limited range of critical approaches to a given show may be detrimental, as Susan Sontag suggests in her influential essay "Notes on Camp": "One cheats oneself, as a human being, if one has *respect* only for the style of high culture" (49). While lines such as "not if Jupiter himself were to open the heavens and dangle his cock from the skies" (Season 1: Episode 3) and the interjection noted in this essay's title suggest that *Spartacus: Blood and Sand* distinctly embodies a camp "love of the exaggerated," the construction becomes problematic when considering Sontag's declaration that "camp is either completely naive or else wholly conscious" (278, 280). *Spartacus: Blood and Sand* would seem to fall somewhere in between these two poles, refusing an interpretation that might imply the show's creators are oblivious to the extravagance of the actors' characterizations or the stylization of the *mise en scène*, but also stopping short of the kind of self-knowingness that might allow for a reading of the show as wholly ironic and distanced in tone. Bearing in mind the nebulous nature of Sontag's use of the term, a more accurate way of understanding the show's camp elements might be found by referring to Sontag's writing on the particular dual nature of some camp artifacts:

> The Camp sensibility is one that is alive to a double sense in which some things can be taken. But this is not the familiar split-level construction of a literal meaning, on the one hand, and a symbolic meaning, on the other. It is the difference, rather, between the thing as meaning something, anything, and the thing as pure artifice [281].

It is certainly possible to read *Spartacus: Blood and Sand* as pure artifice; as an "apolitical" show that, while possessing pretensions of offering serious commentary on the entrenched class system in operation within Roman society, operates more successfully as a visually pleasurable if excessive simulacra of a mass media-inspired version of Ancient Rome (Sontag 279). Conversely, it is likewise possible to read the series as wholly literal, in its intent, in its depiction of violence, in its characterizations, and even in the construction of its fantastic, soap opera-like plots. This dualistic, serio-artificial nature hallmarks *Spartacus: Blood and Sand* and its relationship to its own camp tendencies and sensibilities.

Though most critics were universally condemnatory of the quality of *Spartacus: Blood and Sand*, a slightly more ambivalent view of the show's successes and failures could be found in the acerbic *Guardian* television critic Charlie Brooker's review. While Brooker similarly notes the show's formulaic and repetitive narrative, which "consists of weekly kill-or-be-killed hack-and-slash encounters in the coliseum," the writer is able to appreciate the show's more intentionally lurid excesses on their own, pulp-influenced terms:

> *Spartacus* starts to improve exponentially until somewhere round episode five, where you stop enjoying it ironically and start to enjoy it outright. Yes, it may be the kind of show in which a tattooed warrior gets his face hacked off by a man armed with a hook; it may feature lines like "your wife has been fucked to madness by a thousand vermin cocks"; it may toss in pointless cameos for one-armed topless transsexuals—and all three of these things genuinely happen in the early episodes—but it's also not half bad. In fact I'd go as far as to say it actually gets quite good [Brooker].

In reading such a commentary one is brought back to Sontag's theory of camp, particularly its demarcation as an interpretative reading strategy. Writing in their preface to Sontag's essay in *The Cult Film Reader*, Ernest Mathijs and Xavier Mendik note that Sontag suggests that camp prizes "travesty, *double entendre* [and] unintentional badness" (41). Indeed, Sontag's essay develops this assertion, with the author going on to propose that such an aesthetic practice inherently liberates the individual's approach to cultural artifacts: "The experiences of Camp are based on the great discovery that the sensibility of high culture has no monopoly upon refinement. Camp asserts that good taste is not simply good taste; that there exists, indeed, a good taste of bad taste" (50).

For Sontag this recognition of the operating practices of "bad taste" is integral to any understanding of the camp artifact, chief amongst the characteristics of which are a reliance on visual excess, often as a means of bringing attention to said artifact's constructed nature: "To perceive Camp in objects and person is to understand Being-as-Playing-a-Role. It is the farthest extension, in sensibility, of the metaphor of life as theatre" (41). Indeed, if there is one aspect of *Spartacus: Blood and Sand* that immediately differentiates it from other contemporary television shows, it is its excessive nature. As Brooker notes, the show's depiction of explicit content is frequent, running throughout most episodes: "Roughly every 30 seconds someone gets an axe or sword in the face. Roughly every 20 seconds a woman bares her breasts. Roughly every 10 seconds someone grunts a four-letter word starting with either 'f' or 'c'" (Brooker). An early highlight in this respect is the episode "The Thing in the Pit" (1:4), in which a disgraced Spartacus must fight in the illegal underground pits of Capua and beat the infamous Ixion, a grotesque giant of a man who wields a club and has a tendency to cut off the faces of his fallen victims and wear them as a mask. Before encountering Ixion, Spartacus must defeat a range of lower-level fighters, which he proceeds to do in increasingly brutal ways, including skewering one with a large metal hook and bloodily puncturing the eyes of another. The extent to which this violence is warranted by the concerns of the narrative is a matter of subjective opinion, but it should not be forgotten that HBO's *Rome* was critically lauded, in part, for its authentic depiction of life in the ancient city, an authenticity, which as Jerome De Groot suggests, was achieved by "emphasis[ing] the dirt, squalor, and violence of the city, particularly shown in the explicit language, sex and violence" (199).

Whereas *Rome* may have managed to negotiate its often violent depiction of ancient civilization through claims to historical authenticity, this chapter argues that *Spartacus: Blood and Sand* takes a different route, portraying the acts of the violence between the show's often hyper-masculine central characters in such an exaggerated fashion that a television viewing audience is encouraged to read them as overtly fantastical. Indeed, I would argue that an appreciation of the penchant for excess integral to the pulp genre is crucial to an understanding of *Spartacus: Blood and Sand* as a "successful" text. Thusly, in this chapter I will read the show as effectively borrowing both the Manichean storytelling techniques and visual extravagance that are often found in many video games as one of the most prevalent and popular instances of pulp in the early twenty first century. Of course, many contemporary video games are themselves often indebted to the sort of pulp fiction created by writers like Robert E.

Howard and Edgar Rice Burroughs, and the proliferation of comic book adaptations of their work, which are also reliant on visual and narrative excess. Students of popular culture need only familiarize themselves with hugely popular video game franchises such as *Halo* (Microsoft, 2001–present) and *Gears of War* (Microsoft, 2006–present) to see that the two forms have a long history of feeding into and from each other.

Given that they so often share the same domestic space, with LCD televisions increasingly functioning as visual display units for video gaming consoles, there has been surprisingly little analysis of the growing links between contemporary television and video games. Though a number of scholarly writers, including Geoff King, Tanya Krzywinska, Mark J.P. Wolf, and James Newman, have started to produce work that looks at video games from an academic perspective, widespread mainstream opinion still seems to be that while television is becoming an increasingly valid critical form, in comparison, video games remain inherently lowbrow, unworthy of being considered art, a belief that is perhaps best exemplified by Roger Ebert's declaration as such in the *Chicago Sun–Times*:

> To my knowledge, no one in or out of the field has ever been able to cite a game worthy of comparison with the great dramatists, poets, filmmakers, novelists and composers. That a game can aspire to artistic importance as a visual experience, I accept. But for most gamers, video games represent a loss of those precious hours we have available to make ourselves more cultured, civilized and empathetic [Ebert].

This lack of critical attention obfuscates the influence of video games on today's popular culture, an influence unambiguously reflected in *Spartacus: Blood and Sand*. In fact, *Spartacus: Blood and Sand* stands as one of the first examples of television that actually "remediates" (to borrow a term from Jay David Bolter and Richard Grusin) elements of video games, constructing key elements of the show's design, structure, format, and even characterizations based on common forms found in video games. This is suggested by King and Kryzwinska in their seminal study on the interfaces between film and video games, *ScreenPlay*:

> Forms such as games and cinema exist in complex and multidimensional relationships. In some respects, clear points of similarity can be identified. In others, divergences are sharp. In between, however, lie many shades of overlap, areas of relevance not just to the analysis of this particular conjuncture but to the interrelations between contemporary media forms more generally [30].

While I intend to argue that *Spartacus: Blood and Sand* borrows liberally from the video game form, appropriating the form's aesthetic and narrative structures, I believe that this process of emulation is based on an approximation of generalized video game tropes drawn from a range of "non-genre" video games, including action-adventures, beat-'em-ups, and others, rather than a concerted imitation of any specific video game title or series. Though there have been a number of video games that arguably belong to the sword and sandal genre, such as *Shadow of Rome* (Capcom, 2005), *Conan* (THQ, 2007), and the *God of War* series (Sony, 2005–10), most contain visual and narrative elements that are lacking in *Spartacus: Blood and Sand*, most notably an overtly fantastical aspect to their plots. Rather, *Spartacus: Blood and Sand* borrows more liberally from the generic structure of the video game itself, suggesting that it is the medium — and not any one specific derivation of said medium — that is paramount to not only understanding these structures within the series, but in truly considering their genesis as well.

Such co-option of the video game form is apparent in the second episode of the series, "Sacramentum Gladiatorum" (1:2). This episode picks up the central character Spartacus' story following the betrayal of his Thracian fighting unit by his Roman allies, who subsequently burn Spartacus' village to the ground, attack and rape his wife, and sentence him to death in the gladiatorial arena. Spartacus manages to survive the attacks of the arena's best gladiators and is bought by the gladiator manager Quintus Lentulus Batiatus. This archetypal structuring device is noted in Joseph Campbell's *The Hero with a Thousand Faces*; yet a recurrent plot in which the protagonist is dispossessed of his or her home and familial relations at the start of the narrative by an evil force or individual, and then must attempt to re-acquire them through combat and adventure, is one that is likewise common in video game narratives, where it serves as a handy means of explaining the player-character or "avatar's" motivations in a sufficiently simplistic yet empathetic manner. In this second episode of the series, Spartacus must prove himself worthy of joining Batiatus' band of gladiators. The concept of a character having to acclimatize himself physically and mentally to the quest that lies ahead will immediately remind any avid gamer of the numerous training sequences of many contemporary video games, as King and Krzywinska note: "In the early stages of playing a new game ... a new interface may have to be mastered" (*Tomb* 32). The way in which the show proceeds to visualize these scenes has further echoes of so-called beat-'em-up video games such as *Streetfighter* (Capcom 1987–present) and *Mortal Kombat* (Midway 1992–2009, Warner Bros. Interactive Entertainment 2009–present), in which players pick from a range of avatars and then pit them against one another on a two-dimensional (or more latterly, three-dimensional) plane. Indeed, the episode climaxes with Spartacus having to compete "one on one" against one of Batiatus' best gladiators, Crixus. Crixus' status as the champion of Capua suggestively aligns him with the tougher, more difficult "boss" characters that combat-based video games frequently offer up as staging posts on the player's journey to successful completion (a structural similarity that continues in episodes such as "Shadow Games" [1:5] with the character of the giant Theokoles). This second episode's indebtedness to video game convention is further emphasized through the visual presentation of this climatic battle; Spartacus must face Crixus on a small elevated wooden platform, forcing the men to adopt the face-to-face positioning familiar to any gamer: "Spatial restriction is also an integral feature of many beat-'em-up and wrestling games in which fighting takes place in localized arenas, keeping combatants in close proximity to one another" (King & Krzywinska *Tomb* 77). Spartacus eventually triumphs over Crixus by pushing him off the platform, in a move that emulates the three dimensional beat-'em-up's "Ring Out!" winning conditions, whereby one player forces the other outside the boundaries of the designated play area, and testifies to the series' appropriation of conventions, both narrative and visual, drawn from the culturally lowbrow world of gaming.

The influence of video games is apparent throughout *Spartacus: Blood and Sand*, most noticeably in terms of the show's prominent aesthetic signature elements. While those reviewing the show were quick to point out its use of state-of-the-art filmic techniques—including super imposition, wherein the placement of an image on top of another image creates a new effect; chroma key, which is a process whereby two images are merged together to remove a color or small range of colors; and "Bullet Time," in which virtual cameras are used to create a sensation of variable speed—critics failed to discuss these techniques' relationship to gaming. King and Krzywinska note in their chapter on spectacle in gaming that "qualities such as striking imagery and sound are important sources of pleasure in video games" (*Tomb* 124). They suggest that specific factors such as the visual and aural fidelity of a game are often of vital importance in inducing enjoyment in the player: "The qualities of graphical reproduction on-screen, combined with sound effects, can play a significant part in the establishment of many of the dimensions of games" (*Tomb* 124). This desire for greater levels of spectacle enabled by superior resolution and visual detail in the field of video games seems to be reflected in *Spartacus: Blood and Sand*'s use of super imposition, chroma key, and "Bullet Time," where the techniques serves to create a video game like *mise en scène* that is removed from the more realist tendencies of television through its overt foregrounding of excessive artifice and visual stylization. Where much of contemporary television is characterized visually by a "self-consciously wrought *mise en scène*" and is "art-cinema derivative," *Spartacus: Blood and Sand* is defined by its pulpy, visceral excessiveness, perhaps ironically linking the show to John Caldwell's belief that television since the 1980's has become increasingly "defined by excessive stylization and visual exhibitionism" (Bignell 159, Feuer 145, 352). Indeed, while many commentators criticized the show for what they considered to be its repetitive utilization of techniques like super imposition and "Bullet Time," if *Spartacus: Blood and Sand* is re-considered as a series that is *intentionally* trying to emulate the often excessive visual conventions of video-gaming, then the repeated slowed-down blood splatters, to take one example, begin to seem like an apposite reflection of the central importance of significant and clearly discernible visual feedback in video games and closely resemble the slowed-down impacts of such seminal games as the later entries in the *Fight Night* series (EA, 1985–2009). In video games, it is often thought that the more visceral the indication of the success of a player's action, the more pleasure the player will derive from the game: "feedback can be dramatized on-screen — the spectacular death of an enemy blasted with a powerful weapon, for example" (King & Krzywinska *Tomb* 31).

Here again one is confronted with the relevance of camp. Mathijs and Mendik note that, "Sontag claims that camp is an aesthetic sensibility that is characterized by a high degree of, and attention for stylization, artifice [and] extravagance" (41). Sontag goes on to suggest in her original text that "Sometimes whole art forms become saturated with Camp," proposing that this tendency is more likely to occur in popular art forms such as pop music and cinema than it is in concert music because "it offers no opportunity, say, for a contrast between silly or extravagant content and rich form" (281). It does not seem too much of a leap to suggest that such a reading of popular art forms might be extended to video games, which, with their reliance on visual artifice, can be seen as a logical contemporary instance of Sontag's theories. This is not to say that all video games are camp; yet many of them do seem to embody an approach that echoes Sontag's belief that an extravagant artifice is foregrounded. In the case of many video games, this is often a concomitant factor in the "arms race" of ever increasing graphical advances that result in the promoting of excessive stylization as an effective means to demonstrate the product's technological superiority to that of its competitors.

This particular video game-inflected visual ethos of the show is evident from the pilot, "The Red Serpent" (1:1). As a result of the epic scope of this first episode, the viewer is shown a variety of environments, all of them created digitally with computer graphics; while on one level these backgrounds are meant to resemble "real" geographical locations (the Thracian village, Rome, the arena in Capua,) they are also heavily stylized to the extent that the viewer can be under little impression that they are meant to be considered as mimetically "realistic." Instead, the show appears to bring attention to its own artificiality by imbuing these locales with highly noticeable artistic flourishes— such as the proliferation of autumnal leaves in the orchard outside of the Thracian village — that seem to consciously evoke the "environments" of a video game such as *Okami* (Capcom, 2006) or a comic book panel. Indeed, one could argue that super imposition is an inherently video game aping technique, replicating the form's use of popular processes such as motion-capture, which attempts to capture the physicality of real human beings and map their movements on to in-game avatars, who then operate in landscapes created digitally by video game artists. Motion-capture has been an integral part of many video games since the mid to late 1990s, being used in examples as diverse as the golf simulation *Tiger Woods* series (EA, 1998–present) to the complex and mature serial killer title *Heavy Rain* (Sony, 2010). Chroma key, or techniques that approximate the same sort of visual effect, are also increasingly being employed in video games; in *The Saboteur* (EA, 2009), the player must attempt to wrestle control of France back from the Nazis. The process of freeing areas of France is reflected in a visual transformation from a drab grey landscape drained of color during the German occupation to a colorful and bustling metropolis when liberated. Such perceptible visual techniques speak to the increasingly symbiotic relationship between film and computer graphics, with both forms seeking to capitalize on the advances of the other in order to offer new and exciting creative and commercial possibilities.

While reviews of *Spartacus: Blood and Sand* tended to praise John Hannah and Lucy Lawless's performances as the scheming Batiatus and his wife, they also singled out Andy Whitfield's characterization of the chief protagonist as weak: "Whitfield has the requisite physicality for the title role. Beyond that, it's hard to assess his performance because his character is so consistently two-dimensional" (Garron). Yet, like so much else in the show, Whitfield's acting takes on a different aspect when considered through the auspice of the video game. Whitfield's blankness is ideal for the viewer, who is used to assuming the position of the video game hero. As Joshua Clover suggests of Keanu Reeves' similarly "vacant" performance in *The Matrix*, "This is a bodily leap more than a cathexis; most video games, like most action heroes, ask more for a physical identification than emotional investment" (46). The reading of Whitfield as avatar rather than character is further reinforced in the series' tendency to cut between mid-angle shots of fighters in the gladiatorial scenes with close point of view shots of the fighters' faces meant to depict what is going on inside their helmets. Such editing allows the viewer to share the perspective of the characters, in a manner reminiscent of first-person shooters such as *Half Life* (Sierra Entertainment/Valve/EA, 1998–present) or *Call of Duty* (Activision, 2003), and more specifically combat-based games played from a first person perspective, such as *The Chronicles of Riddick: Escape from Butcher Bay* (Vivendi, 2004) and *Zeno Clash* (Valve, 2009).

The creators of *Spartacus: Blood and Sand* also embrace, with a keen awareness, the homoerotic imagery prevalent throughout many video games (see *Gears of War*) and comic books (see any number of superhero or Robert E. Howard-inspired series) wherein the physically overdeveloped, muscular form of the male body is presented as a pleasurable spectacle for a predominantly male audience. Such images function as a means of imaginative empowerment, a vehicle of identification for those experiencing feelings of powerlessness. The opening of the episode "Legends" (1.3), in which Spartacus is initially dressed in little more than a jockstrap and proceeds to strap on his gladiatorial clothing and armor, sets the tone for what is to follow. Once dressed, Spartacus joins the other gladiators as they train for the arena, allowing, in tenuous narrative terms, for scenes of groups of scantily clad, muscle-bound men grappling with one another, with the profuse use of slow-motion in these scenes allowing for a further emphasis on the male body in the throes of physical exertion. The show's depiction and sexual objectification of the male body is most evident in a scene midway through the episode, when the gladiators' bodies are explicitly put on show for an audience of eager male and female dignitaries as part of the pre-arena festivities organized by Batiatus. The sexualized nature of the display is made explicit when the scene culminates with one of the gladiators being instructed to perform sexual intercourse with a female slave for the viewing pleasure of the assembled Roman luminaries.

While the frequent depictions of semi-clad or naked male bodies might suggest an intentional ploy on the show's part to attract a portion of both a gay male and heterosexual female audience, it is interesting to note that this is perhaps not the primary impetus behind this representation. Instead, it would appear more correct to suggest that *Spartacus: Blood and Sand* employs a type of visual excessiveness with regards to its depiction of the male body as hypermasculine. Functioning in a similar camp manner to the "exaggerated he-manness of Steve Reeves [and] Victor Mature" that Sontag references, this representation highlights its own artificiality, relishing "the exaggeration of sexual characteristics and personality mannerisms" to such an extent that it is no longer threatening to a heterosexual male audience, who can instead take pleasure in the playful amplification on display (42).

While later episodes of *Spartacus: Blood and Sand* see the show maturing somewhat, with the narrative deepening in complexity along with the characterization, the show's continued reliance on the camp excesses of video game aesthetic and narrative conventions results in a program that remains unusual in the contemporary television landscape for acknowledging and foregrounding its own artificiality. The fact is that the show seems quite happy in assimilating the cultural capital of such populist and critically elided forms and has so far proven commercially successful in reaching an audience familiar with such conventions. This may suggest a need for the reassessment of entrenched hegemonic approaches to television studies, one that recognizes the increasingly synergistic and digitized nature of contemporary television and the impact of video games on the pop culture mores of newer generations of television watchers.

Works Cited

Bolter, Jay David, and Richard Grusin. *Remediation: Understanding New Media.* Cambridge: MIT Press, 1999.
Brooker, Charlie. "Charlie Brooker's Screen Burn: Spartacus: Blood and Sand." *The Guardian.* 22 May 2010. 15 Dec. 2010. <www.guardian.co.uk/television-and-radio/2010/may/22/charlie-brooker-screenburn-spartacus>.
Clover, Joshua. *The Matrix: BFI Modern Classics.* London: Palgrave Macmillan, 2004.
De Groot, Jerome. *Consuming History: Historians and Heritage in Contemporary Popular Culture.* London: Routledge, 2008.
Ebert, Roger. "Roger Ebert re-enters the 'games as art' debate." *Guardian.co.uk Games Blog.* 20 April 2010. 10 Dec. 2010. <www.guardian.co.uk/technology/gamesblog/2010/apr/20/roger-ebert-games-as-art>.
Garron, Barry. "Spartacus: Blood and Sand — TELEVISION Review." *The Hollywood*

Reporter. 21 Jan. 2010. 11 Dec. 2010. <www.hollywoodreporter.com/hr/television-reviews/spartacus-blood-and-sand-television-review-1004060949.story>.

Goodman, Tim. "Syfy's 'Battlestar' prequel stylish, compelling." *San Francisco Chronicle.* 22 Jan. 2010. 19 Dec. 2010. <www.sfgate.com/cgibin/article.cgi?f=/c/a/2010/01/21/DDR31BL5VM.DTL>.

King, Geoff, and Tanya Krzywinska, eds. *ScreenPlay: Cinema/Video games/Interfaces.* London: Wallflower Press, 2002.

_____, _____. *Tomb Raiders and Space Invaders: Video Game Forms and Contexts.* London: I.B. Tauris, 2006.

Mathijs, Ernest, and Xavier Mendik, eds. *The Cult Film Reader.* Berkshire and New York: Open University Press, 2008.

Sontag, Susan. *Against Interpretation and Other Essays.* New York: Farrar, Straus and Giroux, 1966.

Spartacus: Blood and Sand. Dirs. Michael Warn, Rick Hurst, Jesse Jacobson. Starz Productions, 2010.

Stuever, Hank. "TELEVISION Preview: Starz's 'Spartacus' offers up a bloody, good time on Friday night TELEVISION." *The Washington Post.* 22 Jan. 2010. 10 Dec. 2010. <www.washingtonpost.com/wp-dyn/content/article/2010/01/21/ AR2010012104590.html>.

Beefy Guys and Brawny Dolls
He-Man, the Masters of the Universe, and Gay Clone Culture

MICHAEL G. CORNELIUS

In 1981, Mattel launched the Masters of the Universe line of action figures, creating a toy-derived sword and sandal fantasy microcosm inhabited largely by a series of muscular, mostly naked he-men marshaled under the figure of the aptly named He-Man himself, the chief warrior for the forces of good and the "most powerful man in the universe," as the figure's packaging modestly noted. Simultaneous to the release of the action figures, Filmation studios syndicated a thirty-minute cartoon of the toy line called *He-Man and the Masters of the Universe*; from a marketing perspective, this was a novel concept, since He-Man was the first series of toys to be launched concurrent to a television show. As Sam Anderson explains: "It [the television show] was basically a long-form, serialized Mattel commercial, the first cartoon ever to be conceived and produced only for the purpose of selling an action figure — a mythology preceded by its own icons (plastic ones, with swiveling torsos and 'power punch action'). In retrospect, it's pretty clear that my love for the show — my quasi-religious immersion — was just a Pavlovian response to aggressive cross-marketing" (Anderson).

The exaggeratedly muscular form of He-Man dominated every aspect of the Masters of the Universe — its packaging, its marketing, the television show and comic books — so much so that it was rare to glimpse at a scene of the series or a page of any of the comics without seeing the hyper-developed pectoral and gluteus muscles of He-Man staring back. Whereas He-Man himself was a drab, stolid Boy Scout–type who always did what was right, fought for social justice, and tossed off the occasionally leaden *bon mot* while doing so, his musculature became the actual cynosure of the show, as his hyper-developed form was continually on display, front and foremost, for all eyes to see. As a result, the enlarged physique of the chief Master of the Universe was not designed to signify He-Man's dominance or virtue; it was not designed as a *signification* at all. Indeed, his muscles were, in fact, what the show and the toy line were ultimately *about*. He-Man's overdeveloped physique was the star of the series, and the man himself was just a skeletal structure crafted to carry that exaggerated musculature into battle for all to admire. He-Man was not fashioned as a simulacrum of exaggerated male masculinity; He-Man's muscles *were* his masculinity. In fact, they constituted his entire identity, the sole and overarching extent of his entire iconic fashioning. For He-Man, he flexes; therefore, he is.

Yet despite the godly otherworldliness and singular nature of He-Man's strength, within the Masters of the Universe toy line, his muscular physique was replicated in hard, tactile plastic for nearly every figure in the series, both good and evil. He-Man's chief nemesis, Skeletor, was a sorcerer, a figure for whom an excess of muscles was hardly relevant, since he relied on magic and guile to combat his foe. Yet, Skeletor's toy body exhibited the same definition as He-Man, since it utilized the same plastic parts to create the same muscular figure. In the Masters of the Universe world, the male form was ceaselessly replicated and transmuted from one figure to the other. Doll manufacturers have long done this, utilizing one form to represent multiple figures. From a pecuniary perspective, this demonstrates a wise business acumen, saving money on molds and parts. Generally, children and even collectors raise no objection if Doll X and Doll Y have the same basic underpinning; their plasticized bodies exist only as a frame to countenance their clothing, hair, and the other accessories that distinguish their identity from the other dolls on the toy store shelf. Barbie is perhaps the ultimate representation of this ability to market sameness in form. Collectors will easily purchase dozens and dozens of the same doll — of the same form, the same plastic structure — in order to amass the paraphernalia associated with the particular look packaged onto the doll (and the packaging itself). Though much has been made of Barbie's representation of the female form, and rightly so, Barbie herself is not her physique, not her plastic curves and molded-over vagina; rather, she is the hair and clothing that cover these aspects of her personage. Her names suggest as much, since Barbie alters identity every time she switches wardrobe: differing personas like Ballerina Barbie, Western Barbie, and Pan Am Stewardess Barbie are differentiated only by raiment, hairstyle, and accoutrement. Her identity is designed to be discerned by how her form is both covered and represented by these accessories. Of course, Barbie is known primarily as a "fashion doll" (Hall 47). Yet the same is true for most other dolls and action figures. GI Joe figures, for example, likewise utilize similar plasticized physiques as their base, but, as with Barbie, the undercarriage is irrelevant; here, clothes (and from a sociophallic perspective, weapons,) truly make the man.

Like GI Joe, He-Man's name is emblematic of his identity; yet, rather than make reference to his clothing, weapons, or occupation, He-Man's name is a double reference to his masculine physique—combining both "he" and "man," noting the masculine twice, while at the same time employing a common term for a strongman or muscleman. Anderson labels He-Man "a half-naked steroidal Aryan cartoon beefcake," an apt description of the character, one emphasizing his bulk and the erotic potential of it ("half-naked," "beefcake") (Anderson). Thus He-Man and his fellow Masters are all about their plastic physiques; raiment and accoutrement matter little. In their world, the body is text, to be read as key signifier in the fashioning of male identity. Interestingly, this reliance upon, and fascination with, the male form in the He-Man toy line is reminiscent of the manner in which the male form is considered as both object of desire and object of subjective fashioning in the gay clone subculture, a subculture that flourished at the same time the He-Man toy line was created. As in the Masters of the Universe, the hyper-developed masculine form is a key marker of the gay clone culture; musculature is crucial for admission into the subculture and acceptance by its membership. Maneuvering successfully through the gay clone world requires musculature; it requires impressive physique. In short, it takes a "he-man." This is not to suggest that Mattel modeled the He-Man line and its reception and representation of the masculine form on the gay clone subculture; however, this happy duality does seem to be suggestive of larger social anxieties and desiderata that the toy line and the clone culture reflect regarding similar attitudes towards the male physique, attitudes that, in many ways, differ from the larger heteronormative continuum present in society at the time. As Karen J. Hall notes, the body gathers "its meaning from historical, social, and geographical contexts" (35). The social context that gave form — literally and figuratively—to He-Man and gay clone culture reflects intriguing notions about the hyperdeveloped male body in this particular moment in history. By establishing the hyperstimulated physique as a model of attainment — as something to desire for one's self and in others—both He-Man and clone culture shape the male form simultaneously as a desirable object of the same-gendered gaze and as an attribute so commonplace in the two microcosmic subcultures as to render the form invisible, or less visible, than would otherwise seem possible for such hulking, out-of-place shapes. The end result is both an idolization and palliation of the enlarged male form and a reconfiguration of contemporary constructs of the masculine overall. Ultimately, the ways and means in which He-Man and gay clone culture both create, sustain, and marginalize the male form suggests that each are rejoinders to masculinity itself, both old-fashioned established forms and newly emerging variations in the late 1970s and early 1980s. They are redactions of and reactions to altering paradigms in the traditional role of the heteronormative male. They are, in fact, more masculine than the newly evolving male of the still-developing men's movement; as men grew more in touch with their feminine sides, these two seemingly disparate cultures—one a sexualized sub culture, the other a fabricated child's fantasia on traditional pepla motifs—both established a male ethos that, in its insistence on hypermasculinity, fetishized and obtunded the male form itself.

On Muscles and Molds

> Men's bodies are detachable ... a man and his body are soon parted.... What men are afraid of most is not lions, not snakes, not the dark, not women. Not anymore. What men are most afraid of is the body of another man.
>
> — Margaret Atwood

The Masters of the Universe line of toys was first designed by Roger Sweet, with a back story created by Donald F. Glut. The early examples of Masters toys, often called the "first wave," are remarkably homogenous in appearance. All of them revel in celebrating the muscularized male form: the pectorals bulge, the abdominals are rippled and rigid, the biceps and triceps strain from overdevelopment. Initially, Masters' toys were crafted from only a few existing molds: there were two chest molds (one smooth and one hairy); one belt/waist undergarment mold (the depicted undergarment was given a textured surface designed to resemble animal fur; hence the fan-given appellative "furry underwear"); and three sets of arm and leg molds (one smooth and muscular, one hairy and muscular, and one smooth and muscular that ended in claws and webbed feet instead of fingers and toes). In addition, all of the initial toys shared the same pose; the left hand was splayed open, as if to slap a foe, while the right hand was curved with the thumb positioned up, designed to facilitate the grasping of whatever weapon was packaged with the action figure. The arms were both curved, to emphasize their muscularity; they could move only up and down, and were easily detached with a small amount of applied torque. The waist swiveled on a tight elastic band, creating a motion designed to mimic a "power punch." The legs were connected to similar bands, which allowed limited mobility in several directions. The figures could balance on their legs, but posing options were severely restricted.

The most significant differentiated piece of any Masters of the Universe figure was its head. Unlike the rest of the body, which was constructed of rigid, firm plastic, the head was much softer, yielding to the touch and somewhat pliable. These heads could rotate, and each was crafted from a different mold, creating a perhaps unnerving paradigm wherein differing heads all shared the same body. While this could be said as emphasizing the nature of the head — and, by extension, the intellect, passions, and ideals held within — in reality, the pliable nature of the head suggested the weakness of the mind as compared to the hardness of the body. This is reflected in the very nature of the toys themselves. He-Man, leader of the Heroic Warriors, was noted chiefly for his strength; the literal "strongest man in the universe," he won contests and saved the day through brawn, not brains. His counterpart was his chief foe, Skeletor, leader of the Evil Warriors, whose intellect and scheming are continually defeated by the sheer he-man-ness of He-Man himself. Peter Schwenger has suggested a correlation between de-intellectualism and maleness when he notes that "self-awareness ... [is] antithetical to [the] idea of the male" (624). Instinct, gut reactions, aggression, violence — this is the world of the male, not logic, coolness, intellect, and awareness. Thus brains were not prioritized in the Masters world; it was brawn that mattered.

As such, the body of each Masters figure was crafted out of a rigid plastic that changed colors for different figures, representing shades of skin or (presumably) ultra-tight clothing. The Evil Warrior Mer-Man was green, for example, reflecting his aquatic home; Beast Man, another evil minion, was orange, his hairy hide perhaps designed to suggest the tawny tone of a lion or tiger. None of the first wave Evil Warriors had flesh-colored skin (Skeletor himself was blue), save for Zodac, who, in the cartoon series, was converted to the side of good (and who also had clawed fingers and webbed feet, suggesting his differentiation from the first wave Heroic Warriors, who all had the shaggy or smooth booted feet). Heroic Warriors were mostly depicted with white faces— He-Man himself, Man-at-Arms, Stratos— and their coloring suggested ultra-tight clothing, save for Stratos, a flying man whose gray, reportedly fur-covered skin was oddly disrupted by the fleshy tones of his face. There is, quite naturally, a presumption of white privilege amongst the coloring of Masters figures; white is good, that old chestnut, while non-white was demarcated by the side of evil. Still, whether the skin was colored tan, blue, green, or orange, all of the figures, good and evil, shared the same physique, and the musculature of each figure was prominently featured and displayed. Sartorial options were minimized in the Masters of the Universe line; He-Man himself only wore a criss-cross "leather" harness that strapped across his chest, emphasizing the chest's enlarged nature, along with his shaggy underwear. Most of the other characters followed suit, wearing uniforms that "revealed" rather than "concealed." Interestingly, for the most part, the Masters' uniforms served no functional purpose (though, on occasion, they had a loop to store the figure's sword, as with Tri-Klops); rather than being an extension of their powers or a reflection of their persona, the clothing placed on He-Man and the other Masters figures was largely designed solely to emphasize each toy's enhanced musculature.[1] Unlike GI Joe, who hid his body behind military fatigues, the sword and sandal pedigree of the Masters of the Universe allowed for the full consideration of the male form in all its plasticized glory.

He-Man was not directly derived from Robert E. Howard's creation of Conan the Cimmerian Barbarian, as some have believed (the popular *Conan the Barbarian* movie, starring Arnold Schwarzenegger, would not be released until 1982, a year after the toy franchise's debut and two years after its initial development). Nevertheless, Conan and his peplum kin are obvious influences on He-Man's appearance. Howard's Conan narratives did not shy away from describing the form of his hero, in all his manly glory:

> [Conan was] a tall man, mightily shouldered and deep of chest, with a massive corded neck and heavily muscled limbs. He was clad in silk and velvet, with the royal lions of Aquilonia worked in gold upon his rich jupon, and the crown of Aquilonia shone on his square-cut black mane; but the great sword at his side seemed more natural to him than the regal accoutrements. His brow was low and broad, his eyes a volcanic blue that smoldered as if with some inner fire. His dark, scarred, almost sinister face was that of a fighting-man, and his velvet garments could not conceal the hard, dangerous lines of his limbs [Howard, *Dragon* 89–90].

Descriptive words like "massive," "giant," and "powerful," commonly applied to Conan, were all designed to convey a sense of his size and strength. Presenting the masculine is important to the sword and sandal genre. In the realm of the barbarian hero, male flesh is an obvious commodity. It signifies power, virility, and dominance. Recent examples of the genre, including Ridley Scott's 2000 film *Gladiator* and the 2010 Starz television network series *Spartacus: Blood and Sand* frankly revel in the fleshy world of the male, allowing the camera to linger on numerous shots of sweaty masculine bodies at work and in repose. This voyeuristic presentation of the male body produces at least one curious side affect; it generates and reduces the male form as the object of the decidedly *male* gaze, since men are considered the primary audience demographic for the sword and sandal genre (as Peter Bondanella observes, "Most audiences [for sword and sandal films] were composed of men" [178]). In those instances where a gendered form is presented as the object of that same gender's gaze— such as in advertisements in women's magazines, where the nearly nude female form abounds, fashioned as such for an overwhelmingly female viewership— the object of the gaze is still constructed as an entity of desire for the surveyor. While the gaze has always had a tendency to deconstruct the human body into its irreducible parts, when the gaze is *heterogendered*, the objective is to make reducible that which the viewer sexually desires, or finds sexually desirable, in others; when the gaze is *homogendered*, however, the object is deconstructed into those components the viewer finds desirable as images of attainment from both a societal and personal perspective for the self.[2] Thus when women gaze upon the lean forms and enlarged breasts of models in women's magazines, they desire those aspects of the model not because they themselves find these women sexually desirable, but rather because they believe others—usually those of the opposing gender—would do so. According to Tricia Sheffield, in instances such as this, the "magazine, its contents, and its readers are ultimately designed to incarnate the male gaze. And what the male gaze is incarnating is normative femininity" (5). In other words, thanks to dominant social conditioning, the socially subjective viewer of the same-gender gaze longs to be the object of the gaze him/herself, and casts the qualities of the viewed object as desirable aspects to be attained by the viewing subject.

For He-Man and the other Masters of the Universe, this suggests a performative aspect to their muscles themselves. These enlarged bodies represent working forms, workmanlike physiques that reflect not only power, desirability, and virility but also wholesomeness and virtue. The strongman has often been cast as a warrior for good (Superman was the homespun, Kansas farm boy do-gooder; his nemesis, Lex Luthor, is the weakling intellect); as such, signification of the barbarian's muscles reflects a social value that is largely deemed beneficial. Manliness is valued, and thus overt and over-manliness must be even more valued. We revere and esteem such musculature. To put it bluntly, big muscles are cool.

Schwenger has noted the importance of the masculine form in the larger role of the male himself in society. Labeling musculature as part of what he considers the "maleness of experience," he writes, "This maleness of experience, at a primary level, must mean the infusion of a particular sense of the body into the attitudes and encounters of a life" (623). The body then provides social and emotional cues for the male's being. It leads him as both a social and sexual figure; the body shapes not only his demeanor and outlook, but the very fabric of his self as well. This is very much true for He-Man, who exists largely to orchestrate the musculature contained upon him. This would suggest that He-Man's body acts as a simulacrum of maleness itself; and yet, as Judith Butler notes,

> The body posited as prior to the sign, is always *posited* or *signified* as *prior*. This signification produces as an *effect* of its own procedure the very body that it nevertheless and simultaneously claims to discover as that which *precedes* its own action. If the body signified as prior to signification is an effect of signification, then the mimetic or representational status of language, which claims that signs follow bodies as their necessary mirrors, is not mimetic at all. On the contrary, it is productive, constitutive, one might even argue *performative*, inasmuch as this signifying act delimits and contours the body that it then claims to find prior to any and all signification [30].

Here Butler suggests that if the body is fashioned first, it is then deconstructed into its signifying auspice based on cultural markers. This may reflect a deliberate fashioning or re-fashioning of the body, and, indeed, bodies can be shaped and re-shaped through diet, exercise, and surgery. Once the desired look is achieved, the body then fits into the cultural signifier that was considered advantageous in the first place. Thus bodies are constructed into specific forms because of what these forms signify, crafting the body as a text that is both deliberately writ and read to present a particular meaning; signs and portents are not attached to shapes, but rather, shapes are created because of existing cultural significations.

Thus He-Man's plastic, molded physique is constructed as a deliberate textual sign to the viewer. His body is meant to be read. Yet what does it say?

Ostensibly, male physique is traditionally associated with markers of desirability to the opposing gender and attracting mates. A recent study examining the correlation between male body attractiveness and those components factors that comprise it begins by theorizing that "(i) a reliable connection exists between body attractiveness and male quality; (ii) male attractiveness is an indicator of some components of fitness such as health and vigour; and (iii) females detect and use this indicator for choosing a mate" (Fan et al. 219). The male body, then, is fashioned to attract females, for the purposes of mating. This corresponds to numerous examples in nature, where male plumage and other like physical attributes are often larger, more colorful, and more ostentatious than their female counterparts possess. These attributes are then used in the process of courting potential mates. The developed male physique suggests the same approach; the more developed the attribute, the more desirable the mate.

However, the end results of the study fail to bear this supposition out. Researchers uncovered that *height* is the most prominent marker of male attractiveness to mating; a developed physique only "can have small, but significant effects on male body attractiveness" (226). Musculature is thus significant but not prioritized; a well-developed but short man would find himself at a disadvantage over a man with an average physique but above-average height. Thus the body text developed in the Masters of the Universe toy line is not suggestive of male desirability to females; these bodies are not made for mating, just as these toys were not made for girls. No, these forms are made for gazing, and here the gazing is done by male eyes.

Guys and Dolls: Fetishizing the Muscular Male Form

> Larry was the omnipresent flannel-shirt-Levi's stud in every bar in New York. Hulking, tall Larry, now, as always, in full uniform: construction boots, bomber jacket, flannel shirt, button-fly jeans with two buttons open to show a flash of jockstrap. The light brown mustache completed the image of every clone on Christopher Street.
> — John Preston, *Mr. Benson*

Male-on-male homogendered gazing suggests, on its surface, male homosexuality, the active act of one male desiring another physically. Indeed, the very action of one male objectifying another through the gaze may be rendered into a homosexual act. Butler notes, "Insofar as heterosexual gender norms produce inapproximable ideals, heterosexuality can be said to operate through the regulated production of hyperbolic versions of 'man' and 'woman.' These are for the most part compulsory performances, ones which none of us choose, but which each of us is forced to negotiate" (237). Socially operated and compulsory forms of heteronormativity suggest the interplay and interaction of males *and* females; since the gaze is often considered an act of sexuality, and often an act of sexual predation, then the homogendered gaze — specifically, a male-on-male gaze without women — can be construed as a homosexual act, and one aggressively masculine at that. Of course, not all gazer/object relationships are sexual in nature — as previously pointed out, some suggest the desire of attainment. Yet to stare at an object — to render a person the subject of one's gaze — is often to suggest either the desire to be *with* (physically) or be *like* (physically) that object. Bounded by dictates of physicality, then, the gaze is necessarily corporeal in its fundamental essence of wanting; whatever the viewer may wish from the object, it is somatic in nature.

Gay clone culture is predicated on a binaristic relationship maintained within the act of gazing; it is, in many ways, mimetic gazing. In clone culture, the goal is to be both subject and subjector of the gaze, others' and one's self. The fashioned male body thus becomes a text to read and a signifier of inclusion into the subculture itself. Like the Heroic or Evil Warriors, one must demonstrate the proper physique to assume membership.

The gay clone was first identified by Martin Levine in his ethnographic study of emerging patterns of identity shifts among gay men in urban areas in the latter 1970s and early 1980s. According to Levine, clones emerged after gay liberation in the 1970s: "When the dust of gay liberation had settled, the doors to the closet were opened, and out popped the clone" (7). Clones were "a specific constellation of sociosexual, affective, and behavioral patterns" (7). Participants in the clone culture relied on both visual and narrative cues to establish their status: physique, social demeanor, sartorial uniformation, and particular linguistic markers all suggested membership in the clone culture. Clones affected a style Levine labels "'butch' rhetoric, which fostered a masculine look through the verbal and visual symbols of macho manhood" (58). Levine's generic description of the stereotypical clone uncannily resembles the description from John Preston, epigraphed above:

> The clone was, in many ways, the manliest of men. He had a gym-defined body; after hours of rigorous body building, his physique rippled with bulging muscles, looking more like a competitive body builders than hairdressers or florists. He wore blue-collar garb — flannel shirts over muscle T-shirts, Levi 501s over work boots, bomber jackets over hooded sweatshirts. He kept his hair short and had a thick mustache or closely cropped beard [Levine 7].

Like the overdeveloped male form itself, clone culture is imitated and performed, reflecting a conscious desire to be like others (Levine 56). This form was reached through the application of sartorial and physical regulations and the appropriation of specialized behavioral codes. Levine writes: "Clones used such stereotypically macho sign-vehicles as musculature, facial hair, short haircuts, and rugged functional clothing to express butchness" (60). Clones utilized distinct uniforms, aping what were considered to be orthodox blue-collar masculine guises of the time period: construction worker, cowboy, policeman, jock, leather man. (The Village People all took their looks from typical clone cultures found in New York City at that time. There seems little doubt that He-Man's criss-cross leather strapping and "furry underwear" would have blended right in.) They also embraced proscriptive behavioral codes that encompassed "... spatial distance, facial inexpressiveness, and loudness ... gay clones displayed reserve, aggression and coarseness in their motions, speech patterns, and facial gestures" (Levine 62). Most significant to the enactment of clone culture was the perfectly formed male physique:

> Clones developed "gym bodies," which denoted the physique associated with weightlifters. A gym body included tight buttocks, washboard stomachs. And "pumped-up" biceps and pectorals. Clones favored this physique because they felt it was the most macho male build [Levine 59–60].

In many ways, this physique was considered the most vocal affront against the stereotypes heterosexuals held about gay men:

> Homophobia often operates through the attribution of a damaged, failed, or otherwise abject gender to homosexuals, that is, calling gay men "feminine" or calling lesbians "masculine," and because the homophobic terror over performing homosexual acts, where it exists, is often also a terror over losing proper gender [Butler 238].

Clone culture was the first social movement displayed among gay men that could be viewed as a direct response to popularly held notions of gay men manifesting a failed masculinity. Vasu Reddy explains:

> Gay masculinity hints at a collection of ideas, attitude and assumptions which culturally determine the way gay men view themselves as men. It is impossible to talk about a gay masculinity as it is something which is absolute; nor is it possible to exclude an understanding of this concept in relation to sexuality, and more specifically, heterosexuality [65].

As a response to heterosexuality, gay clone culture was both defiant and appropriating. It utilized the trappings of traditional masculinity in order to eschew them. It celebrated the hyper-developed male form in order to fetishize it, to render it beautiful. "[U]ntil very recently, the ideas and ideals of masculine beauty have been marginalized," as if male beauty was inessential, unimportant to society (Schehr 78). In many ways, this is true; men controlled the auspices of marriage and mating, and were thus not viewed as commodities in the same manner as women. Women were prized for beauty and demeanor, men for wealth and position. Yet the rise of the feminist movement and gay liberation altered not only the modern perception of manhood but also the ways in which male beauty was demarcated and considered. Suddenly, the beauty of males was not only possible, it was fashionable, desirable, and commercially marketable. Roots of this movement extend back to the very end of the nineteenth century and the new fad for physical fitness, but grew exponentially in the 1970s, when health and physical conditioning for men became both a mania and big business. Movies like *Pumping Iron* (1977) captured this newfound fascination with developing the male form, and its star, Arnold Schwarzenegger (who, not coincidentally, would later go on to play Conan in the film series), became legendry for his bulk. However, much (if not all) of the media surrounding this new version of the male form was designed for the commercial consumption of *men*, not women. Men's fitness magazines, peplum movies, weightlifting competitions — all were designed to attract male capital and male viewers, helping to re-define notions of male beauty for a male perspective and male gaze, not female. Yet if the hyper-developed male corpus is designed to reflect some social notion of male beauty — if, at least, those who see the form desire to attain or possess it — then what does this mean for an audience who, at its construction, is of the same gender as those objects of the gaze? Lawrence R. Schehr, writing on the fashioning of beauty in men, suggests that masculine beauty is ultimately less objective than demonstrative:

> The attributes of masculine beauty, whatever they may be, are invariably translated into the world of the manly, into what is impressive. Again, the English language gets it right: a man is handsome just as a sum of money can be handsome: bigger *is* better. These attributes become cathected onto the body of power so that masculine beauty, instead of being part of an aesthetic, becomes the index of a reinforced ideology of power and phallocentrism [79].

According to Schehr, muscles are attractive because they act as signifiers of larger attributes the male also possesses: wealth, power, status, all of which are associated with, and centered around, the concept of the phallus. For Schehr, the phallus acts as the ultimate symbol of masculinity and virility. One of the reasons the phallus is continually hidden from the outside world, or represented only symbolically, is that its value is diminished if it is exposed. Naomi Schor writes, "To subject the penis to representation is to strip the phallus of its empowering veil, for ... while the phallus can be said to draw its symbolic power from the *visibility of the penis*, phallic power derives precisely from *the phallus's inaccessibility to representation*" (112). Maleness, then — in all its resplendent, "manly" glory — both suggests and represents the imagined phallus, the literal and emblematic embodiment of the essence of male, or of Schwegner's "maleness of experience." The phallus attracts the viewer through its absence, or, rather, through the suggestion of its presence; trappings of masculinity suggest phallic power, entombing and enmeshing notions of male beauty into what is both promised and unseen.

Hyper-developed musculature, however, does not necessarily equate to the phallus; certainly not in He-Man who, unsurprisingly, was not designed anatomically correct. Beneath his shaggy underwear, he is as ineffectual as Barbie, with her molded over vagina, the only difference between them being the size of their missing genitalia. Interestingly enough, the upper raiment of Masters of the Universe figures were designed to come off; the chest plates and faux leather criss-cross bands were removable, allowing for a full appreciation of the developed torso. The shaggy underwear, however, remained firmly in place. This may suggest a conscious presentation of the phallic mystery, but the reality is that no one expected He-Man to be any more intact than Barbie; though his muscles suggest performativity, "down there," he is no man at all.

This would seem counterindicative of gay clone culture, which, as Levine notes, was focused on the "four D's: disco, drugs, dish, and dick" (70). Levine talks extensively of the sexual "roles" found within close culture, using the common labels of "top," "bottom," and "versatile" to suggest "preference" in intercourse (97). In these interactions, the phallus is cynosure to the exchange. Levine goes out of his way to point out that there is no correlation between body mass and sexual role: "many muscular, manly, or hung men were 'bottoms'" (97). This juxtaposes uncomfortably with his description of "versatile" men, however, who "with more masculine, muscular, or endowed men ... become 'bottoms'" (97). In many ways, Levine here falls into his own stereotype, the "failed masculinity" that Butler notes above, and suggests that the more muscles a man has, the more likely he is to take on the role of "top," even though Levine himself says that muscles are no predictor to sexual role moments later. John Preston takes issue with this. In his seminal 1983 novel *Mr. Benson* (which was based on an earlier story of the same name he published in 1978), Preston indicates that one frustration with clone culture is the utter sameness of the individuals contained within it, even in their sexual behavior. The narrator of much of the novel, Jamie, starts by telling the reader, "I had just been cloned and found out that a mustache, a cute ass, and a smile with keys on the right would find me a daddy for the night" (2). Telling the novel in flashback, he chides himself for believing that "when I first came out, I thought *butch* was an insurance salesman in a flannel shirt" (1). When Larry, Jamie's epitome of the male clone referenced in the epigraph to this section, turns out to be a bottom, Jamie laments, "I had never been so disappointed in my whole life" (36). Soon enough, Jamie rejects clone culture: "Weren't there any real *men* left in New York City?" (42, emphasis mine).

Jamie's idea of a *real* man is one for whom his phallus is the locus of his own power, not a symbol of it but an actual source of authority and command. In Jamie's world, the phallus is a literal object of worship; quickly, it becomes the cynosure, the sole reason, of his own existence: "I used to think men in leather and Levis were hot numbers only for weekends. I thought life was really about working, a career, making it after a week climbing the ladder of success. Now I know that success is Mr. Benson's cock, however and whenever I can get it" (1–2). Tellingly, Preston avoids any overt description of Mr. Benson's physique; Jamie considers him "handsome," but never directly describes him (3). Of course not; for Jamie, there is nothing beyond the phallus. Once he rejects clone culture, the body is no longer a text for him to read; for him, there is only the penis.

In moving his character beyond the body, Preston rejects the clone reading of the male physique as signifying masculinity. To him, the fashioned physique is more a sign of weakness, an indication of a detriment, of something missing, seemingly focused on the phallus. Rather than suggesting the phallus or hiding the phallus, the enlarged male form reveals it, and it is lacking. Schwenger suggests that within such exaggerated masculinities there is "a despairing sense of sterility beneath the richness and the vigor" of the hyper-developed muscular form (631). In this reading, slavish devotion to the body suggests a conscious desire to fashion a subjectivity that insinuates phallic power, but, in reality, obfuscates the truth. This hearkens back to Butler's assertion that the body is a performative signifier, and, in this case, what is posited is only a simulacrum — and not a reality — of phallic authority. Adam Isaiah Green argues that "the gay clone ... [is] *more* masculine than his heterosexual counterparts" (535). This overt devotion to masculinity was fashioned as a rejoinder to homophobic constructions of gay masculinity, which until that time had been viewed as an aspect of Butler's "failed gender." The cloned nature of this constructed masculinity, however, suggests that the "failed" view of "gender" was shared by the gay clone himself, not as an internalized form of homophobia but rather as a redaction of and reaction to heteronormative social mores. This enabled the subculture to create a specific construction of masculinity, based on tropes that existed, and to exaggerate them. However, this also suggests not only a predisposition towards the phallus, but also a natural anxiety of it: anxiety because of the abject yearning for the phallus and anxiety created by wondering how heterosexual men would judge the masculinity of the male who desired it. Thus the phallus as a source of anxiety is, in many ways, overtly reflected by clone culture. Embracing the male physique, while still sexually charged, allows for the successful transaction of the male gaze, heterogendered (through admiration) and homogendered (through desire). Yet making the phallus the object of the male gaze renders the gaze untenable for heteronormative society; this creates further tension in the gazing male. Thus clone culture shifts emphasis away from the phallus and towards the body itself. As with He-Man and the other Masters of the Universe, all are allowed to openly admire the physique of the clone; and yet, when we pull back his "shaggy underwear," we wonder if the clone is as lacking in that department as the doll.

Masters of the Masculine Universe: Obtunding the Hyper-Muscular Form

> *If the body could achieve perfect, non-individual harmony then it would be possible to shut individuality up for ever in close confinement.*
> — *Yukio Mishima*

In clone culture, the male form can be seen as a source of erotic desire, but rarely is it sexualized. While the sexuality of the bearer is signified by his musculature and other cultural markers, sex remains obscured, if not outright hidden. At its heart, Levine's "'butch' rhetoric" rejects outright sexualization, at least in public; in aping the trappings of traditional heteronormative men, gay clones create a type of masculine "bluff" when it comes to their sexual behavior. Though they act as overtly "gay" as their culture allows, by mimicking heterosexual males and rejecting the traditional, more "sissified" roles previously allotted to gay men by society, gay clones hide their own sexuality in favor of outward displays of masculinity. Levine notes this by describing the tension that existed between the gay clone and the "feminized" homosexual. He writes: "To the feminized homosexual, what mattered was that one was a homosexual who happened (however inconveniently) to be a man. To the butch [clone], by contrast, one was a gay man — neither was inconvenient, and both were necessary to create gay male identity" (57). Levine here is correct in asserting that clones did not hide the nature of their sexuality; however, whereas the "feminized" homosexual was a constant reminder to heteronormative society of his sexuality (and of male-male sexual behaviors) through his inability to obscure his "feminized" self, the clone's adoption of stereotypically heteronormative masculine behaviors suggests more than a fleeting notion at the construct of "passing." This is not to say that gay clones were interested in being perceived of as "straight"; however, by choosing to adapt the mannerisms and modes of heterosexual men, the appearance and behavior of the gay clone made his sexuality "less" obvious to heteronormative society while making it "more" obvious to those within the subculture itself. Thus camouflaged, the gay clone remained perhaps more palatable to dominant heterosexual society, if only because he recognized constructions of social behaviors within the subculture that he had created. Clone culture thus remains in some ways, on its surface, a very homoerotic world, though not as homo*sexual* as other gay subcommunities, such as the leather world Jamie discovers in *Mr. Benson*, or even the "feminized" homosexual Levine disparages in his study.

Homoeroticism is not lost on *He-Man* and other sword-and-sandal sagas; any work parading that much naked or nearly-naked man flesh is sure to be aware of the self-referents it is making. Yet most works in this genre are highly heteronormative; the presence of women as objects of sexual desire ensures that no disquieting questions are asked about the barbarian sexual identity. Conan had his lovers; their presence not only demonstrated his virility, but also his dominance:

> She was untamed as a desert wind, supple and dangerous as a she-panther. She came close to him, heedless of his great blade, dripping with blood of her warriors. Her supple thigh brushed against it, so close she came to the tall warrior. Her red lips parted as she stared up into his somber menacing eyes.
> "Who are you?" she demanded. "By Ishtar, I have never seen your like, though I

have ranged the sea from the coasts of Zingara to the fires of the ultimate south. Whence come you?"

"From Argos," he answered shortly, alert for treachery. Let her slim hand move toward the jeweled dagger in her girdle, and a buffet of his open hand would stretch her senseless on the deck. Yet in his heart he did not fear; he had held too many women, civilized or barbaric, in his iron–Chewed arms, not to recognize the light that burned in the eyes of this one.

"You are no soft Hyborian!" she exclaimed. "You are fierce and hard as a gray wolf. Those eyes were never dimmed by city lights; those thews were never softened by life amid marble walls."

"I am Conan, a Cimmerian," he answered.

To the people of the exotic climes, the north was a hazy half-mythical realm, peopled with ferocious blue-eyed giants who occasionally descended from their icy fastnesses with torch and sword. Their raids had never taken them as far south as Shem, and this daughter of Shem made no distinction between AEsir, Vanir or Cimmerian. With the unerring instinct of the elemental feminine, she knew she had found her lover, and his race meant naught, save as it invested him with the glamor of far lands.

"And I am Belit," she cried, as one might say, "I am queen."

"Look at me, Conan!" She threw wide her arms. "I am Belit, queen of the black coast. Oh, tiger of the North, you are cold as the snowy mountains which bred you. Take me and crush me with your fierce love!" [Howard, "Queen"].

In the story "Queen of the Black Coast," Conan's love for Belit fuels his rancor against the winged creature that kills her, causing him in turn to destroy the monster. The loss of a man's love is a common trope that can often impel the peplum adventurer to act; both Maximus in *Gladiator* and Spartacus in *Spartacus: Blood and Sand* fight their epic arena battles for the love and honor of their missing spouses, in case we had any doubts about the orientations hidden beneath their leather chest straps and peplumic skirts.

The juvenilization of the sword and sandal epic, however, creates the interesting sub-affect of bringing forth the homoerotic nature of the genre. Juvenilizing the peplum means reducing both the levels of violence and sexuality inherent to the genre; for such a testosterone-fueled narrative, then, eliminating the female sexualized presence creates a condition wherein the eroticized masculine form and traditional levels of sexual energy must be channeled elsewhere. The end result is often a homosocial and at-times homoerotic male grouping, wherein play and practice for battle replace the more aggressive actual combat, thievery, and sexuality that abound in sword and sandal epics. He-Man is a prime example of this, as Anderson notes:

> The best part about rewatching He-Man, after the initial nostalgia-burst, was tracking the show's hilarious accidental homo-eroticism — an aspect I missed completely as a first-grader. In the ever-growing lineup of "outed" classic superheroes, He-Man might be the easiest target of all. It's almost too easy: Prince Adam, He-Man's alter ego, is a ripped Nordic pageboy with blinding teeth and sharply waxed eyebrows who spends lazy afternoons pampering his timid pet cat; he wears lavender stretch pants, furry purple Ugg boots, and a sleeveless pink blouse that clings like saran wrap to his pecs. To become He-Man, Adam harnesses what he calls "fabulous secret

powers": His clothes fall off, his voice drops a full octave, his skin turns from vanilla to nut brown, his giant sword starts gushing energy, and he adopts a name so absurdly masculine it's redundant. Next, he typically runs around seizing space-wands with glowing knobs and fabulously straddling giant rockets. He hangs out with people called Fisto and Ram Man, and they all exchange wink-wink nudge-nudge dialogue: "I'd like to hear more about this hooded seed-man of yours!" "I feel the bony finger of Skeletor!" "Your assistance is required on Snake Mountain!" Once you start thinking along these lines, it's impossible to stop [Anderson].

In Anderson's critique, both Prince Adam's sartorial choices and musculature act as a signifier of a "hidden" sexual desire. As with the gay clone, for He-Man, clothing and physique are designed to relay a message that otherwise can not be sent. In the late 1970s gay men were still socially and legally ostracized in most communities; though clone culture existed in particular ghettoized urban areas, where being openly gay was safer (though not normative), as I have already noted, clone guise and clone physique, derived from traditional aspects of the dominant heteronormative culture, allowed the gay clone both to advertise and to camouflage his self and his intent.

Anderson concludes that He-Man's homoerotic underpinnings reveal "a prime example of how easily an extreme fantasy of masculinity can circle back to become its opposite" (Anderson). To Anderson, homosexuality exists as Butler's failed heterosexuality, its literal "opposite"; too much masculinity, in Anderson's mind, becomes oppositional to the "real" thing, as if He-Man and gay clones are trying too hard to be something they are so obviously not. Yet Anderson here is ignoring both the genesis of each figure and the replicable nature of his masculinity. He-Man and gay clones were not fashioned in opposition to, or as exaggerations of, existing late 1970s tropes of heteronormative masculinity (which, as Butler has pointed out, are only socially fabricated "performances" anyway) (237). Rather, both are fashioned from earlier, more traditional forms of masculine behavior:

> In the traditional male role, masculinity is validated ultimately by individual physical strength and aggression. Men are generally expected not to be emotionally sensitive to others or emotionally expressive or self-revealing, particularly of feelings of vulnerability or weakness. Paradoxically, anger and certain other impulsive emotional expressions, particularly toward other males, are expected or tolerated.
> The traditional male prefers the company of men to the company of women and experiences other men as the primary validator of his masculinity. Though bonds of friendship among men are not necessarily emotionally intimate, they are often strong. In the traditional male role in marital and other relationships, women are seen as necessary for sex and for bearing children, but these relationships are not expected to be emotionally intimate or romantic, and often seem only pragmatic arrangements of convenience. The traditional male expects women to acknowledge and defer to his authority. There is also a strong adherence to a sexual double standard that views sexual freedom as appropriate for men but not women [Pleck 140–141].

Joseph Pleck argues that by the late 1970s a "modern male role" has developed alongside this more traditional mode, not fully supplanting but altering the ways in which society views the role of men within its social milieu. In this new "modern male role" masculinity is validated "by economic achievement and organizational or bureaucratic power" (141). In this instance, "the modern male values the capacity for emotional sensitivity and self expression" (141). As regards to the opposite gender, "women, rather than men, are experienced as the primary validators of masculinity" (141). What Pleck is describing here is a wholly paradigmatic shift in social constructions of masculinity; however, both He-Man and clone culture are dependent upon older methodologies of masculine fashioning. Thus clones are not the opposite of heterosexuals, and He-Man is not "gay"; it is just that their notions of masculinity are out of date.

Socioculturally speaking, both heterosexual and homosexual men are raised in the same way; in essence, they both receive the same fashioning as impressionable youth. Levine raises this point when he writes, "Gay men undergo essentially the same enculturation as heterosexual males" (15). Green agrees: "Hegemonic constructions of masculinity are internalized in early phases of socialization that comes to structure the erotic practices and ideation of straight *and* gay men" (534). Thus at some point gay clones, if they are perceived to be different from the heterosexual men around them in ways beyond sexual activity, must veer off from this social ideation. This difference occurs because clones make the decision to fashion themselves against and along more traditional forms of masculine behavior; their ideas of masculinity were thus not oppositional to the heterosexuality of the day, but rather derived from older forms of the same construct. He-Man works in the same mode; once the wholesome values of juvenile popular culture are imbued with the sword and sandal genre, the character reflects a type of extreme manliness that hearkens back to a prior generation. In both instances, the group nature of clone culture and the Masters of the Universe microcosm works to emphasize and escalate this point. According to Jay C. Wade and Chris Brittain-Powell, men are "dependent on a male reference group for [their] gender role self-concept" (323). The authors continue: "The gender role self-concept is one's self-concept with regard to gender roles and includes one's gender-related attributes, attitudes, and behaviors" (323). As such, "males identify with other males to the extent that they feel psychological relatedness to a particular group of males or to all males" (324). This reflects Pleck's outmoded construct of masculinity being largely validated by other men; the "modern" male finds his masculinity validated by women, but for the gay clone and for He-Man these women, for the most part, do not exist, and their brawny physiques exist to be gazed at and admired by men.[3]

Such group-think reflects what Wade and Brittain-Powell refer to as "Reference Group Dependent status," which "is characterized by feelings of psychological relatedness to some males and not others, a conformist ego identity, dependence on a male reference group for one's gender role self-concept, and thereby rigid adherence to gender roles, stereotyped attitudes, and limited or restricted gender role experiences and behaviors" (325). In such a group, a man would base his construct of masculinity as Pleck suggests the "traditional" male did — on perceptions, instructions (both conscious and subconscious), and validations received from other men:

> He would define his maleness or masculinity based on other like males or his peer group, which would tend to be homogeneous in character. For example, such feelings and beliefs may be present in a man who is a member of a college fraternity, who will only socialize and be friends with other men in his fraternity, and incorporates the fraternity's image of masculinity as his own; or a man who has sexist and prejudicial attitudes because this is what he has learned from other males in his environment with whom he identifies, and to have such attitudes is consistent with being a part of "the group" [Wade and Brittain-Powell 325].

In both the Masters of the Universe toy line and gay clone culture, group mentality is most obviously displayed in the construction of the male form. Gay clones strive to create a form that is both idealized and homogenized; He-Man literally shares his body with the other actions figures in his line. This reciprocal nature of the male form has an interesting effect: it works to lessen the impact of the physique overall. In some ways, this is through sheer numbers; the more something extraordinary is seen, the more common it becomes, and thus the more ordinary it also becomes. This commonality of form also lessens the value of the physique: can He-Man truly be "the most powerful man in the universe" if every other male toy in his line, even those not noted for their physical prowess, reflect the same dimensions? Are we truly to believe the "most powerful man in the universe" has the same bicep size as his chief foe, whose underdevelopment is so emphasized that his face is literally all bone (and no skin)? Howard was always careful to ensure that Conan had few equals in size and strength in his world; indeed, in his works he is prudent to ensure that no human being is ever described as being more powerful than Conan, though a few may be taller or of larger bulk. For Howard, Conan's strength is unique, and it thus becomes an important part of his fashioning. Conan's character definition begins with his strength; that is why only he is allowed it.

Unlike Conan, a dynamic figure with other facets to his characterization, He-Man's entire identity is based on his strength; he exists only when summoned by his alter ego Prince Adam, and only to use his strength to repel the forces of evil. The fact that He-Man must share his physique with the other Masters thus not only works to negate his uniqueness, but also his entire fashioned identity. The same is true of the clone; in embracing the group identity, the individual is subsumed. As Reddy notes, gay masculinity is a response to heterosexuality and "heterosexism" (65). He continues: "Gay masculinity challenges the dominant view of masculinity not by opposing it, but in the way it allows gay people to mediate relationships between individuals" (70). Yet in its desire to allow for social mediation between individuals, clone culture denies the individual being the right of his own individuality. In many ways, denying the phallus denies not only the cynosure of the male sexual act (whether heterosexual, homosexual, or masturbatory), but also the individuality of the male himself. The body can be fashioned; the penis (before the advent of recent surgeries) cannot. Thus we have clones, who Green so aptly labels "cookie-cutter masculine style and affect" (534). The appellative "clone" is no accident here; they are easily replicable, one form — one man — swiftly transmuted into another. Like the Masters of the Universe figures, they share but one or two molds; interchangeable, they abjure individuality, embracing a group mentality and all that it entails while eschewing individuality and the self-fashioning that must result from acknowledging one's own nature. Yukio Mishima's line quoted in the epigraph to this section becomes relevant here: sameness disrupts individuality and identity. Achieving a group ethos can come at the loss of the singular fashioned entity; in the world of both He-Man and the gay clone, as Mishima notes, achieving the perfect male form has come at the loss of individuality. Thus the lack of individuality among these physiques — the very sameness of these forms — obtunds their meaning. Both their power and potential are lessened as their numbers grow. In sharing his musculature with the other Masters of the Universe, in literally sharing his parts, He-Man diminishes his own sense of masterfulness; rather than being viewed as a singular creation, as a whole entity, He-Man is rendered into a gazing subject that is ultimately only about his parts. Far from unique, his body parts are (literally) interchangeable with the other men in his world. This makes him less a man and more a construction whose building materials happen to be muscles. Gay clones suffer from a similar fate; in taking on the trappings of "traditional" masculinity, they ultimately displace notions not only of their individuality but even their own sexual presentation. In becoming more overly erotic, they become more covertly sexual. In fashioning such a group mentality and physicality for themselves, they have worked to both fetishize and diminish the value of their own forms.

Hall writes that the body can be a "symbolic replica of the social forces at play" during the period of its fashioning and construction (35). In this case, both the Masters of the Universe toys and gay clone culture represent a reaction to changing tropes of masculinity and masculine signification. Fascinatingly, despite their demonstrative performativity of man and muscle, they are ultimately both conservative in their representation of old-fashioned and outmoded models of what it is to be a man. And yet both He-Man and the gay clone present rich depictions of the male form in similar and quite different ways. In representing and presenting the hyperdeveloped male physique as they did, both create new notions of masculinity out of old forms and traditional ideas. In crafting such exaggeratedly muscular physiques, both alleviate concerns over the male homogendered gaze and the representation of the phallus as well. In fashioning such replicable bodies, both the Masters of the Universe and gay clone culture diminish the threat of the erotic male by making him more common and relieving heteronormative anxieties over the development and beauty of the male itself. In his study, Levine, paraphrasing Marx, writes as a type of conclusion, "We may create our own identities ... but we do not do it just as we please, but rather we do it from the materials we find around us" (56). For both He-Man and the other Masters of the Universe and gay clone culture, those "materials" just happen to be muscles, and while those muscles may become the cynosure of each groups' individual worlds (for good and for ill), there is no denying the attraction to what Schehr has already pointed out: when it comes to muscles or masculinity, bigger *is* better.

NOTES

1. Later figures occasionally had a full plastic chest plate that did cover their entire torso and upper body; however, these plates were easily removed, thus revealing the toy in its full, thewy glory.
2. The gaze, of course, can have as its objective a sensation other than desire; for example, the object of the gaze can be grotesque, in which case the gaze acts as a mirror of fascination or revulsion (or both). However, critics have long noted that these types of gaze differs from the limited type of gaze being discussed here and, for the purposes of this essay, is not currently under consideration.
3. While these groups are male-centric, they work as units to aid individuals to conform to groupthink and to reflect Pleck's "modern male role."

WORKS CITED

Anderson, Sam. "By the Power of Grayskull! Rediscovering the Heroic Cartoon Beefcake of My Youth." *Slate* 11 May 2006. < www.slate.com/id/2141626/>.
Atwood, Margaret. "Alien Territory." In *Good Bones*. Toronto: Coach House, 1992.
Bondanella, Peter. *A History of Italian Cinema*. New York: Continuum, 2009.
Butler, Judith. *Bodies That Matter: On the Discursive Limits of "Sex."* New York: Routledge, 1993.
Fan, J., W. Dai, F. Lui, and J. Wu. "Visual Perception of Male Body Attractiveness." *Proceedings: Biological Sciences* 272.1260 (2005): 219–226.
Green, Adam Isaiah. "Gay But Not Queer: Toward a Post-Queer Study of Sexuality." *Theory and Society* 31.4 (2002): 521–545.
Hall, Karen J. "A Soldier's Body: GI Joe, Hasbro's Great American Hero, and the Symptoms of Empire." *The Journal of Popular Culture* 38.1 (2004): 34–54.
Howard, Robert E. "The Hour of the Dragon." In *The Bloody Crown of Conan*. New York: Del Rey, 2005.
_____. "Queen of the Black Coast." *Weird Tales*. May 1934. Online. Many Books. <manybooks.net/titles/howardrother08Queen_of_the_Black_Coast.html>
Levine, Martin P. *Gay Macho: The Life and Death of the Homosexual Clone*. New York: New York University Press, 1998.
Mishima, Yukio. *Sun and Steel*. Trans. John Bester. Tokyo: Kodansha, 1970.
Pleck, Joseph H. *The Myth of Masculinity*. Cambridge: MIT Press, 1981.
Preston, John. *Mr. Benson*. San Francisco: Cleis Press, 1983.
Reddy, Vasu. "Negotiating Gay Masculinities." *Agenda* 37 (1998): 65–70.
Schehr, Lawrence R. *Parts of an Andrology: On Representations of Men's Bodies*. Stanford: Stanford Universtiy Press, 1997.
Schor, Naomi. *Bad Objects: Essays Popular and Unpopular*. Durham: Duke University Press, 1995.

Schwenger, Peter. "The Masculine Mode." *Critical Inquiry* 5.4 (1979): 621–633.
Sheffield, Tricia. "Cover Girls: Toward a Theory of Divine Female Embodiment." *Journal of Religion & Society* 4 (2002): 1–16.
Wade, Jay C., and Chris Brittain-Powell. "Male Reference Group Identity Dependence: Support for Construct Validity." *Sex Roles* 43.5/6 (2000): 323–340.

Developments in Peplum Filmmaking
Disney's Hercules

CHRIS PALLANT

Many of the trailers released to promote the recent re-imagining of *Clash of the Titans* (2010) made ubiquitous use of one sequence from the movie in particular: the giant scorpion battle. While its inclusion suggested a degree of continuity with the 1981 movie of the same name, which also saw Perseus battle a nest of scorpions, it also revealed that animation would again play a central role in helping to realize the movie's mythological world.[1] In the 1981 version, Ray Harryhausen's stop-motion animation provided the basis for much of the fantastical action, while in the 2010 edition, computer generated animation proffers the technological bridge into more fantastical realms. In fact, the recent sword and sandal renaissance could not have scaled such epic visual heights had it not been for the contributions made by the many legions of CGI special effects animators. *Gladiator* (2000), *Alexander* (2004), *Troy* (2004), *Kingdom of Heaven* (2005), and *300* (2006) all rely on a multitude of animated components such as synthetic performers, enhanced locations, and three-dimensionally modeled monsters to provide much of their spectacle.

While the use of computer generated animation in these movies is hardly surprising, what is unexpected is the lack of extant scholarship directly concerned with this intersection between animation and sword and sandal filmmaking. Animation shares a longstanding relationship with sword and sandal filmmaking, with Harryhausen being perhaps the most prominent figure in this respect, having produced the iconic stop-motion set-pieces for *The 7th Voyage of Sinbad* (1958), *Jason and the Argonauts* (1963), *The Golden Voyage of Sinbad* (1974), *Sinbad and the Eye of the Tiger* (1977), and the original *Clash of the Titans*. Paul Wells rightly asserts that none of the movies "Harryhausen was instrumental in creating were 'star' vehicles, nor did they enjoy the possibility of being sought after because of their directorial credit" (*Genre and Authorship*

92). Rather, they were "vehicles for the spectacle Harryhausen created" (*Genre and Authorship* 92). This, Wells argues,

> elevates Harryhausen above the normal rigours of live-action film-making, and out of the ghetto of an effects tradition that often refuses to acknowledge the primacy of animation as a form at its heart; a situation echoed in contemporary "blockbuster" film-making where much of the huge spectacle is in some way facilitated by traditional, and more progressive, applications in animation [*Genre and Authorship* 94].

Harryhausen's involvement with sword and sandal filmmaking, however, can be best attributed to the simple but undeniable fact that he was a master of the special affect. In his day, Harryhausen's stop-motion animation was cutting edge, advanced for the time and refined in its ability to create fantastic beasts and beings on the screen. His connection to sword and sandal films is almost accidental then, since he achieved peak productivity and fame during the 1950s and 1960s, when the sword and sandal genre also exploded in popularity.

Creating worlds is key to understanding the role of animation in an affects-driven movie, including those films for which Harryhausen is most famous. Though sword and sandal films are not necessarily as dependent upon the creation of a wholly differentiated terrene as, say, fantasy films are, the use of animation to fabricate and fashion amazing creatures and fantastic feats within the fabric of the sword and sandal film is well documented. In this regard, animation allows the viewer to transcend the dictates of filmic reality, which, in turn, creates the conditions in which the unnatural strongman (usually played by an actor who already possesses an unnatural — or, to be more precise, *hyper*natural — physique) can perform his various acts of astonishing muscularity. Thus animation is the conduit through which reality can be suspended just enough to create the onscreen conditions necessary for the development and function of the strongman figure and the genre as a whole.

Understanding the role of animation in the sword and sandal film is key to understanding the inherent possibilities of the films themselves to fashion figures and schemas that are, quite literally, otherworldly. Thus it stands to reason that feature-length animation would offer filmmakers the most potential and diverse range for fashioning sword and sandal movies. This has not, however, quite proven to be the case. Although a handful of recent feature-length animated productions, such as *Prince of Egypt* (1998), *Joseph: King of Dreams* (2000), and *Ben Hur* (2003), have engaged with aspects of the sword and sandal tradition, their progenitors remain biblical narratives, and their tradition owes more to *The Ten Commandments* (1956) than to *Spartacus* (1960) or even the original *Ben Hur* (1959). In shorter, serialized formats, *He-Man and the Masters of the Universe* (1983–85) and *Hercules: The Animated Series* (1998–1999) represent the longest running and most consistent extensions of the sword and sandal tradition for children's television, though each is—for various reasons—somewhat far removed from the peplumic tradition. Some themed Looney Tunes shorts, such as *Roman Legion-Hare* (1955) and *See Ya Later Gladiator*

(1968), have likewise made occasional use of the genre's identificatory framework. Nonetheless, there has been little opportunity, especially recently, for this genre to develop within feature–length animation. Despite the inherent possibilities feature–length animation proffers the sword and sandal movie, and despite the recent growth, popularity, and seeming box office reliability of the contemporary sword and sandal film, the genre remains largely underdeveloped in this form.

In this context, the 1997 Walt Disney animated feature *Hercules* represents the clearest example of sword and sandal animated filmmaking. Interestingly, unlike many of its animated predecessors, *Hercules* constitutes a surprising renewal of the peplumic filmmaking tradition, embracing both its sword and sandal roots and many key peplumic conventions, including a focus on body culture and the use of camp in interpreting varying aspects of the classical Herculean legend. Despite this use of peplumic motif, or, more precisely, because the film so readily embraces the sword and sandal tradition, a tension is created within the film, a tension focused on the intersection of the dueling genres—Disney animated feature and sword and sandal movie—that inform the making and shaping of *Hercules*. This is an important tension, given the infrequency with which sword and sandal filmmaking, particularly in the peplum tradition, merges with other genres, but it is a tension that the film ultimately leaves unresolved. This generic opposition will ultimately manifest in the film's spin-off, *Hercules: The Animated Series*, whose use of generic hybridity will ultimately inhibit the extension of peplumic tradition found in the original film. Nonetheless, *Hercules* remains a significant achievement in both peplumic and animated filmmaking, an initial foray between two worlds and conventions that seem ideally configured for the other and yet, somehow, have never quite managed to come together in a manner that ultimately proves fruitful to both genres.

Hercules: *Happily After "Ever After"*

For many, the Disney name signifies a realm of children's entertainment predicated on the manufacture of fantasy. Furthermore, this body of work is likely perceived as being aesthetically inflexible, operating, for the most part, within a hyperrealist register that privileges a form of "realism" dependent upon "verisimilitude in ... characters, contexts and narratives" (Wells *Understanding Animation* 23). In fact, Disney's hyperrealism is frequently seen "as the yardstick by which other kinds of animation may be measured for its relative degree of 'realism'" (Wells *Understanding Animation* 25). This aesthetic condition, coupled with the fact that the protagonists in Disney's animated features are, with little deviation, pre-adolescent innocent children, heroines, or anthropomorphic alternatives, has established a generic paradigm that is taken to represent Disney animation *in toto*. However, Disney animation is far more heterogeneous than popular notions of Disney allow for, and *Hercules*, with its peplumic subject matter, serves as a useful illustration of this.[2]

Hercules, the thirty-fifth animated feature to be released theatrically by Disney, chronicles the eponymous hero's early years, relating how, as part of Hades' plot to usurp Zeus (king of the gods and father to Hercules), the young protagonist is rendered mortal. Early in the film, however, Zeus visits his son, telling him that if he can become a true hero he will regain his godly immortality. After a series of failed attempts to assassinate Hercules (unsuccessful because the youthful protagonist has retained his godly strength), Hades is ultimately thwarted by Hercules' selflessness, with Hercules regaining his godly status after sacrificing himself to save the woman he loves.

Released towards the end of Disney's 1990s renaissance, *Hercules* followed a period of box office unpredictability. After *Beauty and the Beast* and *Aladdin* had established a positive trend, taking $351 million and $504 million in worldwide receipts respectively, *The Lion King* became the high watermark of hand-drawn animation, grossing an unprecedented $768 million worldwide.[3] Impressively, it is also estimated that in the years since its release, *The Lion King* has "generated over $1 billion in profits" (Tengler 209). The two movies that followed immediately after *The Lion King*, however, returned much lower box office grosses, with *Pocahontas* achieving $346 million worldwide and *The Hunchback of Notre Dame* $325 million. Witnessing this comparative downturn during a period of growing competition within western animation, Disney's executives would certainly have had cause to re-evaluate the studio's production strategy.

In 1995 Pixar released *Toy Story*, providing a preview of what would quickly become the dominant form of mainstream animation. At the time of its release though, it was "too early to take seriously the possibility that the business landscape for Disney had just undergone a momentous change — that Disney might have unwittingly opened itself up to meaningful competition in animated feature films" (Price 156). Ultimately, writes David A. Price, "Disney still owned feature animation. It had always been so. It would always be so. Disney would dominate computer animation as it had dominated cel animation. Pixar would be the eager-to-please contractor. The stars and the planets seemed to be set in their courses" (156). Also at that time, Disney's executives would have been aware that Twentieth Century–Fox's animation department was developing a feature length hand-drawn animation film, *Anastasia*, that would likely debut in the same calendar year as *Hercules*. Furthermore, two former Disney animators, Don Bluth and Gary Goldman, had been installed as directors for *Anastasia*, indicating that Fox's project would most likely draw on traditional Disney animation both stylistically and thematically.[4] To what extent this competition influenced the immediate trajectory of Disney feature animation is impossible to say, but it is clear that the studio, with the production of *Hercules*, sought to produce something that would extend beyond the limits of conventional Disney filmmaking. Through its aesthetic progressiveness, and, decisively, its distinctive use of peplum convention, *Hercules* did just that.

Like *Aladdin*, *Hercules* actively acknowledged and embraced the "gaze" in a way that Disney had not done since its earliest cartoons (Wells *Animation and America* 110). This is most noticeable during, and immediately after, the "Zero to Hero" musical montage sequence. Disney's musical sequences typically provide an opportunity for the otherwise restricted animators to embrace their creative impulses, though this artistic freedom is usually framed in such a way as to legitimize any departure from the established story world. *Dumbo* was the first Disney animated feature to contain such a sequence, with the "Pink Elephants on Parade" number diverging stylistically from the established story world. Crucially, however, Dumbo is seen to unknowingly ingest alcohol, thus framing the "Pink Elephants" interlude as a drunken hallucination. During the "Zero to Hero" montage, visually, several anachronistic references are made to elements of contemporary material culture, such as American Express, branded soft drinks, Nike Air sports shoes, and, self-reflexively, Disney's own commercial activities, in the shape of a "Hercules Store" filed with Hercules merchandise. However, instead of being confined to the musical sequence—which, by virtue of its gospel rhythm played against the film's ancient Greek setting, is also acoustically anachronistic—these visual anachronisms spill comically into the surrounding story world.

An example of this can be seen when, after a failed attempt on Hercules' life, Hades smashes a vase sporting his nemesis' image, before turning to Pain, one of his minions, to issue an order. Hades is immediately distracted, though, when he notices that Pain is wearing a pair of "Herc Air" sandals. As Hades is berating Pain for his choice of footwear, a slurping noise interrupts him midsentence. A cut reveals Panic, another of Hades' minions, finishing what resembles a Hercules-brand soft drink. This "loosening" of the Disney text, which has become increasingly pronounced in the years following *Hercules*' release, acknowledges, according to Wells, "the increasing prominence of the cartoonal form and a greater trust in the public's ability to embrace its intrinsic vocabulary" (*Genre and Authorship* 110). Examples of this tendency are visible throughout *Hercules*, revealing the extent to which the film's creative team sought to push the boundaries of conventional Disney storytelling. In addition to this, *Hercules* stands out in the Disney canon, not only through its self-reflexivity, but also because it unexpectedly, yet quite literally, re-animated the peplum filmmaking tradition.

The Body: Regulating Signification in Hercules

Robert A. Rushing postulates that "one might plausibly define a peplum as an action-adventure film set in mythological antiquity centered on a spectacular (and frequently eroticized) male body" (241). Although Ron Clements and John Musker, the directors of *Hercules*, embraced the muscularity of their eponymous character, they had to find a way to reconcile this sexually-connotative body image with Disney's censorial approach to sexuality and sexual maturity.[5]

The regulation of Hercules' sexuality echoes what was a common tendency in peplum filmmaking. From the outset, peplum movies featured hyper-muscular characters as a core constituent of their spectacle; however, such sizable performers risked "making the ordinary male body look defective, inferior (in short, symbolically castrated)" (Rushing 241). Taking *Cabiria* as a starting point, Rushing notes how the movie "uses the same tactic that later peplum films do to assuage the male viewer's potential anxiety: the bodybuilding hero is actually marked as a kind of neuter sex, asexual, and actually at the service of the heterosexual romances of the other characters" (241). While Hercules is not consciously depicted as a neuter sex (the main romance in the film is his), the very fact that he is depicted through animation renders him asexual. Not only does his condition as an animated product serve to strip him of any conventionally constructed sexuality, but also the very fact that he is animated potentially endows him with what Sergei Eisenstein termed "plasmaticness." Defined in the context of Disney's early animated shorts, Eisenstein saw animation's plasmaticness as a "rejection of once-and-forever allotted form, freedom from ossification, the ability to dynamically assume any form" (21). It is this hermeneutic freedom, however, that makes the interpretation of masculine bodily culture and sexuality, as depicted in *Hercules*, problematic.

Masculinity is depicted in a largely uncomplicated manner by Disney in the animated features released prior to *Hercules*. Before *Sleeping Beauty* (after which point Disney went through a phase of favoring anthropomorphized characters to humans), masculinity is defined in terms of noble chivalry and romantic appeal, typified by characters such as The Prince (*Snow White and the Seven Dwarfs*), Prince Charming (*Cinderella*), and Prince Philip (*Sleeping Beauty*). In the films of the 1990s, when human characters made a return, depictions of masculinity remain relatively simplistic, albeit with the added binary between hegemonically conservative masculine characters, such as Eric (*The Little Mermaid*), John Smith (*Pocahontas*) and Phoebus (*The Hunchback of Notre Dame*), and characters exhibiting exaggerated hyper-muscular masculinity, such as Triton (*The Little Mermaid*) and Gaston (*Beauty and the Beast*). Masculinity in these later films, despite being depicted as a social construction, nonetheless remains "shaped by and filtered through the patriarchal and conservative metanarratives that dominate the Disney culture industry" (McCallum 117).

Narratologically, *Hercules* could be seen to extend this tradition, depicting a heteronormative construction of masculinity that culminates with Hercules verbalizing his love for Meg, all of which works to contain any overt sexual signification. Visually, however, because Hercules' body is literally sculptured, reflecting the synthesis of renowned caricaturist Gerald Scarfe's conceptual artworks with Clements and Musker's Greco ambitions for the movie, the protagonist's sexuality is less easily contained. Stephen Rebello and Jane Healy note this in *The Art of Hercules: The Chaos of Creation*:

> The Greek ideal says that lines carry movement. Lines should flow, not float, should be anchored in beginnings and endings. Check out Hercules' arm muscle. To sculpt muscle definition, one enormous, flowing line — rather than many internal, short lines — suggests dynamic strength, not sinewy beefiness. A simple, powerful body shape, long and lean in the Greek ideal, denotes his great strength. Such details as the tiny swoop line that defines his knuckles, the triangles to suggest kneecaps, the curlicue that denotes a dimple complement the boldness. Similarly, his hair is confined to only a simple few Art-Deco like lines to suggest a mass of curls. These lines are influenced by the simple graphic patterns of Greek border design [143].

By adopting this style, the film creates a space in which viewers familiar with the art of ancient Greece might, rather plausibly, associate Hercules' stylized depiction with the sexualized and often homoerotic scenes that populated such artworks. This connotation clearly problematizes the conservative and heteronormative masculine sexual identity that the film's narrative seeks to establish. While this construction of masculinity clearly conflicts with Disney convention, this transgressivity, and the regulation of it, was a core ingredient in traditional peplum filmmaking.

Camp Strategies: Subtext in Hercules

Peplum filmmaking has a long history of camp interpretation. Although the hyper-muscular male body of peplum cinema is often configured so as to lack sexual significance, in many instances, it becomes a site of homoerotic tension as a product of camp identification:

> The most striking feature of the later cycle of peplum films, for modern audiences at least, is how easily the asexual bodybuilding hero— or the film as a whole —can appear to be homosexually suggestive (part of what Americans call "camp," the ironic enjoyment of bad or vulgar culture, especially as it appears to offer meaning that were probably not intended by the original authors) [Rushing 241].

Although this Sontagian interpretation, this "love of the unnatural: of artifice and exaggeration," is based on live-action peplum filmmaking, it is equally applicable to *Hercules* (Sontag 275). In *Tinker Belles and Evil Queens: The Walt Disney Company from the Inside Out*, Sean Griffin demonstrates how, by reclaiming the work of the animator, a position often obscured by the Disney studio's artistic and industrial ideologies, it is possible to reveal a camp subtext in *Hercules*. Focusing on the work of Andreas Deja, a supervising/lead animator at Disney since the early 1990s, Griffin writes: "Openly gay, Deja has announced in various interviews that his sexual orientation has had its effect on the characters he draws" (141). Besides his work on the male villains Jafar (*Aladdin*) and Scar (*The Lion King*), Deja has supervised the creation of three hypermuscular characters: Triton, Hercules, and Gaston. Although Triton, Hercules, and Gaston are designed (slightly) differently, "all three spectacularize the male body in a way rarely seen in Disney animation prior to *The Little Mermaid*" (Griffin 142). Viewing Gaston as Deja's *magnum opus* in this context, Griffin observes how "his hairy chest, flexing muscles and stomping around in boots takes on a level of absurdity, ridiculing the hyper-masculinity that Gaston represents" (142). Reacting to the "'body fascism' that became a noticeable aspect of urban gay culture by the 1980s," Deja designed Gaston to symbolize the absurd narcissism of such behavior (Griffin 142). In his study, because Griffin is primarily concerned with legitimizing the reading of homosexual subtexts within Deja's work at Disney, it is understandable that he chooses to focus his analysis on the exaggerated Gaston rather than sculptured Hercules. However, Griffin's decision to ignore the role of gym culture and bodybuilding in *Hercules* is surprising.

As noted earlier, Hercules does not start the movie as a muscle-bound hero; instead, he builds his developed physical appearance only after meeting Philoctetes ("Phil"), who Zeus refers to as "the trainer of heroes" (*Hercules*). This bodily ambition is playfully acknowledged when, immediately before Hercules enters a two-minute montage sequence that sees him transform from a lithe adolescent to a muscle-bound young adult, he poses purposefully behind an immense headless statue. Furthermore, during the montage sequence, Hercules and his companions restore a dilapidated amphitheatre (a site associated with athletic expression), after which Phil turns personal trainer to guide Hercules through step-up, press-up, and single-leg squat repetitions until the sequence concludes with an upwards tilting shot revealing a now hyper-muscular Hercules. After the tilt shot comes to rest in a medium shot of Hercules, we see Phil attempt to measure his protégé's bulging bicep, but as the muscle flexes, to Phil's surprise (and delight), it snaps his tape measure.

This visual metamorphosis not only supports Griffin's subtextual identification of a commentary on male body fascism and gym-culture in Deja's work, but it also overtly acknowledges the bodybuilding tradition that was central to the Italian peplum cycle of the late 1950s and early 1960s. The American bodybuilders featured in many of the Italian pepla were not cast because of their acting prowess; rather their appeal lay in their "size and shape, frozen in moments of maximum tension" (Dyer 167). Filmed holding "a boulder aloft, [or] in a clinch with a lion, these and many other set-ups incorporate not only the posing vocabulary of bodybuilding competitions but also the *mise-en-scènes* of such non-narrative forms as physique photography and the strongman acts" (Dyer 167). Although Hercules' progression from adolescent to muscle-bound adulthood occupies only a small role in the movie, this early chapter in his life provided the basis for a spin-off show: *Hercules: The Animated Series*.

Generic Hybridity: Hercules: The Animated Series

The mixing and hybridizing of genres was a recurrent storytelling strategy employed by the peplum filmmakers of the 1950s and 1960s. Dyer writes:

> Hercules, Maciste and the rest appear in numerous other situations, far removed from their original stories. The whole of the ancient world was drawn upon; new fantasy lands were invented; even the post-classical world was not out of the question, Maciste showing up, for instance, in thirteenth-century Asia (*Maciste alla corte del Gran Khan*), in seventeenth-century Scotland (*Maciste all'inferno*) and Russia (*Maciste alla corte dello Zar*) as well as in non–European ancient worlds, for example, Africa (*Maciste nelle miniere del re Salomone*) and Central America (*Maciste il vendicatore dei Mayas*) [166].

Furthermore, it is this theme of generic hybridity that has underpinned much of the preceding discussion, with *Hercules* representing a filmic space in which the generic traditions of Disney feature animation and the peplum both collide and combine. Although understandings of film genre are necessarily fluid, reflecting the competing and changing cinematic, cultural, and societal influences that shape their development, the practice of combining multiple genres within a single containing story-world can still prove problematic. While *Hercules* explored peplumic tropes within a Disney idiom, the film's overarching narrative helped reconcile these competing genres. When this story world was extended through *Hercules: The Animated Series*, however, the show's heightened cartoonality resulted in a series that focused on Hercules' adolescent years, one which frequently—and knowingly—disregarded the temporal and spatial parameters established in the movie.

"Hercules and the Golden Touch," for example, offers a parodic take on the James Bond franchise. First, important information is established through an introductory theme song (sung by the Muses), which mirrors the typical opening arrangement of a Bond movie. Following this, Hercules visits Icarus to acquire some essential secret agent technology, referencing Bond's reliance on Q. Additionally, Hercules can be heard to paraphrase two of Bond's most iconic phrases, first asking for grape juice, "crushed, not strained," before introducing himself to his female companion as "Lees, Hercu Lees" ("Hercules and the Golden Touch"). Although referentially divergent, "Hercules and the Golden Touch" does not provide any significant temporal or spatial reconfiguration of the landscape established in the original movie. Contrastingly, "Hercules and the Arabian Night" relocates much of the action beyond the already established Grecian space. In this episode, Jafar, after arriving in the underworld, attempts to orchestrate, with the help of Hades, the mutual destruction of their long-time adversaries: Aladdin and Hercules. Consequently, much of the resulting conflict spills over into Agrabah.

The absence of an overarching causality in *Hercules: The Animated Series*, while representative of the cartoon genre as a whole, decentralizes the peplumic tradition as one of the focusing generic paradigms within the series. Instead, referentiality and generic hybridization become the governing principles in *Hercules: The Animated Series*. On a broader level, this hybridity is perhaps most indicative of the developments that had begun to occur within the studio's animation at the turn of the millennium. During this period, with the movies *Tarzan, Fantasia 2000, The Emperor's New Groove, Atlantis: The Lost Empire, Lilo and Stitch, Treasure Planet, Brother Bear*, and *Home on the Range*, the studio's animation diverged, both artistically and narratologically, from Disney tradition to include genres such as science fiction and the Western, and locations such as outer space and the Incan empire of ancient South America.

Conclusion

Ultimately, *Hercules* represents a "Disneyfication" of peplum filmmaking rather than an innovative redevelopment of this genre within the animated medium. This is not to say, however, that *Hercules* represents a typical Disney animated feature; instead, as noted earlier, the fact that the film embraces or supports several key peplumic traditions (such as the muscular male hero, camp subtext, and generic hybridity) marks the movie as a particularly divergent feature in Disney's theatrical oeuvre. As a case study though, *Hercules* is revealing on two counts. First, it highlights how two genres that are perceived to be inflexible, the Disney animated feature and the peplum strain of sword and sandal filmmaking, can, in fact, combine and even develop through generic synthesis. Second, by analyzing the crucial peplumic themes of masculine bodily culture and camp sensibility via *Hercules*, it has been possible to prepare a new critical space — that of animation — in which to address sword and sandal filmmaking.

Notes

1. Given the network of practices and convergent mediums that underpin contemporary digital filmmaking, it is necessary to define precisely how the term animation will be used within this chapter. As Lev Manovich states, "Digital film = live action material + painting + image processing + compositing + 2D computer animation + 3D computer animation" (254–55). This equation remains relevant and applicable to the "live-action" sword and sandal movies identified in this chapter. This quiet, yet common, interpolation of the animated into the live-action should not, however, stop animated filmmaking from being understood in terms of its own formal conditions and artistic devices. Animation, in this chapter, will therefore be used to refer to a moving image that is "artificially created and not recorded from the real world," and which, to varying degrees, foregrounds its very artificiality (Wells *Fundamentals* 7).

2. Disney's animation actually constitutes an incredibly diverse body of work. As I highlight in *Demystifying Disney: A History of Disney Feature Animation*, the studio's animation has adopted many forms over the years, including metamorphic and minimalist shorts of the late 1920s, the surrealist *Destino*, and the highly detailed yet playfully

cartoonish features of recent Disney. On a superficial level, for example, consider the differences in visual style between *Hercules* and the films which immediately precede and follow it in Disney's animated feature canon (*The Hunchback of Notre Dame* and *Mulan*, respectively).

3. All box office data used in this chapter is obtained from www.boxofficemojo.com.

4. Reflecting the sense of malaise felt by the next generation of filmmakers in Hollywood at the end of the 1970s, many of the young animators at Disney, alienated during the production of *The Fox and the Hound*, chose to walk out on the studio in 1979. Bluth, who had wanted the studio to return to the standards of the late 1930s and early 1940s, headed this walkout and established Don Bluth Productions, which subsequently went on to produce animation inspired by Disney's Golden Era (such as *An American Tale* and *The Land Before Time*).

5. While the notion of an animated character connoting sexual maturity may seem like something of a paradox, given the medium's obvious artificiallity, American hand-drawn animation has a history in this respect, with Betty Boop and Jessica Rabbit being the medium's most famous sex symbols. In fact, because the perceived chemistry between Jessica Rabbit and Bob Hoskins' character Eddie Valiant in the film *Who Framed Roger Rabbit?* was so strong, certain scenes had to be reanimated to reassure anxious parents that the cartoon character *was*, in fact, wearing underwear (Clemens and Pettman 66).

WORKS CITED

Aladdin. Dirs. Ron Clements and John Musker. USA. Walt Disney Pictures, 1992.
Anastasia. Dirs. Don Bluth and Gary Goldman. USA. Twentieth Century–Fox, 1997.
Ben Hur. Dir. William R. Kowalchuk Jr. USA. Agamemnon Films, 2003.
Cabiria. Dir. Giovanni Pastrone. ITA. Itala Film, 1914.
Clash of the Titans. Dir. Louis Leterrier. UK/USA. Warner Bros., 2010.
Clemens, Justin, and Dominic Pettman. *Avoiding the Subject: Media, Culture, and the Object*. Amsterdam: Amsterdam University Press, 2004.
Dumbo. Dir. Ben Sharpsteen. USA. Walt Disney Productions, 1941.
Dyer, Richard. *White*. London: Routledge, 1997.
Eisenstein, Sergei. *Eisenstein on Disney*. Ed. Jay Leyda. Trans. Alan Upchurch. London: Methuen, 1986.
Griffin, Sean. *Tinker Belles and Evil Queens: The Walt Disney Company from the Inside Out*. New York: New York University Press, 2000.
He-Man and the Masters of the Universe. Television series. USA. Filmation, 1983–85.
Hercules. Dirs. Ron Clements and John Musker. USA. Walt Disney Pictures, 1997.
"Hercules and the Arabian Night." Dir. Phil Weinstein. USA. Walt Disney Television, 1999.
"Hercules and the Golden Touch." Dir. Phil Weinstein. USA. Walt Disney Television, 1998.
Hercules: The Animated Series. Television series. USA. Walt Disney Television, 1998–99.
Hunchback of Notre Dame. Dirs. Gary Trousdale and Kirk Wise. USA. Walt Disney Pictures, 1996.
The Lion King. Dirs. Roger Allers and Rob Minkoff. USA. Walt Disney Pictures, 1994.
The Little Mermaid. Dirs. Ron Clements and John Musker. USA. Walt Disney Pictures, 1989.
Manovich, Lev. *The Language of New Media*. Cambridge: MIT, 2001.
McCallum, Robyn. "Masculinity as Social Semiotic: Identity Politics and Gender in Disney Animated Films." In *Ways of Being Male: Representing Masculinities in Children's Literature and Film*. Ed. John Stephens. London: Routledge, 2002. 116–132.

Pallant, Chris. *Demystifying Disney: A History of Disney Feature Animation*. New York: Continuum, 2011.
Pocahontas. Dirs. Mike Gabriel and Eric Goldberg. USA. Walt Disney Pictures, 1995.
Price, David A. *The Pixar Touch: The Making of a Company*. New York: Alfred A. Knopf, 2008.
Prince of Egypt. Dirs. Brenda Chapman, Steve Hickner, and Simon Wells. USA. DreamWorks SKG, 1998.
Rebello, Stephen, and Jane Healy. *The Art of Hercules: The Chaos of Creation*. New York: Hyperion, 1997.
"Roman Legion-Hare." Dir. Friz Freleng. USA. Warner Bros., 1955.
Rushing, Robert A. "Memory and Masculinity in the Italian Peplum Film and Zach Snyder's 300." In *Culture et Mémoire: Représentations Contemporaines de la Mémoire dans les Espaces Mémoriels, les Arts du Visuel, la Littérature et le Théâtre*. Eds. Carola Hähnel-Mesnard, Marie Liénard-Yeterian and Cristina Marinas. Paris: Ecole Polytechnique, 2008. 239–246.
"See You Later Gladiator." Dir. Alex Lovy. USA. Warner Bros., 1968.
Sontag, Susan. "Notes on 'Camp.'" In *Against Interpretation: and Other Essays*. London: Eyre and Spottiswoode, 1967. 275–292.
Tengler, Nancy. *New Era Value Investing: A Disciplined Approach to Buying Value and Growth Stocks*. New York: John Wiley and Sons, 2003.
Toy Story. Dir. John Lasseter. USA. Buena Vista Pictures, 1995.
Wells, Paul. *Animation and America*. Edinburgh: Edinburgh University Press, 2002.
_____. *Animation: Genre and Authorship*. London: Wallflower, 2002.
_____. *The Fundamentals of Animation*. Lausanne: AVA, 2006.
_____. *Understanding Animation*. London: Routledge, 1998.
Who Framed Roger Rabbit? Dir. Robert Zemeckis. USA. Amblin Entertainment / Touchstone Pictures, 1988.

Hercules Diminished?
Parody, Differentiation, and Emulation in
The Three Stooges Meet Hercules

Daniel O'Brien

Greco-Roman culture offers many different representations of Hercules, variations on the theme of a super-man or demigod centered on his large muscular body and associated strength. As with other mythological or legendary figures, Hercules was remolded over successive generations, subject to new interpretations that ensured his continuing relevance to different cultures and consequent popularity (Galinsky 2). Jaimee Pugliese Uhlenbrock suggests that the artistic representation of Hercules may date back to the eighth century B.C.E. (7). At various points since its inception, the figure has been depicted as tragic or comic, a lecher or a glutton, an embodiment of metaphysical struggle or a doomed romantic. Hercules could embody extraordinary yet purely physical strength or stand as "an exemplar of virtue ... as a divine mediator, and as the incarnation of rhetoric, intelligence, and wisdom" (Uhlenbrock 19). Hence from this historicized perspective, the common descriptor "Herculean" becomes vague, as the figure himself moves towards varying notions and constructs reflecting the classical imagination, unless the term is understood within a particular and often highly specific context.

Over time, however, the adjective "Herculean" acquired a more standardized meaning, or series of associations, at least in terms of popular currency. In Greco-Roman cultures, representations of Hercules often had negligible connection with notions of morality or ethical behavior. Alastair Blanshard suggests that in Ancient Greece, "people believed that size and heroism went together;" to be a hero meant to be larger than life in the most literal way possible (92). Thus Hercules could employ his strength in ways amoral or immoral without undermining his status. Yet around the fifth century B.C.E., this began to change. G. Karl Galinsky identifies Aeschylus's play *Prometheus Unbound* as marking a significant transformation of Hercules "from the arbitrary perpetrator of excessive force to an ideally motivated and awesome advocate of justice" (42). This new, explicitly moral version of the hero can be characterized as the "Prodican Hercules," from Prodicus' *The Choice of Herakles*, where the latter opts for a life of toil and duty rather than ease and pleasure (Allen and Schwarz 750). Furthermore, the essential act of choosing gave Hercules a new intellectual status, "and intelligence thus became one of the hero's attributes" (Galinsky 102). Thus while the figure of Hercules continued to undergo numerous, and occasionally contradictory, permutations, it is reasonable to observe that the heroic figure associated with super-human strength — in body *and* mind — as well as a foundation of moral certitude has generally been long established and widely recognized in both classical and post-classical tradition. It is this prevalent version of the mythic hero that gives rise to the construct of Herculean masculinity, whereas the qualities and aspects associated with the figure of the Prodican Hercules are ascribed to other, usually exaggeratedly masculine, forms and personages who reflect and imbue the same qualities as the legendary Hercules himself. Thus in the common parlance, describing an individual as Herculean brings to mind those three core characteristics — impressive strength and physique; a strategic sense of intelligence; and a moral probity reflected in a desire to "do" and "be" good — all developed in the individual beyond that of regular men. This form of Herculean masculinity becomes a simulacrum, then, one represented in the flesh by overt muscular development and reflected in the character of the so-ascribed individual through the nobility of both his actions and his sense of what is right and just.

One of the best known depictions, at least in terms of twentieth-century popular culture, of this form of Herculean masculinity is found in the popular 1958 movie *Hercules*, produced in Italy, and the subsequent peplum films that followed its commercial success. The 1958 *Hercules* depicts its title character in a form that valorizes male strength and physical perfection, as embodied by hulking star Steve Reeves, a champion bodybuilder. The majority of peplum films emulated this representation of heroic or super-masculinity with minimal variation, let alone any critical or subversive intent. However, an alternative depiction of Hercules, and by extension his Herculean masculinity, is found in the American-produced film *The Three Stooges Meet Hercules*, released in 1962. This more subversive example of Herculean masculinity was crafted in response to the international success of *Hercules*, its sequel *Hercules Unchained*, and the peplum cycle as a whole. *The Three Stooges Meet Hercules* addresses the standard peplum representation of heroic masculinity through parody, differentiation, and emulation. A parodic interpretation of the peplum has the potential to alter, subvert, and re-encode conceptions of masculinity associated with the genre. *The Three Stooges Meet Hercules* reconfigures Hercules' familiar status, transforming the morally upright hero into a dim-witted thug at odds with his popular filmic representation. At the same time, the positive values associated with the term "Herculean" are transposed to the juvenile male lead, who builds his physique — and character — in accordance with the prescriptions of the American-based bodybuilding culture which influenced the peplum cycle and supplied most of its stars. Thus while *The Three Stooges Meet Hercules* employs parody to invert the values of the peplum and its form of Herculean masculinity, it also simultaneously reaffirms them, mocking that which it likewise endorses. Ultimately, the film demonstrates both the inherent absurdity and irrationality of Herculean masculinity in a contemporary milieu while also confirming society's desire to possess and reflect such figures, to represent not only the ideal virtues of the male, but to evince those values that society believes best reflects on itself as well.

The Three Stooges Meet Hercules is linked to the Italian-produced peplum films on various levels: chronological, thematic, industrial, and economic. It was financed and distributed by Hollywood major Columbia Pictures and filmed in 1961, the mid-point of the peplum cycle and shortly after the American release of *Hercules Unchained* in 1960. *The Three Stooges Meet Hercules* is primarily a star vehicle for its titular trio of comedians, Moe Howard, Larry Fine, and "Curly" Joe De Rita. Howard and Fine, in partnership with, successively, Jerry "Curly" Howard, Samuel "Shemp" Howard, and Joe Besser, starred in 190 short films for Columbia Pictures released between 1934 and 1959. De Rita joined the act in 1958, after Columbia closed down its short subjects department. When the Three Stooges won a new generation of fans— predominantly children — through exposure of their old films on television, Columbia responded to this lucrative market with the feature film *Have Rocket, Will Travel*, a modestly budgeted production that proved a commercial success (Howard 165). Thus the Three Stooges continued to make films until the mid–1960s, mostly for Columbia, and mostly profitable.

The plot of *The Three Stooges Meet Hercules* can be summarized as follows: Moe, Larry, and Curly Joe work at the Ithaca Pharmacy in Ithaca, New York, alongside their friend Diane Quigley (Vicki Trickett). Their boss is the mean-spirited Ralph Dimsal (George N. Neise), who is jealous of Diane's relationship with mild-mannered scientist Schuyler Davis (Quinn Redeker). Schuyler has invented a time machine, which transports him, Diane, and the Stooges back to Ithaca in Ancient Greece, where they encounter the evil King Odius (Neise) and his henchman Hercules (Samson Burke). Odius claims Diane for himself, sentencing Schuyler and the Stooges to become galley slaves. When Schuyler builds his muscles through rowing, the Stooges win their freedom from King Theseus of Rhodes (Hal Smith) by claiming that Schuyler is Hercules and vanquishing the Siamese Cyclops (Marlin and Mike McKeever). After a series of contests, Schuyler defeats Hercules in the arena and makes him promise to reform. Schuyler and the Stooges rescue Diane and take off in the time machine, still pursued by Odius, who is deposited in the Wild West. They return to present-day Ithaca, where Schuyler asserts himself over Dimsal, who enjoys a brief taste of time travel that leaves him punished and humiliated.

As the above outline suggests, *The Three Stooges Meet Hercules* relocates the veteran comedians from a contemporary urban American locale to a classical setting with which audiences would have been familiar, in cinematic terms, from earlier Hollywood epics and the ongoing peplum cycle launched by *Hercules*. Even before the introduction of Hercules as a character, the film plays with ideas of masculinity that link to the Prodican Hercules and the associated physical, intellectual, and moral strength. In these terms, the good-natured yet timid Schuyler falls far short of conforming to an ideal or, indeed, Herculean manliness, and is consequently denied the success, respect, status, and heterosexual relationship that are the province of the fully formed man. The spatial-temporal displacement of the Stooges and their friends to Ancient Greece brings them into direct contact with the real Hercules, which could have facilitated a narrative whereby Schuyler is instructed in the acquisition of true masculinity by the legendary hero himself. However, *The Three Stooges Meet Hercules* confounds this not unreasonable expectation on several levels. While Hercules' physical appearance is similar to the cinematic representation epitomized by Steve Reeves, it soon becomes clear that he is by no means formed from the Prodican mold. Furthermore, this Hercules is amoral, lacking in intelligence, and an outright villain, presenting a parodic form of Herculean masculinity that seems to question the values embodied by the peplum genre and the Greco-Roman hero himself.

Parody Peplum

In *The Three Stooges Meet Hercules*, the latter character is presented initially as conforming to the standard peplum representation of the hero in terms of size, physique, strength, and prowess in combat. Having established a familiar Hercules, the film then subverts this depiction of the character, reconfiguring him as both malevolent and dim-witted. This inversion of Herculean masculinity, which would be a radical, potentially disturbing transformation in a peplum film, sits more comfortably within the comedy genre, where humorous reversals of audience expectations are a familiar device, particularly when referencing another popular genre. *The Three Stooges Meet Hercules* thus operates on the level of parody, which depends on audience recognition of and familiarity with the original text — or texts — being parodied.

There is little doubt that *The Three Stooges Meet Hercules* was made in direct response to the American success of *Hercules* and *Hercules Unchained*. Stooges front-man Moe Howard writes in his autobiography, "The Hercules movies were big hits at the time," a clear commercial incentive for a humorous exploitation of the peplum cycle, allied with an established comedy team whose audience appeal had recently received a considerable boost through television exposure (167). The American promotion for *Hercules* featured such lines as

"See heroic Hercules rip down the Age of Orgy's lavish palace of lustful pleasure!" and "See the Mightiest of Men vs. the Mightiest of Beasts—the killer Cretan Bull!" One style of poster design for *The Three Stooges Meet Hercules* mimicked and parodied this hyperbolic marketing strategy: "SEE what happens when the man of steel meets the maniacs of mayhem!" and "SEE The 3 Stooges make a shambles out of ancient Athens and a wreck out of Hercules!" (Press book 1). A second poster design promoted the film as "The World's SPOOFIEST GOOFIEST SPECTACULAR!" (Press book 2). It is evident that *The Three Stooges Meet Hercules* proclaimed its parodic intent in a clear, unmistakable fashion.[1]

Parody can be characterized as a deliberate imitation or repetition of a specific text with humorous intent. Ingeborg Hoesterey defines parody as "a work of literature or another art that imitates an existent piece which is well-known to its readers, viewers, or listeners with satirical, critical, or polemical intention," suggesting the humorous aspect widely associated with parody is not necessarily among its primary functions (13–14). As with pastiche, parody is dependent for its effect on the audience's awareness and appreciation of the original work. Richard Dyer notes that parody by definition acknowledges the element of imitation involved and works best if the notion of imitation itself is taken into account (*Pastiche* 23). Simple repetition of the target text is in itself insufficient to generate parody; a sense of both difference and distance is also crucial to the effect. Linda Hutcheon defines parody as "a form of repetition with ironic critical distance, marking difference rather than similarity," though I would argue that the latter remains a crucial factor if a sense of the original text is to be retained (xii). Furthermore, the target audience will only engage with the parodic text as intended if, to use Hutcheon's terms, they "share certain assumptions or cultural codes with the encoder" (xiii–xiv).[2] In other words, parody is dependent on frames of reference common to the producer and the intended receivers.

In the case of *The Three Stooges Meet Hercules*, there are clear problems with Hoesterey and Hutcheon's characterization of parody in terms of mono-textual specificity. The film does not parody closely the 1958 *Hercules* film, any subsequent Italian-produced Hercules movie, or even the peplum genre as a whole. Moreover, the extended sequences with the main characters as galley slaves draw on a wider, Hollywood-centered tradition of classical epics, in particular *Ben-Hur*, a then recent, widely distributed and publicized film which would have been familiar to most audiences in 1962. The chariot chase towards the end of the film also invokes *Ben-Hur*, as do the bladed wheel hubs on Odius' chariot and the promotional tag "More fun than a Roman Circus!" recalling the Circus Maximus where *Ben-Hur*'s chariot race takes place (Press book 3). Thus *The Three Stooges Meet Hercules* could be described as a multi-textual parody that plays on ideas, images, and characters from earlier films rather than close textual readings of particular scenes in a specific film. To state it another way, *The Three Stooges Meet Hercules* is more clearly a burlesque of multiple genres as a whole, including the peplum, rather than a spoof of any particular film. This suggests audience familiarity with the conventions of the peplum genre and the forms of masculinity it espouses—gleaned through the popularity of *Hercules* and its successors—as well as the notion that the genre and its masculine values were ripe for parody.

In his book-length study of film parody, Dan Harries states, "Parodic texts simultaneously generate similarity to and difference from their targets in a regularized fashion," echoing the ideas outlined above (8). Harries characterizes the mechanism for maintaining this all-important balance as "logical absurdity," for which "one dimension [is] needed to ensure a logic and another for difference-creating absurdity. This is the necessary oscillation between similarity to and difference from a target that allows parody to maintain either the lexicon, syntax or style while manipulating the others" (9). A parody will manipulate the targeted text's key generic, diegetic, and narrative elements, the order in which they are arranged, and the style in which they are presented. At any given point, the lexicon, syntax, or style of the parody must match closely to its source, or the sense of similarity will be lost. Yet one or both of the other dimensions likewise must be correspondingly and excessively different from the parodied text. If this is not achieved, the new text may be mistaken for imitation or pastiche. While this approach may be overly schematic, suggesting a standardized formula for parody, it has some application to *The Three Stooges Meet Hercules*. In terms of lexical elements, the costumes, props and set design conform adequately to the iconography and generic verisimilitude of both the peplum and the classical epic. Having established a sense of "Ancient Greece," the film then manipulates the lexicon, giving Curly Joe a sundial wristwatch, an incongruous blend of old and new technology that corresponds to Harries' notion of difference-creating absurdity. When the soldiers of Ulysses (John Cliff) flee the battlefield, Larry comments, "The guys in the green skirts chickened out," ridiculing the Greek warriors and their uniform in terms of transvestitism and cowardice (*The Three Stooges Meet Hercules*). Furthermore, his use of a modern American idiom creates a sense of linguistic disjuncture with the setting of Ancient Greece. The character of Achilles the Heel (Lewis Charles), a criminal who runs a protection racket, corresponds to Harries' category of literalization, "a play with the notion that a character's inner qualities can be read by his or her name (literalization through a pun)" (95). In North American slang, the term "heel" is used to denote a disreputable person of dishonest and often criminal intent. In this instance, the name also refers to a figure from Greco-Roman myth, subverting the latter's heroic status through appending his name to a small-time crook. Achilles the Heel also invokes the concept of an Achilles heel, in myth the hero's only vulnerable spot, and in common parlance a literal or figurative weakness.

The spectacle and special effects associated with the peplum are evoked with the appearance of the Cretan Bull, the Nemean Lion, and Cyclops, a one-eyed giant from Greco-Roman mythology. The bull and the lion, which figure in the twelve labors of Hercules and both feature in the 1958 film, are represented with rigid dummies, which could be read as parodic reference to the low-budget props and effects associated with the peplum. The bull is thrown in the air and the lion is swung around by its hind legs, underlining the deliberate artificiality and lack of verisimilitude in their representation. Cyclops is featured in the film *Ulysses*, released in 1954, and a number of pepla, including *Atlas in the Land of the Cyclops* (1961) and *My Son, the Hero* (1962). The generic similarity is subverted with the revelation that this is a Siamese Cyclops, a paradoxical absurdity, as a two-headed Cyclops has two eyes, one in each head, and, therefore, is arguably not a Cyclops. Schuyler's avowedly Herculean fight with a hydra is advertised by a poster which features star billing and an admission charge, a blatant commercialization of the heroic struggle of Greco-Roman mythology that could be equated with the financially-driven peplum films. Schuyler wears a silk robe with "Hercules" emblazoned on the back, an obvious nod to the self-promotion of professional boxers, fighters whose primary objective is the generation of financial reward.

The Three Stooges Meet Hercules conforms broadly with the various definitions of parody outlined above but not in the sense of parodying a specific text. While it might seem logical or expedient for the film to spoof either *Hercules* or *Hercules Unchained*, the peplum epics most familiar to audiences in America and elsewhere, there is little sustained or even tentative attempt to reference characters, scenes, plotlines, or other elements from the Italian productions. For much of its running time, *The Three Stooges Meet Hercules* can be characterized as a general burlesque of various films and genres associated with Greco-Roman legend and history as represented in popular media. Yet the film was made in response to the Steve Reeves Hercules movies and requires, if only on a superficial level, audience familiarity with the character, his exploits, and a general notion of the classical world. More specifically, *The Three Stooges Meet Hercules* plays with the notion of a super or heroic masculinity associated closely with the peplum cycle and therefore presumes a pre-knowledge of genre conventions centered on the concept of Herculean masculine values that informs the film's key parodic strategy.

Differentiation

The Three Stooges Meet Hercules can be appreciated for its broad parody of the peplum and epic genres, alongside the slapstick humor associated with the titular comedians. However, the effect of the film depends to a significant degree on the audience's acquaintance with the figure of Hercules and his representation in the peplum. The North American release of *Hercules* and *Hercules Unchained* ensured at least some aspects of these films were familiar to most viewers, particularly the juvenile audience at whom *The Three Stooges Meet Hercules* was aimed. In casting Hercules, the film followed the standard peplum strategy of employing a bodybuilder with little or no acting experience, in this case the Canadian Samuel Burke. Like many of his peplum contemporaries, Burke underwent both depilation and a change of name. As "Samson Burke," he connoted the physical prowess and masculine potency associated with the peplum genre.[3] The character of Hercules features prominently in the advertising for the film, though Burke is not credited in promotional materials. In one illustration, Hercules is depicted as a figure in repose, suggesting indolence and apathy, another comic subversion of the heroic man-of-action familiar from the peplum.

First appearing around twenty minutes into the film, Hercules performs acts of strength that could be characterized as typically "Herculean" in terms of his standard peplum representation. A low angle medium long shot shows him lifting a man above his head, emphasizing his strength, physique, and prowess in combat. He also lifts two huge boulders, pinning Schuyler's time machine to the ground. Hercules' height, physique, and exposed torso form an extreme contrast with the Three Stooges, elderly, diminutive men whose bodies remain covered throughout the film. One poster design for the film featured the line "Hercules, strongest hero in history, meets weakest weaklings in hysteria," offering a simple contrast of physical strength — and its heroic associations — with physical weakness which, it seems, can only be appreciated in terms of comic potential (Press book 3).

Dyer states that parody employs techniques of likeness, deformation, and discrepancy (*Pastiche* 48). Having evoked an existing and sufficiently well-known text, parody then transforms this similarity in such a way as to subvert the original representation in an extreme fashion that could be termed grotesque. In this instance, Hercules retains his familiar appearance and extraordinary strength, yet the morality and nobility associated with the character in the 1958 *Hercules* are displaced by brutish aggression and subservience to a malevolent patriarch. Hercules could also be seen as an example of what Harries terms misdirection, which operates "by reiterating an expected convention along lexical, syntactic, and stylistic paths and then transforming that convention in a way that is both unexpected and 'inappropriate'" (70). In establishing a Hercules similar to the Steve Reeves incarnation — in terms of appearance, actions, and framing — *The Three Stooges Meet Hercules* can potentially mislead audiences into anticipating this Hercules will not differ significantly from the familiar version. The subsequent reconfiguration of Hercules as a villain could then be termed both unexpected and inappropriate. Even younger members of the audience would appreciate that good guys are not supposed to become bad guys. Moreover, a well-known hero such as Hercules, both a figure from mythology and a recently established cinematic brand-name, embodies only positive attributes, which have here been transformed into negative qualities. This is reflected by the opening credits, which depict Hercules as a statue that is broken by the Stooges, anticipating what happens to his familiar representation in the film.

In terms of physical strength, the spectacular feats associated with the peplum are replaced by Hercules crushing walnuts in the crook of his arm, echoing his earlier demonstrations of strength in intentionally absurd form. On another level, his formerly heroic super-masculinity is reconfigured as aggression directed at a smaller and weaker opponent. During a banquet scene, Hercules traps Curly Joe's head against his flexed bicep, transforming a classic bodybuilding pose into a humorous expression of domination and humiliation. This image also featured in promotional material for the film, permitting audiences to anticipate Hercules' potentially hostile status and, therefore, the subversion of his established persona. A publicity shot featured on the cover of a comic book version of the film highlights Hercules' violent subjugation of the Stooges, underlined by his use of chains, which in *Hercules* symbolized liberation rather than enslavement and oppression (comic book 1).

Hercules is also represented in terms of vulnerability, another parodic inversion, even in his interaction with the diminutive, physically unimposing Stooges. Curly Joe inadvertently hits him in the jaw with an iron bar, while Moe strikes him in the face with a bowl of fruit. The infliction of pain and humiliation undermines Hercules' male potency, dignity, and standing within the tyrannical patriarchy headed by Odius. When Hercules punches all three Stooges in retaliation, Moe bites his fist, attacking directly a prime symbol and tool of masculine power and aggression. This sequence concludes with Hercules running into a wall and knocking himself out, becoming the very instrument of his incapacitation and temporary impotence. However, Hercules can acquire his as-yet unearned popular reputation through the intervention of a third party. Hercules as a man has been inverted and ridiculed; yet the popular conception of Herculean masculinity will be endorsed and validated in the form of the Stooges' scientist friend Schuyler, the stereotypical "weakling" who becomes a super-man through enhancing both his body and spirit.

The Three Stooges Meet Hercules invokes not just the peplum films in its depiction of Hercules but also the American-centered bodybuilding culture, which had existed in its modern form since the early years of the twentieth century. By the 1950s bodybuilding was as regulated and commercialized as many other sports—though its status as a "true" sport is still disputed—and enjoyed a far-reaching, if still relatively niche, international appeal. Thus the comic subversion and parodic misdirection of the film reference the masculine traits associated with body culture as much as the peplum genre that drew heavily on these ideals. While the villainous, thuggish Hercules suggests a negative critique of the mythical/bodybuilder hero, the narrative progression of *The Three Stooges Meet Hercules* offers another form of misdirection. Having ridiculed the built male physique and what it is usually taken to represent, the film performs an about turn and ultimately endorses the bodybuilder as a legitimate and ideal form of masculinity, both ancient and modern.

Emulation

As noted, peplum heroes were often played by bodybuilders, some of whom — Steve Reeves, for example — were champions and celebrities in this specialized field prior to gaining wider fame as screen incarnations of Hercules. Patrick Lucanio asserts: "The major icon of the peplum genre is the bodybuilder; he is so pervasive in fact that ... his very presence defines the genre" (22). While there are pepla which do not employ bodybuilders for their leading men, the genre is invariably characterized by commentators in terms of its "musclemen" stars. This relationship between classical mythology and body culture played a significant role in perpetuating the image of the Prodican Hercules, achieving one of its most notable manifestations in the 1958 film but dating back to at least the nineteenth century.

Anne Bolin defines bodybuilding as "working out with weights to reshape the physique by adding muscle mass and increasing separation and definition of the various muscle groups" (50). It is notable that muscle growth in itself is insufficient to achieve the desired bodybuilder look; the body must also be *shaped* and *honed* to the proper proportions, invoking ideas of sculpture associated with classical statuary. The public display of large, muscular and — by demonstration or implication — strong male bodies had long been a feature of street, circus, and carnival acts. These performances highlighted shows of physical strength or athleticism, claiming artistic legitimacy and respectability through invocation of the Greco-Roman tradition. As Blanshard states, circus strongmen often wore a leopard or lion skin in emulation of Hercules, arguably the best known mythical hero and certainly the one most associated with incredible acts of super-human strength (153). This invocation of the demigod, and the accompanying equation of the built body with both physical and moral strength, offered a new manifestation of the Prodican Hercules. Over time, these classical associations, however tenuous, assumed greater importance. Maria Wyke notes: "As the [nineteenth] century progressed, so circus programs began to include acts that had no pretensions to the display of skills such as weightlifting or equestrianism but were, instead, wholly focused on the representation of classical figures familiar from statues and paintings" (357). As with modern bodybuilding, the *display* of the muscular body, in a legitimate, culturally approved framework, took precedence over any demonstration of this same body's abilities.

One of the first celebrity bodybuilders was the German Eugene Sandow, who made his American debut at the 1893 Chicago World's Fair. Promoting himself as a strongman and physique showman, Sandow offered, in Bolin's phrase, "a new ideal of muscular manhood" (50). In particular, Blanshard identifies Sandow as the first professional strongman to emphasize muscular definition over sheer size or bulk (153). Only a body built according to a prescribed regime could achieve a sculpted look rather than mere muscle mass. The first major bodybuilding contest was held in 1901, in the United Kingdom, and the movement continued to grow throughout the first half of the twentieth century. In 1921, Italian-born champion bodybuilder Angelo Siciliano, better known as "Charles Atlas," launched his "dynamic tension" system of bodybuilding, enjoying international success with his mail order business (Cashmore 141). In 1946 the International Federation of Bodybuilding (IFBB) was founded in America by brothers Joe and Ben Weider.

John F. Kasson notes that Sandow's American debut took place at a time of economic depression and an associated loss of masculine independence and control (23). Those contending with financial and social adversity could at least demonstrate publicly a mastery of their own body, reaffirming their masculinity in the most visible form possible. This attitude chimed with widely shared perceptions of manliness, as R.J. Connell asserts: "True masculinity is almost always thought to proceed from men's bodies—to be inherent in a male body or to express something about a male body" (45). If the muscular body is promoted and accepted as a signifier of strength, power, dominance, and virility, it can withstand any outside threat and maintain its integrity. Kasson argues that, as the early twentieth century progressed, "perceptions of manliness were drastically altered by the new dynamics created by vast corporate power and immense concentrations of wealth" (11). Characterizing manhood in terms of autonomy and independence became problematic, if not impossible, under such conditions, unless an individual could redefine power and status in corporeal terms unrelated to economic realities.

By the 1950s, the American male also had to contend with an unfamiliar threat to his masculine potency. Steven Cohan suggests "the postwar 'free man' had to depend upon the state to preserve his independence in the face of the communist threat, thereby calling into question the myth of rugged, rebellious, and masculine American individuality" (134). Once again, the male body served as the unassailable site of masculine independence and self-sufficiency, reflected in the continuing popularity of bodybuilding during this period. As with the strongman acts of previous eras, 1950s bodybuilding culture often referenced classical iconography for purposes of inspiration and legitimization. The term "Herculean" was employed frequently in specialist magazines, and cover stars were referred to as modern incarnations of Hercules himself. Gideon Nisbet suggests: "To become a bodybuilder was already to emulate Hercules, within a discipline that had always consciously modeled itself on the hero's feats of strength" (48–49). From this perspective, the casting of Steve Reeves in the 1958 film was both a logical progression for the champion and the ultimate endorsement of bodybuilding as a heroizing discipline.

The financial success of *Hercules* in America (and worldwide) indicates its representation of heroic masculinity had resonance for a large number of people. Several commentators on the peplum genre suggest this new form of mythical manliness acted as a salve against traumatic social and economic transformation. Dyer states: "The peplum celebrates a type of male body for an audience to whom it had until now been a source of economic self-worth" (*White* 169). The physical strength and stamina associated with unskilled manual labor had declined steadily in economic value as industrialization increased. Maggie Günsberg suggests the genre promoted "the fantasy that traditional physical prowess was still valuable and even heroic" (181). Faced with numerous social, economic, and political anxieties, consumers of *Hercules* and its successors were reassured of the enduring worth located in their own bodies. In terms of the political situation, Wyke draws an explicit and specific Cold War parallel: "The resulting modern Hercules symbolized the victory of Beauty, Virility, *and* the American Way ... a seemingly natural link was forged between muscularity, masculinity, justice, and the supremacy of the West" (370). While this direct linkage can be criticized as simplistic, the image of the powerful hero defending freedom from oppressive alien aggressors equates the muscular male body with manliness, virtue, democracy, and spirit. *The Three Stooges Meet Hercules* appears to question and subvert this equation through the villainy of Hercules; however, this heroic value is upheld and validated in the form of Schuyler, who must first remodel his body into a truly Herculean form. While most peplum protagonists emerge on screen as fully-formed exemplars of heroic virtue, Schuyler transforms himself into a modern Hercules before the viewers' eyes.

Schuyler is represented initially as an exaggerated contrast to Hercules, a scientist and inventor who values brain over brawn. The objects most associated with him are not a lion skin and a club but a pencil and the rolled blueprint for his space-time machine. He wears thick-rimmed glasses, underlining a lack of physical perfection, and dresses in a dark coat that conceals his upper body. Tall yet awkward, he tends to stoop and bow his head. This lack of physical dominance and assertiveness is equated with a corresponding lack of spirit and courage, demonstrated by Schuyler backing down from a confrontation with Ralph Dimsal, the middle-aged pharmacy owner. Diane regards Schuyler's passivity and unwillingness to engage in physical conflict with Dimsal as an impairment to his masculinity and, consequently, a threat to their potential heterosexual relationship. She reacts to his humiliation at Dimsal's hands with impatience and frustration rather than sympathy. Diane refers to Schuyler as a "jellyfish," evoking a limp, undefined form far removed from the hard, built, and shaped body of the peplum hero (*The Three Stooges Meet Hercules*).

In Ancient Greece, Schuyler does not protest when King Odius places Diane in his chariot, his inaction a tacit acceptance of Odius' superior position in the patriarchal order, even when the prize femininity represented by Diane is at stake. When Odius condemns the Stooges to be galley slaves, Diane exhorts

Schuyler to be a man and intervene. He protests to Odius and is slapped to the ground by the latter, a middle-aged man of unexceptional strength. This illustration of Schuyler's masculine inadequacy echoes in exaggerated form contemporaneous advertisements for bodybuilding courses, where the skinny hero gets sand kicked in his face by a larger, more powerful bully. Indeed, Odius dismisses Schuyler as a "weakling," a term employed widely in the promotion of physique culture, prompting the latter to transform himself according to the prescribed and aggressively marketed methods of the modern bodybuilder.

As a galley slave, Schuyler exchanges his effeminizing Greek robes for rags and grows a beard, a traditional symbol of male maturity and authority. Literally chained to his training apparatus—a wooden bench and an oar—he undergoes a regime of bodybuilding through enslavement, an extreme manifestation of the confinement, repetition and physical duress—bordering on punishment—associated with body culture.[4] This involuntary fitness program produces extreme muscle growth, emphasized by a low angle medium shot, and a shipwreck results in the loss of Schuyler's glasses, the last remaining physical signifier of his "weakling" identity. In one key shot, the camera tracks in on Schuyler's left bicep, accompanied by a trumpet fanfare, an established, if clichéd, signifier of a dramatic or spectacular moment, though here employed for humorous effect. This is followed by a dissolve to a low angle close-up of the bicep, an extreme highlighting of the male physique even by the standards of the peplum, reducing the body to flexed and straining muscle. To emphasize further in parodic form Schuyler's newly acquired strength and masculine potency, he is shown rowing by himself on the left side of the ship, while the other oarsmen sit on the right, struggling to match his pace. Schuyler's newly developed heroic physique becomes the film's main site of spectacle in forms that both reference and parody the peplum genre's highlighting of the built male body. Moe and Curly Joe strip him to the waist to show off his body to King Theseus, a female companion, and the extra-diegetic spectator, acknowledging openly their participation in a "muscle show." This super-masculinity is demonstrated further with a series of bodybuilding poses, leading Schuyler to be taken for Hercules. Thus his change in appearance is accompanied by a shift in identity.

Schuyler's transformation from weakling to super-man is linked not only to the name Hercules but also to objects previously associated with Herculean strength. Early in the film, King Odius states, "No man alive can move those boulders except Hercules" (*The Three Stooges Meet Hercules*). In shifting these same boulders, Schuyler asserts his status as an equal to Hercules in an appropriately physical fashion; if Herculean identity is determined purely in terms of strength, then Schuyler has become Hercules. On a narrative level, he poses as Hercules, defeating a series of opponents for commercial gain. In inter-textual terms, Schuyler's exploits are given a more spectacular representation in the comic book issued to accompany the film's American release. On the most obvious level, unlike the black and white film, these images are in color, as are the pepla, yet the relative freedom from budgetary constraints also means the comic strip version can feature scenes absent from the film. Both the press book and the film mention but do not show a hydra, a creature associated with the labors of Hercules (press book 3). The comic book includes an illustration of Schuyler battling and vanquishing the hydra, underlining both his heroic masculinity and his association with the "good" Hercules of legend (28).

Schuyler's new masculinity is qualified, to an extent, by his perceived lack of fighting spirit. In accordance with bodybuilding literature, male perfection requires strength of mind as well as body, or, as Moe comments, "Now we gotta work on the gumption department" (*The Three Stooges Meet Hercules*). The crucial element in Schuyler achieving full super-masculine potency is Diane, his heterosexual object of desire, who is about to be incorporated into Odius' patriarchal order through the institution of marriage. Led captive into an arena, Schuyler breaks his chains, referencing both *Hercules* and *Hercules Unchained*, his super-masculinity now expressed in body and spirit. Furthermore, this new manifestation of the mythical hero trounces the original in hand-to-hand combat, much as the Prodican Hercules superseded previous representations of the demigod. The built body that was previously undermined and brought into question by association with the bad Hercules is now endorsed and valorized through linkage with a new hero whose truly Herculean potential has been both realized and unleashed.

Conclusion

The representation of Herculean masculinity in *The Three Stooges Meet Hercules* can be characterized in terms of parody, differentiation, and emulation. This depiction is, I argue, a conscious, strategic, and acknowledged reaction to *Hercules* and Steve Reeves' incarnation of the title character. The box-office success of *The Three Stooges Meet Hercules* suggests that, in terms of commercial appeal, Herculean masculinity could be challenged, distorted, subverted, and indeed parodied, so long as this representation reverted to a form familiar from the peplum genre. *The Three Stooges Meet Hercules* ridicules the term "Herculean" only to reaffirm its currency through association with the rebuilt Schuyler and bodybuilding culture in general. The film mocks peplum masculine values, notes itself as different from them, and then recreates them in a pre-existing image. Yet in the end, by mocking Herculean masculinity, *The Three Stooges Meet Hercules* reaffirms it; though the admirable masculine form is given a modern American twist (thanks to the American fascination with bodybuilding culture), the values the film asserts are as ancient as the depiction of the Prodican Hercules himself. By taking on not only Hercules' legendary strength but also the intellectual and moral composition associated with Hercules in both Prodicus' work and the peplum tradition, Schuyler has not only become Hercules in form, but Hercules in deed, as well.

Notes

1. It should be noted that, in terms of contemporary reception, this parody was not necessarily considered successful. The British journal *Monthly Film Bulletin* both acknowledged and dismissed the film's intent: "The script has one or two glimmerings of ideas for parody, but the production is tawdry, the comedy very tired indeed" (121). These perceived deficiencies may undermine the desired effect, yet the attempt itself is of interest.

2. For example, *Dracula: Dead and Loving It* is dependent to varying degrees not only on audience familiarity with the immediate source text, Francis Ford Coppola's *Bram Stoker's Dracula,* but also the previous parodic work of Mel Brooks and star Leslie Nielsen, the Stoker novel, vampire folklore in western culture, and earlier film adaptations of *Dracula*. The title itself only makes sense if the receiver recognizes the name Dracula, knows that Dracula is a vampire, and understands that vampires are living corpses with some level of both self-awareness and emotion and therefore capable of appreciating their "undead" status from a negative or positive perspective.

3. The Samson in the Old Testament is a man of exceptional strength, if questionable moral judgment. He was featured in the influential Hollywood biblical epic *Samson and Delilah*, played by "beefcake" star Victor Mature. Samson reappeared as a character in a handful of peplum and adventure films, notably *Samson; Hercules, Samson and Ulysses*; and *Samson and the Mighty Challenge*. Samson Burke went on to have a modest career in pepla, including starring in another peplum parody, *Toto contro Maciste*.

4. Ratifying the film's connection to this larger body culture, Larry at one point even refers to Vic Tanny, an American bodybuilder and a pioneer of the modern health club. Tanny's business empire was at its peak during the 1950s and early 1960s.

Works Cited

Allen, Robert, and Catherine Schwarz, eds. *The Chambers Dictionary*. Edinburgh: Chambers Harrap, 2002.
Blanshard, Alastair. *Hercules: A Heroic Life*. London: Granta Books, 2005.
Bolin, Anne. "Bodybuilding." In *The Encyclopedia of World Sport*. Eds. David Levinson and Karen Christensen. Oxford: ABC-CLIO, 1996. 50–54.
Cashmore, Ellis. *Making Sense of Sports,* 3d ed. London and New York: Routledge, 2000.
Cohan, Steven. *Masked Men: Masculinity and the Movies in the Fifties*. Bloomington: Indiana University Press, 1997.
Connell, R.W. *Masculinities*. Cambridge: Polity, 1995.
Dyer, Richard. *Pastiche*. London: Routledge, 2007.
_____. *White*. London: Routledge, 1997.
Galinsky, G. Karl. *The Herakles Theme: The Adaptations of the Hero in Literature from Homer to the Twentieth Century*. Totowa, NJ: Rowan and Littlefield, 1972.
Günsberg, Maggie. *Italian Cinema: Gender and Genre*. Basingstoke: Palgrave Macmillan, 2005.
Harries, Dan. *Film Parody*. London: BFI, 2000.
Hoesterey, Ingeborg. *Pastiche. Cultural Memory in Art, Film, Literature*. Bloomington: Indiana University Press, 2001.
Howard, Moe. *Moe Howard and The Three Stooges*. Secaucus, NJ: Citadel Press, 1979.

Hutcheon, Linda. *A Theory of Parody: The Teachings of Twentieth-Century Art Forms.* Urbana: University of Illinois Press, 2000.

Kasson, John F. *Houdini, Tarzan, and the Perfect Man: The White Male Body and the Challenge of Modernity in America.* New York: Hill and Wang, 2001.

Lucanio, Patrick. *With Fire and Sword: Italian Spectacles on American Screens 1958–1968.* Metuchen, NJ: Scarecrow Press, 1994.

Nisbet, Gideon. *Ancient Greece in Film and Popular Culture.* Exeter: Bristol Phoenix Press, 2006.

The Three Stooges Meet Hercules. Dir. Edward Bernds. USA. Columbia, 1962.

The Three Stooges Meet Hercules (comic book). New York: Dell, 1962.

The Three Stooges Meet Hercules (press book). Los Angeles: Columbia Pictures Corporation, 1962.

"*The Three Stooges Meet Hercules*" (review). *Monthly Film Bulletin* XXX, nos. 348–359. London: British Film Institute, 1963.

Uhlenbrock, Jaimee Pugliese. *Herakles: Passage of the Hero Through 1000 Years of Classical Art.* New Rochelle, NY: Aristide D. Caratzas, 1986.

Wyke, Maria. "Herculean Muscle!: The Classicizing Rhetoric of Body Building." In *Constructions of the Classical Body.* Ed. James I. Porter. Ann Arbor: University of Michigan Press, 2002. 355–379.

About the Contributors

Michael G. **Cornelius** is the author or editor of eleven books, including *Nancy Drew and Her Sister Sleuths: Essays on the Fiction of Girl Detectives* (co-edited with Melanie E. Gregg; McFarland, 2008) and *The Boy Detectives: Essays on the Hardy Boys and Others* (McFarland, 2010). For Chelsea House, he has written books on Geoffrey Chaucer, John Donne and other Metaphysical poets, and *Much Ado About Nothing*. Also a novelist (*Creating Man*, Vineyard Press, 2001, and *The Ascension,* Variance, 2007), he is the chair of the Department of English and Mass Communications at Wilson College in Chambersburg, Pennsylvania.

Maria Elena **D'Amelio** holds a degree in literature and film studies from the Catholic University of Milan and a doctorate in film history from the University of San Marino. A graduate teaching assistant at Stony Brook University in New York State, her areas of interest focus on Italian cinema, relations between mythology and popular culture, film theory and history, and gender and genre. She is currently researching Italian peplum and Italian and American melodramas and has published essays in *Non solo Dive: Pioniere del cinema Italiano* (Cineteca di Bologna) and *Metamorfosi del mito classico nel cinema* (Istituto Veneto).

John **Elia** is an associate professor and Thérèse Murray Goodwin '49 Chair in Philosophy at Wilson College in Chambersburg, Pennsylvania. His scholarship is focused on moral virtues such as transparency, self-control, and integrity; he has published on these topics in both academic and popular venues. Some of his favorite recent work has addressed the virtues in popular culture, including, now, the virtue of reverence in the sword and sandal film genre. Besides teaching and writing about philosophy, Elia directs the Wilson Scholars Program at Wilson College.

Andrew B.R. **Elliott** is a senior lecturer in media and cultural studies at the University of Lincoln in the United Kingdom, where he teaches courses in film and television studies. His research focuses on the representation of history on film, popular cinema, and the notions of authenticity and truth. He has published on a range of topics from Vikings and violence to television detectives, and his recent book *Remaking the Middle Ages* (McFarland, 2011) analyzes the semiotic reconstruction of the medieval period.

Kevin M. **Flanagan** is a Ph.D. student in the Critical & Cultural Studies Program in the Department of English at the University of Pittsburgh, where he researches postwar British cinema, ideology, "Birmingham School" cultural studies, and screen comedy. He is the editor of *Ken Russell: Re-Viewing England's Last Mannerist* (Scarecrow Press, 2009). An active critic, his film reviews have been published in *Film & History, Irish Journal of Gothic and Horror Studies,* and *Studies in Australasian Cinema*; his book reviews can be found in *Journal of British Cinema and Television, Journal of the Fantastic in the Arts,* and *Scope*.

Daniel **O'Brien** is a freelance writer and occasional teacher specializing in film and television. Since the late 1980s he has contributed to encyclopedias, dictionaries and other reference works, and written books on such subjects as Clint Eastwood, Frank Sinatra, British science fiction, Hong Kong horror movies, the Hannibal Lecter books and films, Paul Newman, and Daniel Craig. He is completing work toward a Ph.D.

Chris **Pallant** is a lecturer in the School of Creative Studies and Media at Bangor University in the United Kingdom. His research interests include animation, filmmaking technology, screenwriting, and urban studies. His book *Demystifying Disney: A History of Disney Feature Animation* (Continuum, 2011) was written to uproot common misconceptions and bring fresh scholarly definition to a busy field. As a Fulbright Commission winner, he spent the summer of 2010 at New York University and is preparing to co-edit a collection that will develop many of the topics discussed there.

Jerry B. **Pierce** is an assistant professor of ancient and medieval history at Penn State Hazleton. His current work focuses on representations of masculinity and sexuality in films set in the classical period. His forthcoming book *Poverty, Heresy and the Apocalypse: The Order of Apostles and Social Change in Medieval Italy 1260–1307* examines the heretical movement of Fra Dolcino as part of a broader social and political rebellion in northern Italy.

Robert C. **Pirro**'s research has focused on politics and tragedy, Hannah Arendt, and the burden of the German past in the works of émigré German directors in Hollywood. He published *The Politics of Tragedy and Democratic Citizenship* (Continuum) in 2011. He teaches feminist political thought, aesthetic politics, and film and politics in the Department of Political Science at Georgia Southern University in Statesboro and is writing a book on Primo Levi, Lina Wertmüller, and Niccolò Machiavelli.

Larry T. **Shillock** is an associate professor of English and an assistant academic dean at Wilson College in Chambersburg, Pennsylvania. His research interests include critical theory, the history of affect, the modern novel, and classical Hollywood cinema. He writes frequently for *The Bloomsbury Review*. His scholarship has appeared in *Social Epistemology*, *Philological Papers*, and *The Boy Detectives: Essays on the Hardy Boys and Others* (Michael G. Cornelius, ed., McFarland, 2010).

David **Simmons** has published on a range of issues related to twentieth century popular culture, including a monograph, *The Anti-Hero in the American Novel* (Palgrave Macmillan, 2008), and an edited collection on the television series *Heroes* (McFarland, 2011). In the field of television studies he has written chapters on a number of cult television shows, including *South Park*, *Supernatural*, and *Xena: Warrior Princess*. David is currently editing an upcoming collection on British and American contemporary fiction.

Kristi M. **Wilson** is an assistant professor at Soka University of America in Aliso Viejo, California, where she directs the Writing Program and teaches rhetoric and humanities. She founded the Stanford Film Lab and taught at Stanford University for nine years before coming to Soka. Co-editor of *Italian Neorealism and Global Cinema* (Wayne State University Press, 2007), she is the author of numerous articles in such journals as *Screen*, *Yearbook of Comparative and General Literature*, *Signs*, and *Literature/Film Quarterly*. Her anthology *Film and Genocide* is forthcoming.

Index

Accatone 21, 36, 38
Achilles 6, 11, 41, 45–48, 49, 51, 52, 55, 75, 77, 78, 81, 83, 107–112, 116–122, 127, 128, 130, 132, 135, 137, 139, 140, 142; *see also* Achilles the Heel
Achilles the Heel 192
Adam *see* Prince Adam
Aegisthus 141
Aeneas 55
Aeschylus 187
Agamemnon 46, 52–55, 77, 107, 108, 111, 112, 114, 117–120, 125, 127–128, 132, 133, 135–141
Air Force One 117
Ajax 6, 47
Aladdin 183
Alcesti di Samuele 22
Alcestis 22, 23
Alcinous 126
Alexander 5, 175
Alexandros 132, 133; *see also* Paris
Alpers, Hans Joachim 96
Althusser, Louis 62
Altman, Rick 93
Anastasia 178
Anderson, Sam 154, 156, 168, 169
Andromache 48, 130
Andromeda 63, 70
Antoninus 44, 82
Aphrodite 133, 139
Apocalypse Now 115
Apollo 77, 127
Apsyrtus 31, 32, 33, 36
Artemis 137
Athena 81, 118, 126, 127, 130, 133
Atlantis: The Lost Empire 184
Atlas, Charles 197
Atlas in the Land of the Cyclops 193
Atreus 133, 136
Atwood, Margaret 81, 157
Aurelius 69
Aziza, Claude 62

Bacchae 38
Bakhtin, Mikhail 125, 134

Barbie 155, 164, 165
Batiatus 70, 148, 151, 152
La battaglia di Maratona 62–64, 69, 122
The Battle of Britain 114
The Battle of the Bulge 113
Battlestar Galactica 144
Beast Man 158
The Beastmaster 3, 5, 89
Beauty and the Beast 178, 180
Belit 168
Ben-Hur (1959) 64, 176, 191
Ben Hur (2003) 176
Beowulf (2007) 72
Beowulf and Grendel 72
Besser, Joe 189
Blanshard, Alastair 187, 196, 197
Bluth, Don 178, 185
Boagrius 46, 47, 107–109
Bolin, Anne 196
Bolognini, Mauro 21
Bolter, Jay David 147
Bondanella, Peter 4, 5, 6, 14, 159
Boorman, John 2
Das Boot 114, 115, 117, 120
Boyd, Stephen 64, 65
Braedley, Susan 94
Briseis 45, 46, 54, 55, 77, 112, 118, 119, 120, 127, 128, 134, 139, 140
Brittain-Powell, Chris 170
Britton, Andrew 97
Brooker, Charlie 145, 146
Brooks, Peter 129
Brother Bear 184
Bucheim, Lothar-Günther 114
Burke, Samson 189, 194
Burke, Samuel *see* Burke, Samson
Burroughs, Edgar Rice 92, 147
Bush, George W. 113
Butler, David 96
Butler, Judith 160, 161, 165, 166, 169

Cabiria 4, 15, 59, 71, 78, 80, 91, 110, 180
Calchas 127, 137
Caldwell, John 149
Call of Duty 151

207

Callas, Maria 29, 30
Callimaco 63
Calypso 126
Campbell, Joseph 148
Canfora, Luciano 16, 17
Carter, Lin 96
Cascarelli, Don 3
Cassandra 132, 137–139
Castor 126
Centurion 58
Chapman, David 6, 7, 8, 9
Charis 63
Chiron 31
The Choice of Herakles 188
Chopper 67
Christian Democrats (Italy) 20, 21, 30
The Chronicles of Riddick: Escape from Butcher Bay 151
Chryse(s) 77, 127
Chryseis 77, 127, 128, 134, 139, 140
Cinderella 180
Cinecittà 28, 61
Circe 126
Clarens, Carlos 97
Clash of the Titans (1981) 5, 8, 14, 80, 175
Clash of the Titans (2010) 70, 71, 80, 101, 175
Clements, Ron 180, 181
Cline, William C. 92, 93
Clover, Joshua 151
Clum, John M. 43, 44
Clytemnestra 126, 132, 133, 138, 140, 141
Cohen, Steve 197
Columbia Pictures 189
Combs, Richard 97
Commodus 8, 16, 43, 44, 50–52, 53, 54, 63, 113
Conan 7, 75, 76, 78–80, 82, 84, 85, 88–90, 95–102, 158, 167, 168, 171
Conan (videogame, 2007) 148
Conan the Barbarian 3, 5, 10, 68, 76, 79, 85, 88, 89, 92, 95–102, 158, 159
Conan the Destroyer 79, 85, 89
Connell, R.J. 197
Cozzi, Luigi 5
Crassus 16, 44, 79, 82, 105, 106
Creon 17, 32, 94
Cresswell, Tim 127
Crixus 68, 70, 149
Croesus 84
Crowe, Russell 67
Cyclops 189, 192, 193
Cyrino, Monica S. 43, 50

Dalle Vacche, Angela 111
D'Annunzio, Gabrielle 91
Dardanius 64, 65
The Dark Crystal 96
Deathstalker 89
De Camp, L. Sprague 96
The Deer Hunter 115
De Groot, Jerome 146

Deiphobus 139
Deja, Andreas 181, 182
Deleuze, Gilles 106
Della Casa, Stefano 25
Demetrius 64
Demetrius and the Gladiators 64–65
Demodocus 126
DeRita, "Curly" Joe 189, 192, 195, 199
Diane Quigley 189, 198, 200
Dietrich, Marlene 106
Di Stefano, John 36
Dixon, Wheeler Winston 41, 42, 50
Doctore 70
Douglas, Kirk 64, 104
Draba 68
Dumbo 179
Dyer, Richard 17, 183, 191, 194, 198

Ebert, Roger 147
Egan, Richard 64, 65
Eisenstein, Sergei 180
Ellwood, David 23
The Emperor's New Groove 184
Engels, Frederick 31
Eric 180
Eudorus 46
Euripides 29, 32, 33, 37, 38
European Recovery Program (ERP) 23, 24; *see also* Marshall Plan
Excalibur 2

Falco 52
The Fall of the Roman Empire 63, 64, 66, 69, 110
The Fall of Troy 91
Fantasia 2000 184
Farrigno, Lou 5
Fazira 93
Fight Night 149
Filmation Studios 12, 154
Fine, Larry 189, 192
Fire & Ice 96
First Blood 88, 115; *see also* Rambo
First Wave of Peplum Films 4, 14, 122
Flash Gordon (1936) 92
Flesh and Blood 95
Forest, Mark 22
Fourth Wave of Peplum Films 5, 14
Fradley, Martin 45, 51
Francisci, Pietro 4, 22, 28
Freud, Sigmund 119

Gaius 51, 52
Gaius Claudius Glaber 8
Galinsky, G. Karl 187
Garron, Barry 144
Gaston 180, 182
gay clone 12, 156, 162–163, 165, 167, 169–173
Gears of War 147, 151
Gentile, Giuseppe 29
GI Joe 155, 158

Index 209

The Giant of Marathon 20
Ginsborg, Paul 20
Girard, Rene 137
Gladiator 5, 8, 41, 42–46, 50, 54, 55, 58, 66–68, 71, 109, 113, 115, 159, 168, 175
Glauce 32, 33
Glut, Donald F. 157
God of War 148
The Golden Voyage of Sinbad 175
Goldman, Gary 178
Goliath 6, 21, 60
Goliath and the Dragon (La vendetta de Ercole) 19, 20, 23
Goliath and the Sins of Babylon 60
Gorgo 49
Gracchus 52
Gramsci, Antonio 35
Green, Adam Isaiah 166, 170, 172
Griffin, Sean 181, 182
Griffith, D.W. 91
Grusin, Richard 147
Guazzoni, Enrico 4
Günsberg, Maggie 4, 5, 6, 7, 8, 14, 198

Haase, Christine 113, 121
Hades 8, 178, 179, 183
Hagen 68, 69
Haggard, H. Rider 92
Half Life 151
Hall, Karen J. 156, 172
Halo 147
Hannah, John 151
Hargitay, Mickey 22
Hark, Ina Rae 50, 64, 67, 68, 104, 105, 106, 109
Harries, Dan 192, 194
Harrison, John Kent 132, 133, 134, 135, 138, 140, 141
Harryhausen, Ray 175, 176
Have Rocket, Will Travel 189
Hayek, F.A. 95
He-Man 154–156, 158, 160, 163–166, 168–173
He-Man and the Masters of the Universe 5, 12, 154, 167, 176
Healy, Jane 181
Heaven Can Wait 96
Heavy Rain 150
Hector 9, 41, 45, 47, 48, 52, 55, 77, 78, 81, 83, 112, 116, 117, 118, 130, 139, 140
Hecuba 130, 132, 139
Helen of Troy 11, 47, 52, 112, 124–142
Helen of Troy (1956) 131
Helen of Troy (2003) 11, 131–142
Hephaestus 137
Hera 127, 130, 133
Hercules 6, 8, 15–26, 28, 29, 37, 46, 60, 78, 82, 178, 187–191, 193–201
Hercules (1983) 5
Hercules (Disney, 1997) 12, 177–182, 184–185
Hercules (*Le fatiche di Ercole*, 1958) 4, 15, 16, 28, 60, 93, 188, 190, 192–196, 198, 200

Hercules Against the Moon Men 60
Hercules Against the Tyrants of Babylon (Ercole contro i tiranni di Babilonia) 17, 18, 21
Hercules and the Captive Women 21
Hercules in the Haunted World (Ercole al centro della terra) 18, 19, 20
Hercules: The Animated Series 176, 177, 182–185
Hercules Unchained (Ercole e la regina di lidi) 4, 17, 19, 20, 94, 100, 188, 189, 193, 200
Hermione 126
Herodotus 40, 84
Heroes 144
Heston, Charlton 64
Hitchcock, Alfred 105
Hitler, Adolf 114, 115
Hoesterey, Ingeborg 191
Home on the Range 184
Homer 11, 72, 75, 79, 81, 83, 113, 116, 117, 125, 127–134, 138, 139, 141–142
Howard, Jerry "Curly" 189
Howard, Moe 189, 190, 195, 199, 200
Howard, Robert E. 88, 96, 147, 151, 158, 159, 171
Howard, Samuel "Shemp" 189
Hughes, Bettany 127
The Hunchback of Notre Dame 178, 180
Hundra 89, 100
Hutcheon, Linda 191

Icarus 183
Iliad 11, 46, 76, 77, 107, 109, 111–113, 116, 118, 121, 124–131, 133, 134, 136–140
In the Line of Fire 117
Ingraham, Chrys 41
Intolerance 91
Invasion U.S.A. 89
Iphigenia 132, 137, 140, 141
Iris 129, 130, 140
Italian Communist Party (PCI) 21
Ixion 146

Jafar 182, 183
James Bond film series 183
Jameson, Frederic 124
Jason 29, 31, 46, 78
Jason and the Argonauts 175
Jocasta 29
John Rambo 88
John Smith 180
Johnson, Paul 72
Joseph: King of Dreams 176
Juba 45, 68

Kasson, John F. 197
Kellner, Douglas 87, 88, 89, 92, 94, 97, 101
Kern, Ronni 132, 138, 141
King, Geoff 147, 148, 149
Kingdom of Heaven 67, 71, 75
Kniebe, Tobias 113, 116

Knives of the Avenger 93
Koestenbaum, Wayne 30
Kraken 8, 71
Krom 98
Krzywinska, Tanya 147, 148, 149
Kubrick, Stanley 68, 70

The Labors of Hercules see *Hercules (Le fatiche di Ercole,* 1958)
Laertes 131
Lagny, Michèle 110, 122
The Last Days of Pompeii (Gli ultimi de Pompei) 4, 91, 110
The Last Legion 68, 69, 71
The Last of the Mohicans 2
Lattimore, Richmond 128
Lawless, Lucy 151
Laxton, Meg 94
Leda 126
Lee, Christina 66
Leonidas 9, 40, 41, 48–49, 51–53, 55, 64, 65, 76, 78, 79, 82, 84, 85
Leprochon, Pierre 122
Levine, Martin 162, 165, 167, 170, 173
Lilo and Stitch 184
The Lion King 178, 182
The Little Mermaid 180
Livius 63, 64, 66
Looney Tunes 176
Lord of the Rings (1978) 96
The Lord of the Rings (2001) 71
The Lost City 92
Lotman, Jurij M. 124
The Loves of Hercules (Gli amori di Ercole) 18–22
Lucanio, Patrick 4, 91, 93, 94, 196
Lucia 64
Lucilla 44, 50, 51, 55, 63
Lucius 51, 55
Luke Skywalker 89

MacDonald, Marianne 31
MacIntyre, Alasdair 78, 84, 85
Maciste 4, 6, 15, 17, 18, 21, 22, 60, 61, 78, 89, 90–92, 110
Maciste 91
Maciste, Gladiator of Sparta 21
Maciste in Hell 91, 92
Maggi, Luigi 4
Man-at-Arms 158
Manfredi, Valerie Massimo 68
Mann, Anthony 109
Mann, Michael 2
Manovich, Lev 184
Mansfield, Jayne 22
Marcellus 64
Marcus Aurelius 55, 63
Mariniello, Silvestra 30, 33, 34
Marshall Plan 16, 22–24
Masters of the Universe (toy line) 154–158, 160, 161, 164, 166, 170–173

Maté, Rudolph 64
Mathjis, Ernest 145, 150
The Matrix 151
Mattel Toys 154, 156
Mature, Victor 64
Maximus 8, 9, 41, 42–46, 48–51, 54, 55, 66–68, 109, 168
McArthur, Colin 93
McDowell, Deborah E. 8, 13
Medea 29–38
Medea 9, 29–38
Medium Cool 87
Meg 180
Megara *see* Meg
Mendik, Xavier 145, 150
Menelaus 47, 112, 124–129, 131–133, 135–139, 141
Mer-Man 158
Milius, John 3, 88, 96, 97, 98, 100
Miller, Toby 28
Ming the Merciless 93
Mishima, Yukio 166, 172
Mr. Benson 161, 165, 167
Mitchell, Gordon 22
Mortal Kombat 148
Mulvey, Laura 104–106
Musker, John 180, 181
Mussolini, Benito 18, 19
My Son, the Hero 193

National Fascist Party (Italy) 4
Neale, Steve 61, 63, 93
Ned Kelly 2
Nemesis 126
Nestor 47, 108, 112, 114, 118
The Never Ending Story 120
Newman, James 148
Nisbet, Gideon 55, 197
Norris, Chuck 89

Odius 189, 191, 195, 198–200
Odysseus 46, 47, 75, 81, 83, 117, 118, 126, 128, 131, 135, 141, 142
Odyssey 76, 77, 90, 124–127, 130, 131, 134, 141
Oedipus 29, 34
Oedipus Rex 29, 30, 34
Okami 150
Osric 99

Pagano, Bartolomeo 4
Pain 179
Panic 179
Paoella, Domenico 61
Paris 47, 52–55, 120, 124–6, 128–134, 136–141
Park, Reg 22
Pasolini, Pier Paolo 9, 21, 29–38
Patacci, Claretta 19
Pathfinder 101
Patroclus 46, 47, 51, 77, 112, 117, 119, 139, 140
Patrone, Giovanni 4, 91, 110
Pavone, Carlo 19

Peleus 46, 112
Penelope 81, 130, 131, 138, 141
The Penelopiad 81
Percy Jackson and the Olympians: The Lightning Thief 14
Perseus 8, 14, 70, 71, 75
Petersen, Wolfgang 5, 11, 106–122
Phillipides 20, 62, 63, 122
Philoctetes 182
Phoebus 180
Pitt, Brad 113
Pixar 178
Pocahontas 178, 180
Pollux 126, 133–135
Poseidon 131
Prager, Brad 115
Preston, John 161, 162, 165, 166
Priam 52, 54, 112, 125, 128–130, 132, 138–140
The Prince 180
Prince, David A. 178
Prince Adam 169, 171
Prince Charming 180
Prince of Egypt 176
Prince of Persia: The Sands of Time 101
Prince Philip 180
"Prodican Hercules" 188, 190, 196, 200
Prodicus 188, 201
Prometheus Unbound 187
Propp, Vladimir 128, 134, 135, 136
Protas, Allison 3
Proximo 43, 44
Pumping Iron 164

"Queen of the Black Coast" 168
Quo vadis? (1913) 4, 91

Ralph Dimsal 189, 198
Rambo 68, 69; see also *First Blood*
Rambo *see* John Rambo
Reagan, Ronald 88, 97, 99, 101
Rebello, Stephen 181
Red Sonja 13, 86, 89, 96, 100
Reddy, Vasu 163, 171
Reeves, Steve 4, 20, 22, 62, 188, 190, 193, 194, 196, 197, 200
The Robe 66, 72
Rocky 66, 89
Roman Legion-Hare 176
Rome 146
Romper Stomper 67
Romulus 68, 69
Roosevelt, Franklin Delano 23
Rubin, Gayle 31, 32, 36
Rushing, Robert A. 179, 180
Russo, Vito 42
Ryan, Michael 87, 88, 89, 92, 94, 97, 101

The Saboteur 150
Saetta 6
Samson 6
Samson and the Mighty Challenge 60

Samson in King Solomon's Mines 93
Sandow, Eugene 196, 197
Sarpedon 77
Savinio, Albert 22, 23
Scar 182
Scarfe, Gerald 181
Schehr, Laurence R. 164, 173
Schein, Seth L. 125
Schenk, Irmbert 7, 8, 14, 122
Schliemann, Heinrich 142
Schor, Naomi 164
Schuyler Davis 189, 190, 193–195, 198–201
Schwarzenegger, Arnold 13, 66, 98, 158, 164
Schwenger, Peter 15, 160, 164, 166
Scott, Gordon 22
Scott, Ridley 5, 42, 67, 68, 109, 159
Second Wave of Peplum Films 5, 8, 10, 14, 110, 122
See Ya Later Gladiator 176
Segal, Lynne 43
The 7th Voyage of Sinbad 175
Shadow of Rome 148
Sheffield, Tricia 159
She-Ra: Princess of Power 5
Sholay 2
Siciliano, Angelo 197
Sinbad and the Eye of the Tiger 175
Skeletor 155, 158
Sleeping Beauty 180
Snow White and the Seven Dwarves 180
Snyder, Zack 5, 40, 48
Solon 84
Son of Hercules in the Land of Darkness 60
Son of Samson (Maciste nella Valle dei Re) 17, 21
Sontag, Susan 144, 145, 146, 150, 152, 181
Sophocles 29
Spartacus 44, 66, 68, 80, 83, 104–106, 109, 176
Spartacus (film character) 6, 21, 64, 68, 76, 78, 79, 82, 84, 85, 105, 168
Spartacus (television series character) 8, 11, 70, 146, 148, 149, 151
Spartacus: Blood and Sand 8, 11, 70, 83, 144–152, 159, 168
Spinazzola, Vittorio 16, 28
Stack, Oswald 36, 37
Star Wars 89
Stone, Oliver 5, 102
Stratos 158
Streetfighter 148
Studlar, Gaylyn 106, 11
Subotai 97, 100
Sweet, Roger 157
The Sword and the Sorcerer 89, 96

Tarzan 184
The Ten Commandments 176
Teocrito 63
Teorema 34, 38
The Terminator 66, 68

Tessari, Duccio 18
The Testament of Maciste 91
Thaur 6
Theokoles 148
Theseus 6, 134, 136
Theseus of Rhodes 189, 199
Thetis 111, 127, 130, 137
Third Wave of Peplum Films 5, 10, 14
300 5, 40, 41, 44, 48–50, 52, 53, 55, 76, 80, 83–85, 101, 175
The 300 Spartans 64
The Three Musketeers 90, 93
Three Stooges 189, 190, 194, 195, 198
The Three Stooges Meet Hercules 12, 188–201
Thulsa Doom 7, 80, 93, 97, 98
Thundarr the Barbarian 5
Tiger Woods 150
Time Bandits 96
Tiresias 85
Toy Story 178
Treasure Planet 184
Tri-Klops 158
Triopas 46
Triton 180, 182
Troy 5, 11, 41, 44, 45–48, 50, 52–55, 106–122, 142, 175
Truman, Harry S 22, 23
Turner, Susanne 44
20th-Century–Fox 179
The Two Gladiators (I due gladiatori) 16
Tyndareus 126, 133–136

Uhlenbrock, Jaimee Pugliese 187
Ulysses 6, 192
Ulysses 193
Undersea Kingdom 92
Ursus 4, 6, 71
Usai, Paolo Cherchi 91, 92

Valeria 79, 97, 98
Van Damme, Jean-Claude 67
Van Watson, William 33
Varinia 82
Varro 70
Verdicchio, Pasquale 38
La viaccia 21
Viano, Maurizio 30, 32, 34, 35, 36
Village People 163
von Sternberg, Josef 105, 106

Wade, Jay C. 170
Walt Disney Company 177–185
Warner, Michael 36
The Warrior and the Sorceress 100
Weider, Ben 197
Weider, Joe 197
Wells, Paul 175
Wexler, Haskell 87
White, T.H. 58
Whitfield, Andy 151
Winckelmann, Johann-Joachim 116
Wise, Robert 131
the Wizard 98
Wolf, Mark J.P. 147
Wolf, Martin 112, 113
Wood, Robin 97
Woodruff, Paul 75–77, 84, 85
Wyke, Maria 196, 198

Xerxes 40, 53, 54, 55

Zeno Clash 151
Zeus 126, 127, 178, 182
Žižek, Slavoj 60
Zodac 158

www.ingramcontent.com/pod-product-compliance
Ingram Content Group UK Ltd.
Pitfield, Milton Keynes, MK11 3LW, UK
UKHW042000140426
5217IPUK00015B/891